PAX ATOMICA

Mark Cioc

Pax Atomica:

THE NUCLEAR DEFENSE DEBATE IN WEST GERMANY DURING THE ADENAUER ERA

Columbia University Press
New York   1988

Columbia University Press
New York   Guildford, Surrey
Copyright © 1988 Columbia University Press
All rights reserved

Library of Congress Cataloging-in-Publication Data

Cioc, Mark.
  Pax atomica: the nuclear defense debate in West Germany during the Adenauer era.
  Bibliography: p.
  Includes index.
  1. Germany (West)—Military policy. 2. Nuclear
warfare. 3. Germany (West)—Politics and government.
I. Title.
UA710.C54 1988   355'.0217'0943   87-32550
  ISBN 0-231-06590-6

Book design by Jennifer Dossin
Printed in the United States of America
Hardback editions of Columbia University Press books are Smyth-sewn and printed on
permanent and durable acid-free paper

For my parents,
Charles and Beatrice Cioc

CONTENTS

Contents

ILLUSTRATIONS

MAPS

DOCUMENTS

Illustrations

ACKNOWLEDGMENTS

MOST of my doctoral research was done during a visit to West Germany from 1981 to 1983. Several institutions made this project possible: the Council for European Studies, the Friedrich-Ebert-Stiftung, the Forschungsinstitut der Deutschen Gesellschaft für Auswärtige Politik, the Institute for the Study of World Politics, and the United States Arms Control and Disarmament Agency. The Ford Foundation and Stanford University's Center for International Security and Arms Control also provided welcome scholarly and financial assistance.

For their guidance in the preparation of this manuscript, I want to thank Gerald Feldman, Alexander George, Catherine Kelleher, Walter McDougall, and Hinrich Seeba. I also wish to acknowledge the invaluable editorial assistance of Gordon Harvey, Ehud Havazelet, and George Lee. The maps were designed and drawn by my father, Charles Cioc. Thanks also to Manfred Schneider for his help in photographing and replicating the political cartoons. Michelle Carter deserves special praise for her support and criticism, not to mention for taking time away from novel writing and Grateful Dead concerts.

Finally, the writings of four participants in the 1950s' nuclear debate—Karl Jaspers, Helmut Schmidt, Helmut Thielicke, and Carl-Friedrich von Weizsäcker—had a far-reaching influence on my analysis of the nuclear controversy. I thank you all.

ABBREVIATIONS

AB Akten der Kirchlichen Bruderschaft im Rheinland, Landeskirchenamt, Düsseldorf
ABC atomic, biological, chemical
ASD Archiv der sozialen Demokratie, Friedrich Ebert Stiftung, Bonn
BA FDP Bundestag Archiv, Bonn
BA-MA Bundesarchiv–Militärarchiv, Freiburg
BHA Bundeshauptausschuss, Politisches Archiv der Friedrich Naumann Stiftung, Bonn
BK Büro Kloppenburg, Evangelisches Zentralarchiv, Berlin
BRD Bundesrepublik Deutschland [Federal Republic of Germany (FRG) or West Germany]
BV Bundesvorstand, Archiv des DGB-Bundesvorstandes, Düsseldorf
BVA Bundesverteidigungsausschuss (or Bundesausschuss für Verteidigungsfragen), Politisches Archiv der Friedrich Naumann Stiftung, Bonn
BW Bundeswehr
CDU Christlich Demokratische Union [Christian Democratic Union]
CNA Committee against Nuclear Armaments [same as KgA]
CND Campaign for Nuclear Disarmament
CSCE Conference on Security and Cooperation in Europe
CSU Christlich Soziale Union [Christian Social Union]
DDR Deutsche Demokratische Republik [German Democratic Republic (GDR) or East Germany]
DFU Deutsche Friedens-Union [German Peace Union]
DGB Deutscher Gewerkschaftsbund [German Federation of Trade Unions]
DP Deutsche Partei [German Party]
EDC European Defense Community
EKD Evangelische Kirche Deutschland [Evangelical Church of Germany, or Protestant Church]
EM Erich Mende Bestand, Politisches Archiv der Friedrich Naumann Stiftung, Bonn
EO Erich Ollenhauer Nachlass, Archiv der sozialen Demokratie, Friedrich Ebert Stiftung, Bonn
EZB Evangelisches Zentralarchiv, Berlin
FAZ *Frankfurter Allgemeine Zeitung*
fdk *Frei Demokratische Korrespondenz*
FDP Freie Demokratische Partei [Free Democratic Party]

Abbreviations

FE	Fritz Erler Nachlass, Archiv der sozialen Demokratie, Friedrich Ebert Stiftung, Bonn
FNA	Franz Neumann Archiv, Berlin
FNS	Politisches Archiv der Friedrich Naumann Stiftung, Bonn
FR	*Frankfurter Rundschau*
FRG	Federal Republic of Germany [Bundesrepublik Deutschland (BRD), or West Germany]
FRUS	*Foreign Relations of the United States*
FS	Fraktionssitzung, FDP Bundestag Archiv, Bonn
FVP	Freie Volkspartei [Free Peoples' Party]
GB/BHE	Gesamtdeutscher Block/Bund der Heimatvertriebenen und Entrechteten [All-German Block]
GBV	Bundesvorstand (Gesamt), Politisches Archiv der Friedrich Naumann Stiftung, Bonn; and Gesamt Bundesvorstand, DGB-Archiv
GCND	German Campaign against Nuclear Death [same as KdA]
GDR	German Democratic Republic [Deutsche Demokratische Republik (DDR), or East Germany]
GHA	Gustav Heinemann Archiv, Archiv der sozialen Demokratie, Friedrich Ebert Stiftung, Bonn
GVP	Gesamtdeutsche Volkspartei [All-German Peoples' Party]
HW	Helene Wessel Nachlass, Archiv der sozialen Demokratie, Friedrich Ebert Stiftung, Bonn
ICBM	intercontinental ballistic missile
ICFTU	International Confederation of Free Trade Unions
IG	Industriegewerkschaft [Industrial Union]
INF	intermediate-range nuclear force
IRBM	intermediate-range ballistic missile
JCS	U.S. Joint Chiefs of Staff
KAS	Konrad Adenauer Stiftung, Rhöndorf
KB	Karl Bechert Nachlass, Archiv der sozialen Demokratie, Friedrich Ebert Stiftung, Bonn
KdA	Kampf dem Atomtod [same as GCND]
KgA	Komitee gegen Atomrüstung [same as CNA]
KPD	Kommunistische Partei Deutschlands
KI	Karl Immer Nachlass, Landeskirchenamt, Düsseldorf
KJ	*Kirchliches Jahrbuch für die Evangelische Kirche in Deutschland* [church yearbook for the EKD]
LA	Landesausschuss [state committee]
LKA	Landeskirchenamt, Archiv der Evangelischen Kirche im Rheinland, Düsseldorf
LO	Landesorganisation [city/state organization]
LV	Landesvorstand [state executive committee]
MBFR	Mutual and Balanced Force Reduction
MC	Military Committee
MIRV	multiple independently targetable reentry vehicle
MLF	multilateral force
MR	Manfred Rexin Papers, private collection of Manfred Rexin, West Berlin
NATO	North Atlantic Treaty Organization
NPG	Nuclear Planning Group

NRW North Rhine-Westphalia

NSC National Security Council

NZZ *Neue Zürcher Zeitung*

ÖTV Gewerkschaft Öffentliche Dienste, Transport und Verkehr [Transportation Union]

PA Parlamentsarchiv, Abteilung Wissenschaftliche Dokumentation des Deutschen Bundestages, Bonn

PN Peter Nellen Nachlass, Archiv der sozialen Demokratie, Friedrich Ebert Stiftung, Bonn

PV Parteivorstand Bestand, Archiv der sozialen Demokratie, Friedrich Ebert Stiftung, Bonn

SAC U.S. Strategic Air Command

SACEUR Supreme Allied Commander Europe

SDZ *Süddeutsche Zeitung*

SED Sozialistische Einheitspartei Deutschlands [Socialist Unity Party]

SHAPE Supreme Headquarters Allied Powers Europe

SPD Sozialdemokratische Partei Deutschland [Social Democratic Party]

TCC Temporary Council Committee of NATO

TDA Thomas Dehler Archiv, Politisches Archiv der Friedrich Naumann Stiftung, Bonn

VA Verteidigungsausschuss, Parlamentsarchiv, Bonn

VDPG Verband Deutsche Physikalische Gesellschaft [German Physics Society]

VfZ *Vierteljahrshefte für Zeitgeschichte*

WCC World Council of Churches

WDS Wolfgang Döring Stiftung, Düsseldorf

WM Walter Menzel Nachlass, Archiv der sozialen Demokratie, Friedrich Ebert Stiftung, Bonn

WPC World Peace Council

ZS Zeitschrift-Sammlung, Bundesarchiv, Koblenz

PROLOGUE

It remains to be seen whether the *pax atomica* turns
out to be a genuine peace, followed by an easing of
tension between the United States and the Soviet
Union. It is entirely conceivable that the superpowers,
armed with atomic weapons, may confront each other
for a long time. Indeed, they might keep their fingers
on the trigger of unlimited atomic war for decades.

—Axel von dem Bussche,
Das Parlament (April 21, 1954)

HORTLY after the 1957 West German election, Chancellor Konrad Adenauer spoke with the foreign press. The conversation turned again and again to the divisive issue of the moment: NATO's plan to station medium-range missiles in West Germany and convert the Bundeswehr into a nuclear-capable army. Twelve years after Adolf Hitler's death the word "Germany" still evoked images of militarism, genocide, and reckless nationalism. With Central Europe occupied and the former Reich divided, no one welcomed a German military resurgence, especially a nuclear one. "Perhaps you must accept these weapons," one journalist conceded, "but at least you should take as few as possible." The chancellor replied: "Instead of saying 'as few as possible,' why not talk about taking 'as many as are necessary.' That is the precise phrase."[1]

Adenauer's plea for Western solidarity deftly disarmed the critic. Yet his remark left much unanswered. How many Euromissiles sufficed to deter the Soviet Union from attacking Western Europe? What military rationale did a nuclear-capable Bundeswehr have? During the past forty years, one NATO doctrine has displaced another, ranging from "massive retaliation" to "flexible response." One dispute has followed another, from the 1950 decision to create the Bundeswehr to the "two-track" decision of 1979. Major public debates have twice erupted in West Germany over NATO's nuclear strategy; the more recent debate, from 1977 to 1987, was a sequel to that of the Adenauer era.

Since 1945, German territory has been militarily occupied by the United States, Soviet Union, Great Britain, and France. Not only were they the major victors in World War II, they were also, by 1960, the first nuclear powers. These nations redrew the map of Europe, molded postwar Germany, and took control of Central Europe's destiny. They held numerous conferences on the "German question"—from Teheran (1943) to Potsdam (1945), from Moscow (1947) to Geneva (1955)—but they never reached an accord, or signed a peace treaty. In the wake of the Berlin blockade (1948–1949), two Germanies emerged: the Federal Republic (West Germany), a heavily industrialized region with over fifty-five million citizens, and the Democratic Republic (East Germany), with a population under twenty million. Germans (like the Koreans and the Vietnamese in their turn) felt the superpowers' presence more acutely than other nations in the world; "cold war" connoted "civil war" and the risk of "global war."

North Korea's surprise attack on South Korea in June 1950 spotlighted the possibility of Communist aggression in West Berlin, West Germany, and Western Europe. At the New York Foreign Ministers Conference in September, NATO decided that a West German defense contribution was imperative. Once the initial war scare subsided, however, the European governments let it be known that they feared a revival of German militarism almost as much as they feared the Soviet army. At France's insistence, the European Defense Community Treaty (May 1952) defined West Germany as a "strategically exposed area," meaning that NATO could refuse to license armament factories there. NATO also forced Adenauer to forswear the production of atomic, biological, and chemical (ABC) weapons, as well as the delivery system "triad" (missiles, submarines, long-range bombers). Similar restrictions (known collectively as Adenauer's nonnuclear pledge) were added to the 1955 Paris Treaties, which allowed West Germany to join NATO. Adenauer turned necessity into a virtue. "I do not like to feel fractious or quarrel," he stated at the October 2, 1954, London Foreign Ministers Conference, "therefore, I am prepared to declare, on behalf of the Federal Republic, that we will voluntarily renounce the manufacture of A, B, and C weapons, not on the reasons of strategically exposed zones, but quite voluntarily!"[2]

The NATO restrictions effectively curtailed Germany's reemergence as a great power. Ironically, Adenauer's nonnuclear pledge did not resolve the nuclear issue, but rather complicated U.S.–West German relations and confounded intra-alliance military planning. West Germany lay along the Iron Curtain, yet no chancellor had control over NATO's nuclear stockpile. NATO's most extensive nuclear infrastructure was placed in West Germany (an estimated 3,400 warheads and 240 facilities), as visible proof of America's commitment to Central Europe's defense. But the presence of so many nuclear weapons turned West Germany into NATO's powder keg. Would the United States risk a Soviet nuclear strike against North America in order to defend West Germany? Would the Americans and Russians fight a proxy war in Europe? Did the superpowers view Central Europe as a nuclear no-man's-land?

West German citizens have always felt more dependent on the United States, more subject to the vicissitudes of NATO's defense posture, more endangered by a superpower conflict than their Western neighbors. Security issues have swung elections, determined coalitions, and toppled chancellors.

SCHOLARS concerned with the security controversies of the 1950s generally divide the decade into three phases: the rearmament debate (1950–55), the army legislation controversy (1955–56), and the nuclear debate (1957–61). In the first phase, NATO established the Bundeswehr. In the second phase, the West German government codified its civil–military relations, creating the first German army ever to come under complete parliamentary control. In the final phase, NATO's nuclear defense doctrine came under scrutiny.

This chronological framework, however, disregards the critical role of nuclear weapons in all phases. Plans to rearm Germany were tied to the chancellor's nonnuclear pledge. Had the Western powers suspected that West Germany harbored serious ambitions of creating a national nuclear deterrent, they would have halted the Bundeswehr's creation. Once NATO introduced nuclear-capable systems on West German soil in 1953, discussion of nuclear weapons preempted the debate over army legislation within the German parliamentary body, the Bundestag. Even before it became clear, in 1957, that NATO planned to train Bundeswehr troops in the use of nuclear-capable systems, and that the United States would station missiles in Western Europe, the nuclear specter had begun to cast its shadow over West Germany's domestic politics.

West Germans debated NATO's nuclear doctrine in cafes and beer halls, in theaters and on the radio. The discussion aroused conservatives and socialists, Communists and capitalists, theologians and laymen. Rhetoric overleaped reality on more than one occasion. Contrary to rumor, NATO never gave the Bundeswehr direct access to nuclear warheads; it had only offered to train German soldiers in the use of nuclear-capable systems. These systems were under West German control, but the nuclear warheads remained in American hands. Yet there was a pervasive misperception that the Bundeswehr had been transformed almost overnight from a conventional army into a powerful nuclear war machine, and that ex-Nazi generals had their fingers on the nuclear trigger. Serious discussion of NATO's defense choices was rare, especially from 1957 to 1959. "There was a total division, a total tearing apart that revealed all the old wounds," one observer noted with only slight exaggeration. "There seemed no basis for consensus; it was impossible even to talk—you were either for or against and that was that."[3]

The worst of the "old wounds" was the military's role in the demise of the Weimar Republic (1919–1933) and the advent of the Third Reich (1933–1945). Opponents of nuclear weapons instinctively feared the new Bundeswehr; never in history had Germans produced a pro-democratic army. By contrast, nuclear proponents distrusted extraparliamentary agitation, viewing it as a mass-organized movement not dissimilar to that of the Fascists of the 1920s. Both sides greatly overestimated West Germany's political frailty. Yet perhaps the healthiest sign of all was that the memories of Weimar (parliamentary instability, economic ruin, social conflict) haunted every politician in West Germany. No one wanted to repeat the horror of Fascism.[4]

Throughout the decade, Adenauer held the allegiance of West Germans. Even as his opponents increased, so did his popularity. In 1957, voters gave the chancellor's coalition—composed of the Christian Democratic Union (CDU) and its Bavarian sister party, the Christian Social Union (CSU)—an absolute majority. This event was unprecedented in German history. But a majority was not a consensus, for it did not guarantee bipartisan (or, in the case of West Germany, tripartisan) support. During most of Adenauer's fourteen-year tenure as chancellor, he battled an opposition that sought a new direction in the country's defense affairs. Not until 1960 did the Social Democratic Party (SPD) and Free Democratic Party (FDP) accept the premises upon which the chancellor's security policy rested. Two factors contributed to the conversion. International developments from the Korean War to the Berlin Wall (August 1961) confirmed the division of the world into hostile camps. Reunification, the paramount goal of the SPD and FDP, became ever more unlikely; by the end of the decade, opposition leaders had grasped the hopelessness of their cause. Second, the new American administration of John F. Kennedy shared many of the defense concerns of the SPD and FDP. Opposition leaders saw an opportunity to revise the least-savory aspects of NATO's doctrine, while silently acceding to a nuclear defense.

The temptation to compare the nuclear debate of the 1950s with the more recent controversy is difficult to resist. Both disputes began with the deployment of American-made nuclear warheads on European soil. Western European governments welcomed the arsenal because it strengthened deterrence, while a portion of the populace opposed deployment on the grounds that it increased the likelihood of a superpower confrontation in Europe. Both debates spilled into the streets, as West Germans wrestled with the geostrategic, political, and moral implications of NATO's defense posture. But the Adenauer-era debate was not merely a precursor to the recent nuclear controversy. The converse is more nearly true. The furor over the 1979 two-track decision was an aftershock to the debate of the 1950s: it was under Adenauer that West Germans sought to regain their confidence and prove themselves worthy of the West's trust.

PAX ATOMICA

the irony
of a forward defense

INTRODUCTION

It is cold comfort for any citizen of Western Europe
to be assured that—after his country is overrun and
he is pushing up daisies—someone still alive
will drop a bomb on the Kremlin.

—President Dwight Eisenhower
(March 1953)

NATO was the United States' first formal European pact since
1778. The foremost goal of the alliance was the "containment"
of the Soviet Union behind the Iron Curtain. American leaders presumed that a similar commitment to Britain and France in 1914 or
1939 would have deterred both Kaiser Wilhelm II and Adolf Hitler
from embarking on a global war.[1]

By joining NATO, the United States committed itself to a "forward defense" of Western Europe. President Truman (1945–1953)
deployed a portion of the Strategic Air Command (SAC) at European bases, and stationed six army divisions along the Iron Curtain.
Yet throughout the early years America's forward defense strategy
was largely bluff. NATO members were well aware that the Soviet
army, operating from bases in East Germany and Poland, was positioned for a quick strike into Western Europe. Even U.S. war plans—
Pincher (1946), Halfmoon (1948), Offtackle (1949)—depicted the

ease with which Western forces could be driven back at least to the Pyrenees mountain range between France and Spain.[2] The Soviet Union's first A-bomb test (August 1949) further underscored the West's vulnerability, depriving the United States of its greatest military asset, the nuclear monopoly.

During the last two years of the Truman administration, National Security Council directive NSC-68 guided American defense policy. NSC-68 was a precursor to "flexible response" doctrine (adopted by NATO in 1967): it foresaw a Western defense structure capable of responding to all levels of aggression, of applying force "proportional to the extent of the mischief."[3] Hydrogen bomb research began, as did experimentation with low-yield nuclear weaponry. America trebled its defense budget, increased its troop strength worldwide, and tightened its military alliances with nations lying on the periphery of the Soviet Union.[4] The United States set a fast pace for European rearmament, insisting on a large West German army. "Unless the military strength of the Western European nations is increased," NSC-68 stated, "on a much larger scale than under current programs and at an accelerated rate, it is more than likely that those nations will not be able to oppose even by 1960 the Soviet armed forces in war with any degree of effectiveness."[5] At the 1952 NATO Lisbon conference, U.S. leaders pushed for a NATO army of ninety-six divisions, and announced their intention of constructing more European air bases. America's representative, General Alfred Gruenther, proposed a motto for the conference: "Praise the Lord and Pass the Infrastructure."[6]

Adenauer pressured the Western allies for a swift implementation of the forward defense strategy. West Germany was long and narrow; Soviet tanks were eighty miles from Frankfurt, a few "tank hours" from the industrialized Ruhr region. "German territory must not be viewed as a forefield with the intent of utilizing the Rhine River as the primary line of defense," wrote West Germany's security advisers in October 1950:

Wherever possible, the defense must be led offensively. This means that, at the outset, we must counterattack everywhere that is feasible. This method will impress the Soviets tremendously, and warn them to be cautious. There is no natural boundary east of the Rhine, no line that is suitable for a defense (except for the Thuringian forest, which lies in Soviet hands). Even with fifty divisions it would be impossible to achieve a stationary defense of the eight-hundred-kilometer border from Passau to Lübeck. Only a mobile fighting command can successfully hold the region from Elbe to Rhine. . . . We must strive with all our means so that the battle gets pushed back onto East German soil as soon as possible.[7]

SPD chairman Kurt Schumacher (1945–1952) was even more outspoken. "It would be irresponsible," he stated, "if we were to offer Germany as a theater of war for the purpose of covering an allied retreat."[8] The Germans, he added, "do not fit the role of partisans or that of a rearguard for a new Dunkirk."[9]

From December 1952 to December 1956 NATO Military Committee directive MC-14/1 guided official defense policy. MC-14/1 called for a forward defense with conventionally equipped armed forces, in conformity with NSC-68, the Lisbon goals, and the West German government's priorities. In practice, however, it was never implemented: most member states were too weak to sustain large defense budgets; the Europeans were reluctant to permit a West German army; British and French troops were occupied with colonial revolts. In August 1954, after four years of planning, the French legislature refused to ratify the European Defense Community. West Germany subsequently joined NATO directly, but another decade elapsed before the Bundeswehr approached full strength. At NATO's Supreme Headquarters Allied Powers Europe (SHAPE) in Fontainebleau, plan after plan was scrapped as it became clear that the necessary troops would be mustered much more slowly than Truman's advisers expected. NATO resembled, said one observer, the Venus d' Milo: "all SHAPE and no arms."[10]

President Dwight Eisenhower (1953–1961) knew Western Europe's defense dilemmas first-hand. Not only had he overseen the liberation of occupied Europe during World War II, but he had also served as NATO's first Supreme Allied Commander Europe (SACEUR) from 1950 to 1952. Ike's fiscally conservative advisers concluded that NSC-68 was too exorbitant to implement globally, MC-14/1 too overtaxing to implement in Western Europe. They took a "New Look" at America's defense expenditures, with the intent of reducing America's troop strength in Western Europe. They also put greater reliance on a nuclear arsenal, arguing that it offered "a bigger bang for a buck." The resulting strategy, codified in a new National Security Council directive, NSC-162/2, was dubbed "massive retaliation" doctrine. It went through various permutations, but one feature endured: at the global level, American nuclear superiority was pitted against Soviet conventional superiority. Since nuclear stockpiles were less expensive than large standing armies, the doctrine was salable to the American public.[11]

As before, U.S. leaders stressed the need for large NATO ground and air forces, deployed along the Iron Curtain. "Some areas are so vital that a special guard should and can be put around them," wrote Secretary of State John Foster Dulles:

> Western Europe is such an area. Its industrial plant represents so nearly the balance of industrial power in the world that an aggressor might feel that it was a good gamble to seize it—even at the risk of considerable hurt to himself. In this respect, Western Europe is exceptional. Fortunately, the West European countries have both a military tradition and a military potential, so that through a European Defense Community, and with the support by the United States and Britain, they can create an adequate defense of the continent.[12]

There was, however, a twist to NATO strategy as envisaged by the Eisenhower administration: the term "conventional" no longer signified nonnuclear armed forces; "conventional" now meant both nonnuclear and low-yield nuclear weapons as distinguished from America's "strategic" forces carrying large-yield A-bombs and the newly developed H-bombs. "The United States," Dulles told NATO leaders, "considers that the ability to use atomic weapons as conventional weapons is essential for the defense of the NATO area in the face of the present threat. In short, such weapons must now be treated as in fact having become conventional."[13] At the December 1954 NATO Council meeting, Dulles secured European approval of massive retaliation doctrine. "We have determined," SACEUR General Gruenther (1953–1956) told the press, "that our strategy in the center requires the use of atomic weapons, whether the enemy uses them or not, and we must use atomic bombs to redress the imbalance between their forces and ours and to achieve victory."[14] In December 1956, NATO adopted MC-14/2, which officially redefined the strategic rationale for ground troops on the continent. NATO's nuclear arsenal (especially SAC) functioned as a "sword," its conventional forces as a "shield." The ground forces along the Iron Curtain served as a "trip wire" for nuclear war; their purpose was to stave off a Soviet invasion long enough for the West to prepare a nuclear counterthrust as far eastward as possible.

America was not the only NATO member to choose the nuclear path. Even before the Eisenhower administration adopted the New Look, Prime Minister Winston Churchill's military advisers announced that the British were also planning to reduce their defense budget. Their blueprint, "Global Strategy," was a version of massive retaliation doctrine. Written shortly after Britain detonated its first atomic device in 1952, it argued in favor of a nuclear arsenal. After the Suez debacle (1956), the plan was fully implemented: defense expenditures for the British army and navy were cut and Britain came to rely primarily on its long-range, nuclear-capable V-bombers, the "Great Deterrent."[15] The French soon followed suit—in part to bolster NATO's credibility while depriving the Anglo-Saxon countries of their hegemonial role in the Western world, in part to guarantee military superiority over the West Germans. Prime Minister Pierre Mendès-France funded a full-scale nuclear research project in December 1954. Under Charles de Gaulle's leadership, the French detonated their first prototype in 1960. As with America and Britain, massive retaliation became the strategic doctrine of the *force de frappe.* "The French atomic force," de Gaulle asserted, ". . . will have the sombre and terrible capability of destroying in a few seconds millions and millions of men. This fact cannot fail to have at least some bearing on the intents of any possible aggressor."[16]

Instead of fulfilling the Lisbon goal of a large conventional army (with 54 divisions earmarked for Central Europe), NATO came to rely on atompower to defend Western Europe along the Iron Curtain. The number of front-line NATO divisions dwindled from 21 (1954), to 18 (1956), to 16 (1958), due largely to British and French

MAP 1

American Defense Lines vs. a Soviet Attack
on Western Europe & Evolution of NATO's Defense Strategy

	1945–1950 defense line
° ° ° ° ° 1950 provisional defense line NSC-68	▲ ▲ ▲ ▲ 1953 Rhine defense line
•••••••• 1956 trip wire defense line	+ + + Iron Curtain & forward defense line

troop withdrawals. As the number of soldiers decreased, the number of nuclear warheads increased. The United States deployed several 280-mm. atomic cannons in West Germany in 1953; Corporal and Honest John rockets were brought to Europe soon thereafter. In 1958, the United States offered the West German government nuclear-capable Matador cruise missiles, surface-to-air Nike Hercules, and F-104 fighter bombers. Because these systems fired both atomic and conventional warheads, they were considered "dual capable." They were also under "dual key": the United States kept strict control over the nuclear warheads, but West Germany took control of the delivery systems.[17]

The New Look lent credibility to NATO's forward defense posture. The Rhine River became the provisional defense line in 1953, and a "trip wire" defense line was implemented by 1956. Once the Bundeswehr was at full strength, a defense along the Iron Curtain would become feasible (see map 1).

Ironically, the forward defense strategy boomeranged on the West Germans: it transformed Central Europe into a potential nuclear battlefield. The New Look also drastically altered the military rationale for front-line soldiers, assigning them the task of staving off a Soviet assault long enough for NATO to drop nuclear warheads above them. Bundeswehr troops became the footsoldiers of NATO, the atomic cannonfodder of a future war. Nor did the New Look offer much solace to West German citizens. Central Europe was densely populated; a nearly continuous string of large cities, towns, and villages lined the inter-German border. If Eastern bloc troops attacked Western Europe and NATO responded with nuclear weapons, civilian casualties would be high, regardless of how "limited" the war remained. Massive retaliation was a "deterrent": by brandishing the nuclear sword, NATO sought to frighten the Soviets from attacking in the first place. But if war nonetheless occurred, nuclear weapons would most likely devastate the region they were supposed to defend (see map 2).

As West Germans discussed the pros and cons of rearmament, they found themselves caught in a paradox. America's nuclear arsenal added to the West's deterrent capability and made it feasible for NATO to halt the Red army before it rolled over Western Europe:

MAP 2

West German Population Centers
Near Iron Curtain Countries
(1980 Census Estimates)

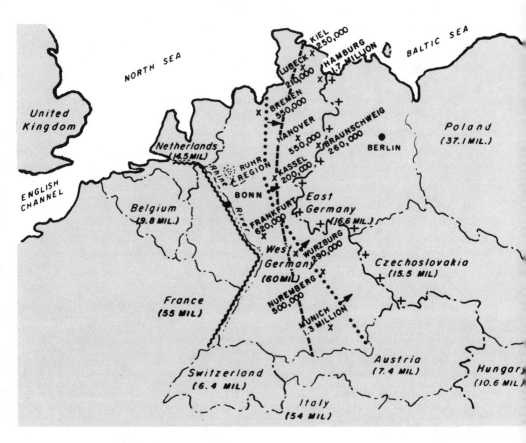

EVOLUTION OF NATO'S
DEFENSE LINES

+ + + Forward defense line

------- Trip wire defense line

~~~~~ Rhine defense line

Area within 65 miles of inter-German border. Nearly 25% of West Germany's population lives in this region.

North Rhine-Westphalia (including the Ruhr region) has a population of 17 million.

but it also meant that a future European war would be the continuation of the last—with more devastating consequences. This dichotomy lay at the heart of West Germany's security dilemma, baffling parliamentarians as they struggled to lay the foundation of the Bundeswehr.

1

THE NUCLEAR ARSENAL
OF DEMOCRACY

Alliances, to be sure, are good, but forces of one's
own are still better.
—Frederick William of Brandenburg
Political Testament (1667)

THE thought of rearming Germany is spreading like a drop of oil,"
wrote correspondent Paul Sethe in July 1950. For the previous
five years, the Western occupiers had preached the gospel according to Potsdam: de-Nazification, demilitarization, democratization.
Then came the Korean War. Suddenly, rearmament and rehabili-
tation were the watchwords of the day. "Germans will be allowed
to wear the Stahlhelm again," Sethe predicted, "although they never
asked to."[1]

West Germans showed little enthusiasm for rearmament. Over half
the populace opposed the creation of the Bundeswehr in 1950.[2] Many
perceived the need to provide for their own defense, but they were
hesitant to entrust their political leaders with such a grave task so
soon after the recent catastrophe. Further, they resisted the diver-
sion of budgetary resources for military purposes while hunger still
gnawed and the debris of the previous war lay about them. Gov-

ernment leaders encountered a pervasive *ohne mich* (count me out) sentiment among voters and youth, as well as active opposition from some church leaders, labor spokesmen, and left-wing intellectuals.

Germans cherished reunification; it took little imagination to realize that a commitment to the Western alliance jeopardized a settlement with the Soviets. The West German government tried to claim that rearmament offered the West diplomatic leverage over the Soviet Union. But this only concealed the contradiction between rearmament and reunification under the guise of "negotiating from strength." West Germany's options were easily stated, yet the choice was difficult: security at the price of division, or reunification at the risk of security.

The task of convincing the populace to choose security over reunification fell to the chancellor. Adenauer had a dozen variations on one basic speech, designed to drill the dictates of international affairs into the minds of a war-weary populace. "The Western world finds itself in a truly great danger," the chancellor told the Bundestag in late 1950:

> West Germany is a part of the Western world, and due to its geographic situation, it is more exposed to that danger than other lands. At the present time, negotiations with the Soviets for the purpose of normalizing relations can only promise success if the Soviets know that their negotiating partner is strong enough to make aggression risky. This strength can only be maintained if the *Western world* organizes its *defense together.* The Western powers are agreed that this strength will only suffice if Germany also contributes. The German people cannot refuse, not only because it guards us against a lethal danger but also because we have duties to fulfill to Europe and the people of Western civilization.[3]

The Politics of Rearmament, 1950–1953

ADENAUER'S attitude reflected his lifelong view of Germany's role in Europe, and Europe's role in world affairs. As mayor of Cologne in the 1920s, he had devoted himself to Franco-German rapprochement: the cold war buttressed these attitudes. He emerged from political obscurity in 1949 not only as the first West German chancellor but also as one of Europe's foremost proponents of Western integration.[4]

Adenauer was deeply concerned by the expansionist drive of the Soviet Union. His mission was threefold: to create a Western-style democratic state allied to France; to lay the political and economic foundations for cooperation among Western European powers; to make West Germany a respected and equal partner among the Western allies by collaborating closely with the United States.[5] The chancellor's activities in the formative years of the republic displayed his unanimity with the occupying powers. The concord, of course, was partly dictated by necessity; he needed Western economic and political capital in rebuilding his devastated country. But more than simple opportunism motivated Adenauer, who was driven by a deep affinity for Western culture, democratic politics, economic liberalism, and religious tolerance. Kurt Schumacher, the acid-tongued opposition spokesman, labeled him the "Chancellor of the Allies," a biting phrase that dogged him for the rest of his life.[6] But Schumacher obscured Adenauer's tenacious defense of the political rights of West Germans. "All right, then," U.S. High Commissioner John J. McCloy interjected during the 1952 rearmament talks with the chancellor. "This is now the 122nd concession the Allies have made to the Germans."[7] Within a decade, Adenauer had returned his country to a near-equal status among the Western powers.

Adenauer used the future German army as leverage to regain German sovereignty, while pulling his country into the Western alliance. Adenauer had little instinct for military affairs, and he was generally ill informed about nuclear strategy. His statements often displayed an odd mixture of prescience and nonsense. "It has been said that the present Western advantage in Europe lies in the United States' possession of the atomic bomb," he said in an interview in the *New York Times* in August 1950. "However, one must foresee the time when the Russians will consider themselves in a position to retaliate with atomic bombs. When that time comes, as with poison gas, possession of the atomic bombs on either side would be neutralized and once more military power would rest on the size and equipment of the ordinary air and ground forces."[8] He never tired of reiterating the dangers of localized Communist aggression in a divided nation. He was committed to the idea of a large conventional NATO army, and held onto the Lisbon prescriptions long after the Truman era had ended. He failed to perceive—until Admiral Radford and Dulles jolted him out of his slumber in 1956—that the line separating conventional and nuclear weaponry had become blurred, that NATO strategy relied on the early first use of nuclear ordnance, that NATO's "conventional" forces would be nuclear-capable. "I never met a statesman," SACEUR General Lauris Norstad (1956–1962) allegedly said of Adenauer, "who understood so little about strategic issues, even after they had been explained to him."[9]

The chancellor's conservative party—the Christian Democratic Union/Christian Social Union (CDU/CSU)—was forged largely out of the Weimar Catholic Center Party; but it also spanned the gamut of political conservatism, Catholic and Protestant alike. While conservative leaders shared Adenauer's vision of a rehabilitated Germany firmly tied to the West, some party spokesmen balked at the chancellor's preoccupation with Western integration at the expense of reunification. Not until the Korean invasion did most conservatives come to perceive political neutrality as dangerous, reunification as illusory, and military integration as the only feasible way for West Germany to meet its security needs. By 1950, Adenauer had no rivals within his party, and he kept a tight rein over the government during his fourteen years as chancellor. Many a political friend and foe chafed under Adenauer's autocratic rule. His attitude was often so dictatorial, his methods so high-handed, that the unsavory oxymoron, "Chancellor Democracy," has been used to describe his style of leadership.[10]

Gustav Heinemann, Minister of Internal Affairs (1949–1950), came to symbolize resistance to Adenauer's lordly domain over the conservative party. A devout religious leader, he was troubled by the partition of Germany, not the least because it caused a de facto division within the Protestant church. He quit the government in protest against Adenauer's "Security Memorandum" (August 29, 1950), which the chancellor had written without the full consultation and consent of his cabinet. Heinemann founded a rival party, the All-German Peoples' Party (GVP), which promoted the cause of political neutralism. After the GVP fared poorly in the 1953 elections (1.2 percent of the vote), he joined forces with the Social Democrats. For the remainder of the decade, he sought to convince West Germans that nuclear weapons were immoral.[11]

The small Free Democratic Party (FDP), heir to Germany's national-liberal tradition, formed a coalition with the CDU/CSU from 1949 to 1956. FDP leaders vigorously defended German prerogatives vis-a-vis the occupation powers. They led the battle for veterans' rights and the return of German war prisoners. The FDP's most spectacular political coup—accomplished despite strong opposition from Adenauer and the French government—was to force a plebiscite in the Saar, which led to its return to Germany. Most FDP leaders shared Adenauer's Western orientation and his vision of a unified Europe. Along with their CDU/CSU partners, they secured passage of a constitutional amendment, allowing the creation of an army; further, they assisted in the preparation of NATO defense treaties and cosponsored the Bundestag's defense legislation.[12]

Like the CDU/CSU, the liberals had one prominent dissenter—Karl Georg Pfleiderer, a deputy from Baden-Württemberg. In mid-1952 he outlined his own plan for reunification. The Pfleiderer Plan differed little from those proposed by the Western allies in 1946 and 1947, plans that had long ago been shelved. He championed a reunified Germany with an elected parliament and small national army, in good national-liberal tradition. The rest of the plan consciously evoked the Locarno spirit of 1925. A rehabilitated Germany would join the United Nations as a unified country and enter into a European security pact. Though FDP leaders rejected the plan when it was announced, they embraced it when they quit the conservative–liberal coalition in April 1956.[13]

A myriad of forces shaped the attitude of the Social Democratic Party (SPD) toward rearmament. Some of these are best cast in the negative (antimilitarism, anti-Fascism, anti-Communism), others in the positive (pro-democracy, pro-West, pro-nationalism). Kurt Schumacher, the SPD's first postwar chairman, kept himself fully abreast of NATO military strategy. Though Schumacher championed reunification, he posed no fundamental opposition to a new army. He made rearmament conditional upon a full return to political sovereignty, insisting on a Western defense strategy capable of adequately defending Germany in the event of war. His foremost complaint with the NATO defense posture (which at the time still envisaged a pull back to the Pyrenees) was that it did not protect German territory from Soviet tanks.[14]

The differences between Schumacher and Adenauer were more tactical than fundamental. Adenauer, always fearful of Soviet expansionism, utilized the cold war to implant West Germany into the Western defense bulwark. Schumacher thought largely in terms of the superpower stalemate, which he felt offered Germany some maneuverability as yet untested by Adenauer. The chancellor saw NATO as the best avenue for securing Germany's political and strategic interests, whereas Schumacher demanded that NATO formulate a strategy for defending Central Europe as a precondition for German rearmament. Adenauer wanted to tie Germany's political fate to the West; Schumacher was more concerned that the West share Germany's military risks.[15]

After Schumacher's death in 1952, Erich Ollenhauer was appointed party chairman (1953–1963). Like Schumacher, he preferred to postpone indefinitely the thorny defense decision. But like the socialist antimilitarists of the late nineteenth century, he appealed strongly to pacifist feeling within the SPD's rank-and-file, where sentiment against the army ran strong. Under Ollenhauer, the cardinal goal of the SPD's defense politics was the creation of a European-wide security pact. He forged a large domestic coalition against Adenauer's defense policy, holding intraparty factions together under an antirearmament banner.

The German Federation of Trade Unions (Deutscher Gewerkschaftsbund, or DGB) was an umbrella organization for West Germany's sixteen major unions. Under the leadership of Hans Böckler (1949–1951), the DGB remained neutral on the question of rearmament. Böckler shared Adenauer's predilection for a Western alliance; he was willing to support a democratically organized army, so long as the government yielded to some of the DGB's economic demands. "Will the DGB support the creation of a new army?" Adenauer allegedly asked him. "Will the government pass the Metalworkers' codetermination bill?" Böckler reportedly replied. Böckler's pragmatism, however, was not shared by the DGB's six million workers, who looked upon the army with great distrust. His successors—Christian Fette, Walter Freitag, and Willi Richter—followed the lead of the SPD. "The Federal Congress," stated the DGB's 1954 resolution, "rejects a defense contribution as long as all avenues for negotiation have not been explored that might contribute to German unification and mutual understanding among all humans."[16]

The Catholic church, to which 45 percent of West Germans belonged, gave widespread support to Adenauer's rearmament policy. Catholic dissenters, led by Eugen Kogon and Walter Dirks, the editors of the *Frankfurter Hefte,* found themselves isolated, even within Catholic workers' and youth groups.[17] The politics of the Protestant movement was more complicated. Composed of Lutherans and Calvinists from both sides of the Iron Curtain, the Protestant church was the sole remaining all-German institution. The church, therefore, remained officially neutral on all issues that affected East German–West German relations. But many churchmen, including the Bundestag President Eugen Gerstenmaier, were openly in favor of rearmament. Other churchmen, led by the Church Brethren, a group of politically active pacifists, were passionately opposed to the new army. At each of the yearly synods, Protestants wrestled with the moral implications of modern warfare.[18]

During Adenauer's first term in office, the defense debate occurred in two phases. From 1950 to mid-1952, Adenauer encountered a widespread "count me out" attitude among the populace, but little active opposition. No consensus existed among the major political parties, but leaders were favorably disposed toward Western European integration. The Korean War convinced them that some sort of West German military contribution was necessary, even though opinion varied as to how best to approach the problem. Though reunification was the most loudly proclaimed long-range goal, there were few who wished to see their country reunited by the Soviet army.

During the difficult negotiations over the European Defense Community in March 1952, Joseph Stalin proposed a four-power agreement on German reunification. The Stalin note called for a nonaligned German government run by non-Fascist political parties (though there was no mention of free elections). The note also demanded the gradual withdrawal of foreign troops and the neutralization of Germany, allowing only a token local defense force. NATO leaders generally interpreted the Stalin note as propaganda. They pointed out that neutralization proposals had been on the agenda at earlier four-power conferences. These proposals had always faltered over the question of free elections. The Americans and British were inclined to plumb Stalin's intentions, but Adenauer strongly opposed any negotiations with the Soviets: if the Western powers took the note seriously, Germany would face neutralization; if the note was propaganda, the delay might undermine the whole European Defense Community. Whether Stalin's offer was sincere or not, it was a sensational propaganda success for the Soviets; it blatantly appealed to German nationalism. The note electrified West Germany's rearmament foes, and caused a wellspring of discontent over the manner in which Western leaders dealt with German reunification. The chancellor's foreign policy suddenly looked hollow, leaving him vulnerable to the charge of having "missed the opportunity" for reunification.[19]

From mid-1952 to autumn 1953, Adenauer and the CDU/CSU faced more severe domestic criticism than ever before. There were debates within the religious community and discussions among labor leaders over the chancellor's military policies. Factions within the FDP demanded a more forceful reunification policy (it was at this time that Pfleiderer proposed his plan). Ollenhauer's ascendancy in the SPD put the party on a more pacifist course, and, with the 1953 federal elections in sight, in a more polemical mood. Stalin's death (March 1953) convinced the SPD that the Kremlin would seek detente with the West; the Soviet army's intervention in the East German general strike (June 1953) buttressed Adenauer's view that Stalin's successors would not change course. These factors conspired to ensure a lively debate in the Bundestag over the European Defense Community, and led to a highly charged election campaign.

"The German people in their entirety feel allegiance to Western culture and Western freedom," Ollenhauer noted in his Bundestag address, in which he summed up the oppositions' misgivings over the government's defense policy. "Upholding the West is the prerequisite for a meaningful existence in this world. When freedoms are endangered, we must attempt to protect and defend them." But ratification of the European Defense Community, he argued,

> would not heighten the Federal Republic's security. The necessity of the treaties is always justified on the grounds that only a policy of strength can maintain the peace. Let me tell you: from a German point of view, this is the most cowardly argument of all. It has afflicted the sense of reality in the Federal Republic; it has awakened false hopes in the Soviet zone; it has obscured the fact that membership by the Federal Republic in the defense community will further isolate and intimidate the Germans in the Soviet zone for the foreseeable future.[20]

It was a foregone conclusion that the Bundestag would ratify the European Defense Community: 225 CDU/CSU and FDP deputies voted in favor, 165 opposition members against. More importantly, the government followed up this victory with an election sweep in September 1953, planting the chancellor more firmly in the saddle. The CDU/CSU was the only party to raise its electoral percentages; it captured 45.2 percent of the vote, as compared with 31 percent in 1949. The FDP secured 9.5 percent, a drop from its previous 11.9 percent. The SPD received 28.8 percent, a fractional decline (.4 percent) from four years earlier. A host of tiny parties also lost in strength, including the German Party (DP) and the All-German Block (GB/BHE), capturing 3.3 percent and 5.9 percent of the vote respectively. The Communist Party (KPD) dropped from 5.7 percent to 2.2 percent, thereby losing its voice in parliament. The CDU/CSU received 243 Bundestag seats, just short of the absolute majority. The FDP received 48 delegates, while 151 mandates went to the SPD.[21]

Three years elapsed between the Korean War and Bundestag passage of the European Defense Community. Domestic controversy characterized the period; but in the end, the chancellor prevailed over his critics and convinced citizens to choose security with the West over the pursuit of national unity. "No one can now argue any longer that the German people's attitude to the treaties and the defense contribution is negative," Adenauer declared in his opening address to the new legislature. "The 'count me out' standpoint which was of some significance about two years ago and of which the entire opposition, from the Communists to the supporters of Dr. Heinemann, took advantage, has been abandoned and has yielded to a realistic assessment of the German situation."[22]

But the domestic debate was far from over. While the Bundestag deliberated on the European Defense Community and argued the pros and cons of a half-million-strong army, the Eisenhower administration was stoking the fires. The United States no longer conceived the European army as a conventional deterrent against the Eastern bloc's troops; it now viewed them as a "shield" which would temporarily defend Europe until NATO's nuclear "sword" (SAC) was activated. The American New Look aggravated the domestic discord, giving the opposition parties both a strategic grievance against NATO and an issue with immense emotional appeal.

The defense controversy had only begun. West Germans would debate NATO's nuclear policy for the remainder of the decade.

The European New Look, 1953–1956

THE New Look arrived in West Germany by sea, in the form of 280-mm. cannons. Designed for divisional artillery, the cannons could fire both conventional and atomic shells at a range of twenty miles. The Americans had planned to deploy them in mid-1953, but Adenauer delayed shipment until after the September elections. Their presence, he feared, would offer the SPD political ammunition in the battle over Western integration.[23] A few days after his reelection, the cannons made their journey down the Rhine River amidst a fanfare of publicity. A curious sight, massive and cumbersome, they attracted press speculation as to their purpose and capabilities, which the U.S. army only vaguely revealed.[24]

No public discussion or parliamentary debate on the nuclear issue took place in West Germany for the entirety of Adenauer's first term. For many months into the Eisenhower administration, Germans discussed rearmament within the framework of NSC-68 and the Lisbon goals. The advent of tactical nuclear weaponry and the alterations in American strategy went largely unnoticed, even though the New Look had immediate implications for Europe's defense. The arrival of nuclear-capable artillery triggered an abrupt change. At the SPD's request, the Bundestag Defense Committee held several secret sessions on NATO policy. The SPD sought answers from the government on a variety of questions: What was the government's attitude toward the New Look? Was it true that other countries had rejected deployment of nuclear warheads on their soil? Could West Germany, according to existing treaties, decline the atomic artillery? What implications did the atomic cannons have for NATO strategy?[25]

Theodor Blank, chief of Adenauer's nascent defense ministry, sent Adolf Heusinger and Johann Adolf Graf von Kielmansegg to the Bundestag Defense Committee hearings.[26] At the first meeting, Kielmansegg told the committee that the West German government had not been contacted by American or NATO authorities about deployment. He did not know whether other countries had known of the deployment, or if they had rejected the American request. Blank Office personnel had not even seen the cannons until their public unveiling in Mainz a short while before. Kielmansegg did not know the total number expected, or where the Americans had stationed the battalions, though he did suggest the most logical site was the left bank of the Rhine around Kaiserslautern. Preliminary information indicated that six cannons had arrived. West German officials, he asserted, had no authoritative information on the cannon's capabilities; they had gleaned their facts from American and European military journals and press reports. Kielmansegg characterized the weapons as battlefield artillery for front-line use against tanks and troops. As to the broader implications for NATO strategy, he would not venture beyond a vague statement: "In general it must be said that we welcome any strengthening of the defense capability directly on the front, that is, at the point where the first blow is absorbed, and that as far as we can judge, atomic artillery undoubtedly signifies an essential strengthening of that point."[27]

Adolf Heusinger assured the Bundestag Defense Committee that NATO still believed in the value of a conventional defense. He told the committee in July 1954:

The destructive power of large-yield weaponry renders unlikely an all-out war between the two nuclear powers. For that reason the Soviets will play with the thought of small conflagrations, where the risk of nuclear war is not great. If a war between the superpowers nonetheless breaks out, then it is also possible that both sides will renounce the use of nuclear weapons, at least temporarily. Precisely this point is crucial, because now and again one encounters the thought of wanting to base the whole success of an eventual war solely upon nuclear weapons. It is absolutely necessary not to neglect other fields of armaments. The days of a highly modern army and navy are by no means gone.[28]

NATO, Heusinger stated in February 1955, needed a three-tiered defense structure. "We need weapons of deterrence, and these are nuclear warheads. We need a defense capability which can halt enemy troops on the ground. We need reserves which can be assembled in the event of war, in case nuclear weapons are not used at all in the fighting."[29]

Heusinger did not consider West Germany the sole, or even most likely, battlefield for any future war. He argued that the area stretching from the Persian Gulf to the North Pole was a unified war theater, with four potential battle zones: the Caucasus, Central Europe, the Balkans, and Scandinavia. He surmised that the Soviets would bypass Central Europe entirely, and, with a huge pincer-like movement, engulf the continent via Norway and the Balkans. If the Soviets began a nuclear war, they would strike England first, in order to weaken her industrial capacity. He suggested that they would direct a second strike against the European Atlantic harbors in order to knock out the West's supply routes. Only thereafter might West Germany become a target, depending on whether the Soviets felt they could achieve their objectives without recourse to a nuclear attack (see map 3).[30]

SPD leaders were skeptical of Kielmansegg's and Heusinger's analyses. The deployment of atomic cannons in Kaiserslautern suggested that NATO's provisional front line ran along the Rhine River; the weapon's short range implied the atomic shelling of German soil by NATO forces in the event of war. All available evidence indicated that both Soviet and American military planners viewed

MAP 3

Heusinger's Conception of a Soviet Attack (1955)

Finland

Norway

Sweden

Denmark

USSR

Ireland

United
Kingdom

LONDON

Netherlands

BERLIN

Poland

WARSAW

Belgium

BONN

East
Germany

PARIS

Lux.

Rhine River

West
Germany

Czechoslovakia

France

VIENNA

Switz-
erland

Austria

Hungary

Rumania

Italy

Yugoslavia

Bulgaria

Spain

Corsica

ROME

Albania

Sardinia

Greece

Sicily

Algeria

Tunisia

☀ Nuclear attack

+ + + Iron Curtain   ◄▪▪▪▪ Naval forces approach   ◄━━ Ground forces route

Central Europe as the main battlefield. "Please imagine concretely," the SPD's security expert, Fritz Erler, told the Defense Committee, "what it would mean if, with a few shots, a city such as Frankfurt or a part of the Ruhr were destroyed. These weapons are not just directed at the enemy. Their use would also entail massive destruction of the surrounding area where the enemy might happen to be, in this case a part of the Federal Republic."[31]

NATO's 1954 field exercise, "Battle Royal," further aroused the SPD's suspicions. Battle Royal pitted two defending divisions armed with sixteen atomic shells against four conventionally-equipped invading divisions along a fifty-mile line in northern Germany. The maneuver portrayed, in miniature, a Soviet tank assault in Central Europe. The defense "utilized" ten of its sixteen atomic shells in a successful attempt to confine the enemy to a twenty-mile advance. Three of the ten shells "struck" massed enemy divisions; the remaining either missed their targets or struck dispersed troops. Each shell "devastated" a one-mile radius, all ten "contaminated" a thousand square miles of German territory.[32] "I have gained the impression," stated the SPD leader, Carlo Schmid, "that the maneuver's leaders simply considered the area in which they operated as a kind of carving board, as a realm only for soldiers in which one could do as one wished. Apparently they totally ignored the civilian population and its activities during the maneuver. . . . Hasn't anyone done any thinking at all about civilian losses caused by the use of such atomic weapons?"[33]

The SPD's concern was shared by a military critic within the Blank Office, Bogislav von Bonin. As Planning Chief from 1952 to 1953, Bonin had been given the task of creating a twelve-division army within two years, in accordance with the Lisbon goals. He correctly judged the timetable unfeasible, and warned vehemently against an overhasty assemblage of untrained, poorly equipped troops. Bonin assumed the Soviets would concentrate their forces in Central Europe, launching a tank assault through East Germany in an attempt to capture the Ruhr region. West Germany's paramount concern, he argued, should be the creation of a temporary defense force along the Iron Curtain where allied ground force levels were still insufficient to protect German territory. He worked out an "emergency plan" for the defense of German territory by a small volunteer army.

This militia would hold the line with anti-tank weapons until allied reinforcements arrived (see map 4).[34]

After SHAPE forced Bonin's dismissal as Planning Chief in 1953, the Blank Office sent him to France, England, and America, where he discussed NATO strategy with allied authorities. He concluded that the New Look did not meet West Germany's defense requirements. Upon returning to Bonn, he reformulated his plan and presented it to Heusinger. The new Bonin Plan foresaw a volunteer force of 125,000 to 150,000 men, equipped with some eight thousand anti-tank guns, for deployment along the five-hundred-mile inter-German border to a depth of thirty-five miles. Bonin still banked on allied willingness to rescue Germany should its defenses collapse, but he came to stress the need for an autonomous force, backed up by armored battalions and a national reserve. He demanded, moreover, the "creation of a neutral, all-German state lying between the two blocs, upon whose territory there were to be no foreign troops, no foreign air bases, and above all no atomic weapons."[35]

Bonin conveyed his plan to Adelbert Weinstein, the mercurial military correspondent for the *Frankfurter Allgemeine Zeitung*. He also enlisted the support of the Foreign Office, the Ministry of All-German Affairs, and a select group of generals and political leaders. When *Der Spiegel* (a weekly news journal famed for its access to inside information) leaked the plan to the public, the Blank Office dismissed Bonin on the grounds of insubordination.[36]

The Bonin Plan had many alluring features, not least the goal of reintroducing a sharp firebreak between conventional and nuclear defense. By allocating money and equipment for nonnuclear needs, it promised to raise the nuclear threshold and permit, at least in the opening rounds, a conventional defense. It sought to protect local areas conventionally and thereby reduce the risk of nuclear war. But the plan also had some serious shortcomings. It presumed a nonnuclear attack from the East bloc, a Soviet tank assault unsupported by effective air power and infantry. It also presumed NATO's intrinsic willingness to defend German territory. If these assumptions proved false, the Germans were back to square one should the Soviets crush the sparse German troops in the early phase of an all-out war. By reducing the risks to the Soviets, the Bonin Plan made war more tempting; such a war might escalate to the nuclear level

MAP 4

**Bonin's Conception of a Soviet Attack
(1955)**

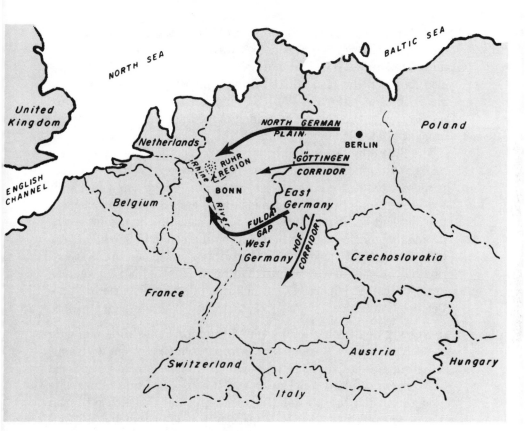

regardless of original intent. "Russia doesn't fear German divisions," Blank explained, "as much as it fears European solidarity and Western strength."[37]

Bonin's solution may have had some military shortcomings, but Bonin's penetrating critique of the New Look lent ammunition to the SPD when the Bundestag debated the Paris Treaties. Negotiated at the Foreign Ministers Conference of October 1954, these treaties superseded the moribund European Defense Community (which the French parliament had refused to ratify the previous August). The new differed from the old in two ways: West Germany was permitted to join NATO, and there was no European army. The treaties also loosened the restrictions on the armaments industry and nuclear facilities, allowing West Germany to engage in aircraft production (with the exception of long-range bombers) and the development of atomic energy plants.

The SPD opposed the Paris Treaties on the grounds that NATO strategy did not offer security for West German citizens. "Nowhere is there a binding clause," Erler stated, "in which one can say in good conscience: here it is unambiguously agreed upon and planned that the Federal Republic will be defended with the goal of maintaining its human existence in the event of a conflict."[38] While CDU/CSU government spokesmen clung to antiquated notions of security, he charged, new weaponry had revolutionized NATO, rendering a successful defense of Central Europe impossible. Erler told the Defense Committee:

> Nobody denies that a strategic conception looks different *with* twelve German divisions than *without* twelve German divisions, but there is still an objection—which we have already discussed in earlier committee debates—and it goes along these lines: one cannot reach Mars *without* a spaceship; but that doesn't mean one can reach Mars *with* a spaceship. One cannot defend Germany *without* twelve German divisions; but that doesn't mean one can actually defend Germany *with* those twelve divisions. That is the problem around which everything here revolves.[39]

The government admitted that NATO was currently only able to defend West German territory at the Rhine. But the chancellor claimed that once it reached full strength, the Bundeswehr would make a forward defense feasible. "As long as we do not belong to NATO," Adenauer told the Bundestag, "we are the European battlefield in any hot war between Soviet Russia and the United States. Once we are in the Atlantic organization our land won't be the battlefield any longer."[40] Heusinger invoked the domino theory to explain the strategic rationale of the Bundeswehr. "The decisive pivotal point is West Germany. If Germany falls, then the whole front from the Persian Gulf to the North Pole breaks asunder. If Germany falls, Denmark stands alone, allowing the East out of the Baltic. One can assume what the consequences would be without sounding pessimistic: Holland could not be held, or, I dare say, France. Then the Mediterranean falls and the enemy reaches Italy."[41]

Adenauer had no trouble winning the battle. The Bundestag ratified the Paris Treaties in February 1955, as did the other NATO members, and they went into effect in May. But his orations on behalf of NATO came back to haunt him a short time later in connection with "Carte blanche" (June 23–28, 1955), a military maneuver designed to test the efficacy of massive retaliation doctrine with NATO tactical air forces. Carte blanche was the largest air exercise, and the first simulated massive nuclear attack, held over Western European territory. Since an East-West axis was unfeasible, NATO pitted the "North" against the "South," using the Main River as the Iron Curtain. The Second Allied Tactical Air Force played the North (or Soviet army), the Fourth Allied Tactical Air Force the South (or NATO). Each side possessed 200 Hiroshima-size "A-bombs," with strategic weaponry in reserve. Nearly 3,000 aircraft from eleven nations flew over 12,000 sorties, "dropping" 335 A-bombs in a battle zone stretching from Italy to Norway.[42]

Carte blanche posed four distinct challenges: whether NATO's tactical air force could withstand a Pearl Harbor-type air attack; whether command and control centers could function after a surprise attack; whether radar and other defensive means blunted the assault; and whether the West could retaliate massively after a first strike.[43] The "war" opened with a pre-dawn strike by the North at the major airfields and command centers in the South. The attacking forces dropped 25 atomic bombs, "destroying" six air bases. The South hastily assembled its forces, retaliating with 24 A-bombs on the aggressor's territory. Wave followed wave until the South had dropped 161 bombs, the North a few more. The exercise entailed the near total "destruction" of the armed forces of both sides; supply lines were obliterated, most soldiers killed, few air bases left functional. The "natural" course of events went more swiftly than expected, for the first two days proved decisive. To give airmen experience in the tactics of nuclear war, the judges extended the battle by "resurrecting" demolished airfields and other targets shortly after they had been "struck."

As measured by the gauge of massive retaliation, Carte blanche was a success: NATO had survived and counterattacked effectively without calling in America's strategic forces; the Western world's deterrent credibility was still intact. "The conclusion which Germans should draw from this exercise," claimed one Blank Office spokesman, "is that through the creation of a German air force we can contribute to an essential increase in NATO's air capabilities and thus further enhance its deterrent power."[44] But many West Germans took cognizance of the fact that two-thirds of the "bombs" had fallen on their territory. Statistics published by *Der Spiegel*—presumably acquired through governmental channels—estimated 1.7 million West Germans "dead," 3.5 million "wounded."[45] Grim as they were, the statistics did not tell the full story. More complete figures would have had to include fallout effects, hunger, and eventual starvation. "We no longer talk of fighting or winning a war," one British commander candidly admitted to reporters. "In an all-out atomic war there would be no winners and no losers and little left to assess."[46] Weinstein summed up the sentiments of many: "The first billions which are earmarked for rearmament would more wisely be spent securing the populace against a nuclear attack. If it is politically impossible to prohibit atomic bombs, then at least the protection of the populace against such warfare ought not to be treated as a negligible factor."[47]

By coincidence, the Bundestag began debating the Volunteers Bill while the Carte blanche exercises were underway, the jets streaking overhead casting an eerie shadow over the proceedings. The Volunteers Bill authorized the creation of a six-thousand-strong skeletal force as a prelude to conscription; it was the first of many defense bills that came before the Bundestag in 1955 and 1956. The Volunteers Bill passed the legislature with little difficulty. But Adenauer's bland assurance about West German security made the government appear perversely indifferent to the Damoclean sword dangling over the nation. The SPD chided the chancellor for having deceived the public into thinking Germany would not become the battle zone in a future war. "Everyone knows that in the age of atomic warfare," Ollenhauer stated in his Bundestag speech, "neither the six thousand volunteers nor the twelve divisions which the Paris Treaties oblige us to recruit, can or will represent any contribution to the security of the Federal Republic's citizens."[48]

The only government spokesman to fare well in the debate was Franz Josef Strauss, Bavaria's young parliamentary pugilist. Strauss was more in tune with the New Look than with his own government. By championing the government's political rationale for a defense contribution without resorting to outdated military arguments, he tackled the SPD on its own turf. "The political meaning of the NATO air maneuver was to demonstrate to the Soviets NATO's capacity to slice off their outstretched atomic arm," he told the Bundestag. "The possible consequences ought not to be minimized. It should not be claimed that the aggressor would not cause horrible carnage. But according to the maneuver's results, the enemy could not win the war any longer, even in its first phase." Herein lay the silver lining of the Carte blanche cloud. "The Soviets must reckon that the strategic retaliatory power of the Americans would force them within a brief period to halt an attack on Central Europe."[49]

Unlike other government leaders, Strauss wasted few words defending the Bundeswehr as a conventional counterweight to Soviet forces. The twelve divisions interested him primarily as a buttress to the nuclear might of the West:

Making this observation does not mean we are pursuing American policy, or that we are racking our brains over the problems faced by U.S. strategists concerning their own security. But we are thankful to be anchored in an integrated security system in which we all sit in the same boat, and in which even the would-be aggressor cannot attack without deadly consequences, so long as our defense foundation cannot be rocked. Unfortunately, that is the thin thread upon which our security hangs. . . . For us it is no longer of importance whether the United States would win the last showdown. For us it is only important that our defense readiness render the first battle hopeless to the aggressor.[50]

Strauss' speech was nothing less than the most forthright defense of massive retaliation doctrine yet heard in the Bundestag. It exposed a fissure among conservative policymakers, ushering in a year-long party battle for control over the defense ministry and strategic policy. While Blank, Heusinger, and Adenauer continued to defend the twelve divisions as a conventional buttress in line with the Truman era, Strauss profiled himself as the Dulles of Germany, the defender of a nuclear deterrent.

The greatest shortcoming in Strauss' argumentation lay in the confusion of grand strategy with local consequences. Nothing in the Carte blanche exercise suggested that all NATO members "sat in the same boat." On the contrary, Germany had comprised the main battlefield, while the other European powers remained largely unaffected and North America unscathed. By robbing the government of its fig-leaf—that a conventionally equipped Bundeswehr would soon rectify this situation—Strauss exposed the chancellor to even more severe criticism from the SPD.

When the Bundestag debated the Universal Military Conscription Bill in mid-1956, the SPD remounted the political offensive. Erler and Helmut Schmidt, the party's young defense expert, had just returned from a fact-finding mission at NATO headquarters. SACEUR General Gruenther had confirmed that the chancellor's justification for a Bundeswehr rested on an illusion. Gruenther told them that a defense against a Soviet assault entailed "an immediate use of nuclear armaments" by the NATO powers. No plans existed to alter strategy once the German contingents were ready: "The Atlantic organization will utilize tactical atomic weapons regardless of whether the half million men are available or not." The U.S. army, moreover, would soon withdraw troops from the continent for budgetary reasons. Finally, NATO planned to train the Bundeswehr in the use of modern weaponry and to equip the troops for a nuclear war.[51] "General Gruenther said first of all: in order to fulfill the plans, 500,000 German soldiers are needed," Erler told the Bundestag in July. "Secondly, he said these 500,000 soldiers are needed in the event of a Soviet invasion, in order to force the Soviets to concentrate their forces, thereby making the use of nuclear warheads possible in the first place. And now you are going to claim that the Atlantic Alliance will move away from the use of nuclear warheads when there are 500,000 German soldiers!"[52]

As if to underscore the SPD's argument, the *New York Times* leaked the Radford Plan in mid-July. According to the report, Admiral Radford, chairman of the U.S. Joint Chiefs of Staff (JCS), planned a 800,000-man reduction in U.S. troop levels over the next four years. The JCS considered an American–Soviet conventional confrontation over Europe unlikely, and the danger of a second Korea in Germany minimal. The U.S. army, therefore, faced a 450,000-man reduction, a large portion of which would come from the divisions stationed in Europe. Though the Radford Plan proved to be more speculation than fact, a message came through loud and clear to the West Germans: the JCS were willing to use Bundeswehr soldiers, not American soldiers, as atomic cannonfodder along the front line.[53]

The Radford Plan acutely embarrassed the chancellor, for it seemed to confirm the SPD's claim that the United States had abandoned the last vestige of a conventional defense of Europe. But more than domestic nightmares robbed the chancellor of his sleep. He considered the Radford Plan a retreat by the Eisenhower administration into "atomic isolationism," a return to a Fortress America mentality.[54] He wrote:

> Regarding the debate unleashed by Americans over the relationship between conventional and nuclear weapons, I would like to stress emphatically that I consider wrong a shift towards emphasis on atomic weapons for the present. . . . I am of the opinion that everything primarily depends upon localizing possible smaller conflicts. For that we need divisions with conventional weapons. Their number must be sufficient to hinder a small conflagration from immediately unleashing an intercontinental rocket war. . . . I unequivocally declare myself against a shift in weaponry in favor of atomic weapons.[55]

In a talk with CIA Director Allan Dulles, the chancellor expressed his concern over Europe's chronic defense weakness. With French troops committed to North Africa, the British reducing their forces on the continent, and the West German army in its infancy, NATO could not withstand American troop reductions. A nuclear buildup, coupled with demobilization, was politically and militarily untenable.[56] Adenauer eventually secured a promise from the Americans to halt their troop withdrawals on the continent. This assuaged his fear of U.S. isolationist trends, aiding him in his political battle with domestic critics.[57] But after winning the battle against Radford's troop reductions, he lost the war against NATO's nuclear strategy. Allan Dulles told him America had allocated its resources in favor of a nuclear defense. Overt Soviet aggression against NATO territory necessitated immediate nuclear retaliation.[58]

The SPD watched with interest as the chancellor swallowed the bitter pill of the New Look. The primary victim of the Radford crisis was Defense Minister Blank, who came under heavy criticism for his alleged incompetence and ignorance. Why had Blank failed to foresee this crisis? Why had the chancellor remained so ill informed? Blank gave a comprehensive account of Bundeswehr planning when the Defense Committee reviewed the defense budget in October 1956. He accused his critics of giving the public the false impression "that we were the last Mohicans who had not yet grasped that America now belonged to the White Man, as if we were the last who had not yet grasped what was happening in the world of weapons technology, military organization, and structure." He told committee members that the New Look had long ago begun to affect West German defense planning. Bundeswehr troops would be trained in the use of so-called "multipurpose" weaponry, capable of taking both nuclear and conventional armaments. "Let me declare to you: neither the defense minister nor any of the Bundeswehr commanders would ever equip a German soldier—or send him into battle— with weaponry inferior to that possessed by other armies or a potential enemy." But he warned strenuously against sole reliance on a nuclear defense, reiterating the defense ministry's long-held support for a flexible conventional and nuclear defense.[59]

But the Bavarian had already won Blank's scalp: in October, Strauss secured the post of defense minister. Strauss immediately gave the Bundeswehr a New Look. He reduced the length of conscription service from eighteen to twelve months, as he had advocated for years. He also reduced the buildup pace. Instead of putting a half million soldiers in uniform by 1958, he promised NATO only 120,000 soldiers by the end of 1957, 350,000 by 1961. Both decisions exacerbated the West's manpower shortage, evoking protests from NATO. But Strauss argued that the changes allowed the Bundeswehr to place a premium on "quality" over "quantity," without overstraining the economy. Since the chancellor had halted American troop withdrawals, Strauss had little incentive to follow Blank's timetable.[60]

In December 1956, the NATO Council gave final trussing to the European New Look (MC-14/2). Policymakers agreed to a twenty-six division front line, composed of twelve West German, five French, five American, and four Benelux contingents, all equipped for nuclear warfare. Northern Europe housed nuclear-capable U.S. airborne divisions. The figures told the tale: NATO had become top-heavy at the nuclear level. "If we want to defend ourselves in the event of a general war, then we must do it with atomic weapons," SACEUR General Norstad told the German Defense Committee in March 1957. "There is no alternative solution."[61]

THE stockpiling of nuclear warheads on West German soil increased the discord between the CDU/CSU and SPD without altering the general contour of the Bundeswehr debate. SPD leaders, long wary of Western defense politics, saw their worst fears confirmed: NATO possessed a carte blanche over Germany's destiny. The CDU/CSU, by contrast, became more and more convinced that West Germany's geographic vulnerability rendered it dependent on a potent nuclear deterrent and Western solidarity.

Similar fissures divided West German military leaders. Bonin revealed that NATO strategy neglected the disproportionate vulnerability among the allies, especially those along the Iron Curtain. But the Bonin Plan was a German reunification proposal dressed in military garb; it called for a small nonnuclear, volunteer army, equal in size to the East German army. Bonin did not offer the West an alternative to the New Look, for he took little cognizance of global strategy or the security of other NATO lands. Nor did his plan offer much hope of defending West Germany along the Iron Curtain. A military force of 150,000, equipped with antitank weapons, was not likely to stop the Soviets, let alone assist NATO in deterring a massive assault. "When Russian troops reach the border," Strauss allegedly said of the Bonin Plan, "they will die of laughter."

Heusinger, taking a larger view of NATO strategy, placed a premium on allied unity, deterrence, and adequate ground forces. He viewed West German security solely as part of an overall Western defense against a Soviet onslaught. But he painted a far rosier picture of Germany's fate in an all-out war than most other strategists, German and non-German alike. Most foresaw a nuclear holocaust in Central Europe as Soviet troops moved westward. Heusinger suggested that the nuclear exchange would take place largely over West Germany's head. Central Europe, he argued, would be the main booty, but not the primary victim, of a superpower confrontation. Heusinger thought in terms of large conventional forces and flexible options open to NATO, in conformity with NSC-68 and MC-14/1. But his analysis stood in crass contradiction to the logic of the New Look, which assumed the West's permanent inferiority in conventional troops. He championed a strategic conception that relied on the West's deterrent capability, but failed to grapple with the obvious fact of West Germany's special vulnerability. Heusinger had added the atom bomb to his mental arsenal without integrating its fallout into his logic.

Until the Radford crisis, the West German government saw tactical nuclear weapons as a temporary expedient rather than a permanent substitute for manpower. The chancellor and his advisers assumed NATO would once again move toward a conventional strategy as Europe built up its ground forces. "The defense of the West here in Europe," Heusinger told the Bundestag Defense Committee in February 1955, "is simply not possible without the German contribution, unless one decides that the whole defense will rest solely on nuclear weaponry." NATO, he added, needed two distinct plans. The first plan would determine strategy if the utilization of nuclear weapons were prohibited, the second if utilization were permitted. When one SPD delegate asked whether there actually *were* two plans at NATO headquarters, Heusinger replied: "They must exist. Were I in the position of responsibility, I would say: I must prepare for both cases."[62]

West German leaders faced the same dilemma as their American counterparts. A defense that highlighted flexibility was ideal (NSC-68, for instance); but due to manpower shortages and budgetary constraints, NATO was unable to enact such a plan. Massive retaliation doctrine (NSC-162/2) made a virtue out of necessity; it maximized the West's deterrent credibility. Nuclear proponents did not neglect conventional strategy entirely ("You don't swat a fly with a cudgel" was Strauss' terse answer to the question of how the West would respond to a limited border dispute along the Iron Curtain);[63] but neither did they see a conventional defense as anything but a prelude to nuclear war.

Like America, West Germany was still struggling with the implications of the New Look. More than any other NATO member, it had to grapple with the fundamental issue of whether the New Look offered peace and security, or whether it had transformed Central Europe into a nuclear no-man's-land in the East–West struggle.

2

THE WAR AT HOME

All paths of Marxism lead to Moscow.

—CDU campaign poster (1953)

Christ did not die for the sins of Karl Marx.
He died for us all.

—Gustav Heinemann (January 1958)

As the 1957 Bundestag election approached, nuclear strategy took its turn, like Persephone in Hades, as a captive of domestic politics. West German leaders, of course, always conducted their battle with an eye to public opinion. Yet until the December 1956 NATO meeting, the nuclear debate rarely broke the confines of political and military circles. NATO strategy remained something of a mystery to most citizens, and the furor over Carte blanche was short-lived (a poll of September 1955 indicated that less than half the populace had heard of the exercise).[1] No event illustrated public passivity better than the much publicized "Paulskirche movement" (January 1955), a brief protest campaign begun at Frankfurt's venerable Saint Paul's Church. It never became a "movement"; it was sensational primarily because SPD leaders, overcoming their misgivings about extraparliamentary agitation, sponsored the event.[2]

Adenauer's popularity dipped in mid-1956, then rose again after the Soviets crushed the Hungarian revolt (October 1956). There was, therefore, little chance that the CDU would look for a new chancellor-candidate, or that the Bundeswehr per se would be an election issue again. The problem for the government lay in the cumulative effect of the debate over NATO strategy. The public airing of defense issues gradually channeled the "count me out" sentiment into an antinuclear crusade. The Radford crisis had hurt the chancellor domestically more than any other event of the previous year, exposing him to ridicule from the SPD. Strauss' year-long battle with Blank for the post of defense minister gave West Germans the impression that Adenauer was losing control over his own cabinet. Strauss' unconcealed desire to acquire as many nuclear weapons as possible for the Bundeswehr awakened fears that the West German government intended to play the role of a great power again.

Three events further threatened to undermine the CDU/CSU's defense policy and weaken the government's prospects for reelection: the FDP's adoption of an antinuclear plank; Adenauer's "artillery statement"; and the "Göttingen 18" controversy.

Election Politics

THE CDU/CSU and FDP had slowly been parting ways since 1953. The chancellor sought the FDP's advice only on rare occasions, when he needed Bundestag votes to secure passage of constitutional amendments. Under Thomas Dehler's leadership (1954–1956), the FDP attacked the chancellor's defense policy and began profiling itself as the party of reunification.

The CDU/CSU–FDP coalition unraveled in the wake of the Geneva summit (July 1955). British Foreign Minister Anthony Eden proposed an all-German government and a Europe-wide security pact, in which Central Europe would be transformed into a buffer zone between East and West.[3] The Eden Plan came to nought, largely because the Kremlin refused to countenance free elections in Germany. The Soviet Union's objective, Eden wrote in his memoirs,

tional agreement on nuclear weapons. Over half (51 percent) opposed a nuclear-capable Bundeswehr. A majority of the populace (56 percent) felt nuclear weapons enhanced the danger for Germany in the event of conflict in Europe.[12] The FDP's clause gave vent to all these concerns: "In order to eliminate the danger of an atomic war between Germans on German soil, we demand general disarmament. In order to avoid prejudicing the ongoing disarmament negotiations, the equipping of the Bundeswehr with nuclear weapons and the production and stockpiling of these weapons on German soil ought not to occur. Care facilities and protection for the civilian populace must also be dealt with at once."[13]

As the FDP took the antinuclear path, a new round of controversy erupted between the two larger parties. On April 2, 1957, the SPD demanded a Bundestag debate over the European New Look (MC-14/2). "What is the Federal Republic doing to reduce the danger of Germany being drawn into a nuclear war?" the SPD resolution queried. "Furthermore what is it considering doing to protect Germans in the Soviet occupation zone from the danger of an atomic conflict?"[14]

The chancellor, interpreting the SPD's challenge as the opening round of the election campaign, held a press conference a few days later to clarify the government's nuclear policy. The question-and-answer session culminated in Adenauer's most famous faux pas, his "artillery statement." The press asked three interrelated questions. Did the government plan to equip the Bundeswehr with atomic weapons, and would it purchase nuclear-capable missiles from the United States? Would the Bundeswehr be equipped with atomic warheads, even if the East German army remained conventionally equipped? Did the presence of nuclear weapons in West Germany, or the possession of tactical warheads by the Bundeswehr, increase the danger of a Soviet nuclear retaliation that would lay waste to Central Europe?[15]

Adenauer told the press that the government planned to equip the Bundeswehr with American-made tactical atomic weapons, assuming that there was no progress in arms control or alterations in NATO policy. "Tactical atomic weapons," he stated, "are basically nothing but the further development of artillery. It goes without saying that, due to such a powerful development in weapons technique (which we unfortunately now have), we cannot dispense with having them for our troops. We must follow suit and have these new types—they are after all practically normal weapons." He noted,

> It is a different matter as regards the large-yield weapons, but as you can see by looking at Britain, this whole development is in flux. Great Britain announced last week that it intends to become a nuclear power which means that we will then have not only the United States and Soviet Union as nuclear powers but Britain too. This whole development is in total flux, and we Germans cannot halt this process. We must adapt to the developments. The only thing we can do, and we are doing it everywhere, is to help assure that a relaxation of tensions somehow and in someway comes to the fore. I am firmly convinced that a renunciation of these weapons—a unilateral decision by this or that country alone not to accede to the developments in modern weapons techniques—signifies no relaxation of tensions.[16]

In making this extended excursion into nuclear strategy, Adenauer reckoned with a rebuttal from the SPD and FDP. He did not, however, expect a response from eighteen of West Germany's famous nuclear physicists, most of whom were affiliated with the government's Ministry of Atomic Affairs. "Tactical weapons are basically nothing but the further development of artillery." "They are after all practically normal weapons." The phrases caught in the throats of the "Göttingen 18" as they read the morning papers. The scientists delivered a response—the "Göttingen Manifesto"—to the press on April 12, 1957:

> Today a tactical nuclear weapon can destroy a smaller city, while an H-bomb can make an area the size of the Ruhr temporarily uninhabitable. Through the dispersion of radioactivity from H-bombs, the entire population of the Federal Republic could probably be extirpated. . . . We believe that a small country like the Federal Republic best guarantees its own safety, and contributes to world peace, by expressly and voluntarily renouncing the possession of nuclear weapons of any sort. Under no circumstances would the undersigned be willing to participate in the production, testing, or use of atomic weapons in any way.[17]

A fortnight later, Albert Schweitzer appealed (via Oslo radio) for an end to nuclear testing. Schweitzer was not only the incarnation of the "good German," he was also an SPD partisan, so his statements were regarded as a veiled attack on West Germany's defense policy.[18]

The Göttingen 18 and Schweitzer appeals offered the press a month's worth of headlines that bridged the New Look controversy to the upcoming parliamentary debate. Nearly all newspapers expressed admiration for the courage and determination of the scientists. Since it was an election year, the temptation for the party press was too great to miss; it was an ideal opportunity for polemical exchange. The CDU/CSU journals, echoing the chancellor, criticized the eighteen "sorcerer's apprentices" for wandering into political waters too deep for them.[19] SPD journals backed the Göttingen scientists fully, and the party used the May Day celebrations a few weeks later to march against the government's position on nuclear weapons.[20]

The Göttingen controversy lent the opposition parties new ammunition in the May 1957 Bundestag debates, as well as the federal election campaign. The SPD demanded a prohibition on nuclear deployment in Central Europe, a non-proliferation treaty, and a test ban. "The time-worn perception," Erler told the Bundestag, "cannot be repeated often enough: in any conflict with these weapons there is no victor and vanquished, there is only vanquished. . . . The balance-of-terror, which today keeps the peace, will continue to exist whether the Bundeswehr receives nuclear warheads or not."[21] The FDP argued that Germany's unique fate as a divided nation necessitated a unique role within NATO that did not prejudice reunification. The liberals also claimed that conventional weapons, not nuclear warheads, offered West Germans their only chance for an effective front-line defense. "Every German now knows," Mende told his party colleagues, "what tactical nuclear weapons mean for the densely-populated Central European realm, namely to turn every city into a thousand-fold Auschwitz. . . . Whoever calls for the utilization of tactical atomic weapons on German soil must know that the consequence is the destruction of what remains ours after World War II."[22]

CDU/CSU leaders (in an effort to defuse the Göttingen 18 and

Schweitzer appeals) denied the existence of any final plans to nuclearize the Bundeswehr. "The federal government has not up to
this moment requested equipping the Bundeswehr with nuclear
weapons," Strauss declared. "Nor have they been offered to us, nor
forced upon us. It is our expressed wish that this eventuality be
taken care of by an arms control agreement."[23] The government also
denied the immediacy of the problem. "When one hears posed the
question of nuclearizing the Bundeswehr," Adenauer said in a major Bundestag address, "one is supposed to believe that tomorrow
or the next day the whole Bundeswehr will be equipped with nuclear weapons from that point on. Not one syllable of this charac-
terization is true."[24] The government linked the New Look to the
fate of the London Disarmament Conference, which was underway
at that time: "The nuclearization of the Bundeswehr is not a matter
for decision at this point. It is closely connected with the success
of arms control negotiations."[25]

The chancellor's strategy of calling the nuclear issue *nicht aktuell*
(not topical, not urgent) worked political wonders. The CDU/CSU
easily defeated the SPD's May Bundestag resolution, then trounced
the SPD and FDP in the September elections. Adenauer sidestepped
nuclear questions, and asked voters instead whether they felt safer
in the bosom of the CDU/CSU and NATO, or whether they wished
to risk their security on the untested hypotheses of the opposition
parties. The September elections, he told voters, "revolve around
the question as to whether Germany and Europe remain Christian
or become Communist," and he predicted "Finis Germaniae" in the
event of an SPD victory.[26] Such rhetoric paid rich dividends. The
conservatives kept the loyalty of the middle classes and the religious vote (including Catholic workers). They also won the loyalty
of a sizable portion of German immigrants (the 9 million expellees
from Eastern Europe and the 3 million refugees from East Germany).
Altogether, the CDU/CSU received 15 million votes, as compared
with 12.4 million in 1953 and 7.4 million in 1949. The percentage
gains were striking: 31 percent (1949), 45.2 percent (1953) and 50.2
percent (1957). For the first time in German electoral history (dating
back to 1871), a single party captured the absolute majority.[27]

The SPD did slightly better than in the past, receiving 9.5 million
votes, a gain of 1.5 million from 1953 and 2.5 million since the first

election. These figures did not translate into large percentage gains, since the number of registered voters had grown considerably over the years, but they nonetheless testified to the steady strength of socialism: 29.2 percent (1949), 28.8 percent (1953) and 31.8 percent (1957). The FDP fared poorly against both larger parties. It gleaned only 2.3 million votes, a loss of 300,000 from the 1953 elections and 500,000 since 1949. In percentage terms, the party dropped from 11.9 percent (1949), to 9.5 percent (1953), to 7.7 percent (1957), an electoral erosion that brought them ever closer to the 5 percent abyss.[28]

The 1958 Bundestag Debates

AS Adenauer entered his newly won electoral paradise, however, he discovered that he was back in the garden of Anthony Eden, with nuclear neutralism tempting the populace. Nuclear "disengagement zones" had entered strategic parlance with the 1955 Geneva summit, and nearly one hundred proposals followed Eden's. The best known disengagement plan, named after Poland's Foreign Minister Adam Rapacki, was introduced at the United Nations on October 2, 1957. Rapacki's initiative was integrally linked with the chancellor's election victory two weeks earlier. He submitted his proposal as a way of reviving the London Disarmament Conference, which had recently ended in failure. The West German government, he claimed, was revanchistic, and a nuclearized NATO would turn Europe into a powder keg. To avoid this danger, Rapacki declared Poland's willingness to prohibit nuclear weapons on its own soil, provided that both German states renounced the production and stockpiling of these weapons on their territory. Rapacki later expanded his proposed zone to include Holland, Belgium, Czechoslovakia, and Hungary, and he linked denuclearization to Soviet and U.S. conventional troop withdrawals on the continent.[29]

The Rapacki Plan had a major attraction to the West: since twothirds of the proposed denuclearized zone encompassed Eastern bloc territory, it heralded less Soviet influence over Eastern Europe. But

Western leaders rejected the proposals, as the "end of Europe" (Adenauer), "complete nonsense" (Paul Henri Spaak), and as "the same futile—and lethal—attempt to crawl back into the cocoon of history" (Dean Achenson).[30] Decisive for them was the Soviet Union's geo-strategic advantage on the European continent. Two days after the Rapacki Plan was announced, moreover, the Soviets launched the first Sputnik satellite, heralding the day of intercontinental missiles. A Soviet withdrawal meant far less than an American withdrawal, since the Soviets were geographically close to Central Europe. If they chose to violate the buffer zone, they could operate along interior lines and mass large armies on their territory before overrolling the continent. NATO's conventional troops in France and Britain would be deprived of maneuvering room, air bases, and geographic depth for a counterattack, thereby turning the whole western European coast into a potential Dunkirk. The West's geo-strategic disadvantage was so obvious that Western leaders felt the implementation of the Rapacki Plan would make Europe the political hostage of the Soviet Union.

Rapacki unveiled his plan at the moment when America was preparing to sell nuclear-capable Matador cruise missiles to West Germany. The timing was, of course, not accidental: it made the German government appear politically intransigent and militarily greedy in the eyes of the opposition, thereby fostering domestic discord. The SPD and FDP, seeing fertile ground for another reunification initiative, demanded a Bundestag debate to discuss the Rapacki Plan. The FDP posed two main questions: Did the federal government intend to promote a nuclear-free zone in Central Europe as a first step toward detente? Was the federal government prepared to accept a militarily thinned-out zone along the lines mentioned by the Pfleiderer and Eden plans?[31] The SPD also introduced a resolution demanding that the Bundeswehr renounce the use of nuclear-capable systems; that the West German government renew its nuclear renunciation pledge; that East Germany remain denuclearized. Like the FDP, the SPD demanded immediate negotiations designed to effect the "withdrawal of foreign troops from a realm designated as atomic-free."[32]

When the Bundestag debated the Rapacki Plan in January 1958, the SPD and FDP conspired to put Dehler and Heinemann back-to-back toward the end of the discussion. This meant that two of the government's bitterest foes (both former cabinet ministers) monopolized nearly three hours of prime-time radio to indulge in a massive attack on the chancellor. Dehler accused Adenauer of doing "everything humanly possible to hinder reunification." The government, he charged, had pursued only the twin goals of U.S. friendship and nonrecognition of East Germany, while neglecting the goal of reunification. He drew a parallel between the Stalin note (March 1952) and the Rapacki Plan: "The chancellor explained to us at that time: it is a diversionary tactic! That is exactly what he is saying today. I trusted him then. . . . I stayed in the government. I am ashamed of myself!"[33]

As befits a man with indistinguishable political and religious beliefs, Heinemann told his countrymen that each German had a Christian duty to work towards reconciliation and reunification, utilizing the plight of the Protestant church to illustrate the unbearable hardship of a divided nation. But Heinemann gave more than a political sermon. He outlined in succinct form the ideas that were to guide him several years later as Federal President (1969–1974) during the detente era:

> Our political task since the last war has been and continues to be a two-fold one, and that means, in other words, that it is a good deal more difficult than the CDU presents it to us. It is a two-fold task, namely to combine a hard, unshakeable "no" to the totalitarian system with a "yes" to being the neighbor of Eastern peoples ruled by totalitarianism. We must manage to combine them, this "no" and this "yes" at one and the same time. I have never criticized the chancellor for seeking a settlement with our Western neighbors. That was imperative. But I have always criticized him—and do so again today—for having combined a Western reconciliation with a new hatred for the East.[34]

Heinemann addressed the nation with deftness and subtlety, Dehler with shrill agitation. Both electrified the audience of millions. In an attempt to recapture the offensive, several government spokesmen went to the podium, but none could undo the damage: the debate ended in the early hours of the morning as a complete rout for the CDU/CSU. Not surprisingly, the government sought revenge.

They called for yet another Bundestag debate in March, devoted to the issue of nuclearizing the Bundeswehr.

The government's 1958 "March Resolution" defended the policies pursued by Adenauer since 1949, while imploring the superpowers to pursue general disarmament and arms control. It expressed satisfaction with West Germany's defense contribution to NATO, citing world Communism as the enemy of peace in Europe and the world. It demanded nuclear weapons for the Bundeswehr in accordance with NATO policy, unless the two superpowers reached a mutually acceptable agreement over Europe in the near future. The resolution stated:

> The Bundestag has determined that the Bundeswehr serves solely for the defense and maintenance of peace, therefore the federal government is charged with the task of continuing to build up a German national defense within the framework of NATO until the time when general disarmament is agreed upon. In keeping with the demands of this defense system, and in view of the armaments of the possible enemy, the armed forces of the Federal Republic must be equipped with the most modern weapons in order that they can undertake the tasks assigned to them by NATO and contribute effectively to maintaining the peace.[35]

The March Resolution was in certain respects a "two-track" proposal (similar to the one passed by NATO in December 1979), linking an arms control initiative with nuclear modernization if no successful negotiations occurred. The 1958 resolution foresaw a NATO buildup of medium-range missiles and tactical weaponry to counteract the planned Soviet deployment of SS-4 and SS-5 missiles. In arguing their case in the Bundestag, government spokesmen never demanded the nuclearization of the Bundeswehr. Instead, they always highlighted the necessity of balanced force reductions, a peace treaty, and a reversal of the arms spiral through negotiations.

While the two-track approach reflected the genuine feelings of the chancellor and his party, the March Resolution nonetheless had a disingenuous aspect: there were no arms control talks underway, nor did Western leaders plan to revivify the moribund London conference. The most recent proposal under discussion in the East, the Rapacki Plan, was unacceptable to the West for military reasons;

and the West's foremost precondition for further negotiations—free elections throughout Germany prior to a settlement over reunification—was unacceptable to the East for political reasons. It was this stalemate in negotiations, coupled with the fear that the Soviets enjoyed a missile lead, that fostered NATO's five-year buildup in the first place. The government reversed the order of events, presenting the March Resolution to the public as a last effort to stave off a nuclear buildup through negotiation: in reality, it originated in the recognition that the superpowers had failed to find a mutually acceptable settlement.

The March Resolution was a pretext to avenge the January debacle, a way of parading nuclear politics once again before the public under circumstances of its own choosing. By chance, it occurred exactly twenty-five years after the Reichstag passed the Enabling Act (March 23, 1933), which had allowed Hitler to destroy the last vestiges of the Weimar Republic. Adenauer's March Resolution was therefore an open invitation to a four-day verbal battle, a challenge to see which side could best besmirch high politics with oratorical excess.

"Let me declare to you," Defense Minister Strauss said in a provocative Bundestag speech,

> that we do not want to equip the German army with tactical nuclear weapons. We do not want to produce these weapons. We are open to a prohibition of nuclear weapons based on controls and a balance of conventional forces. Our allies are free to make such declarations with certainty of German support. But we are not willing to weaken the West's defense potential through our "no," so that an aggressor can hope one day to capture all of Europe without risking a third world war.

The Bundeswehr needed an air defense, Strauss argued, because the Soviet Union was capable of dropping H-bombs on Central Europe with supersonic bombers. West German soldiers, moreover, needed nuclear-capable weapons systems because the Eastern bloc had them. "I do not see why the same weapons in the hands of the Soviets are supposed to be somehow less harmful and dangerous than if they are in our hands, when we are struggling for our very lives and the maintenance of our freedom," he said in summing up the

The Politics of Nuclear Weapons

Vorwärts (August 19, 1955)

The Policy of Strength
CAPTION: ". . . but how do we get back to
unification?"

Meinungs-Austausch

Vorwärts (June 22, 1956)

CAPTION: An Exchange of Opinions
Adenauer: More American than the Americans
Dulles: More European than the Europeans

Hoppla, jetzt kommt Franz Josef Strauß aus Bayern

Vorwärts (November 30, 1956)

The Atomic Danger
CAPTION: "Yippee. Now it's Franz Josef Strauss of Bavaria's turn."

Bald gibt es echte Bömbchen . . .

Vorwärts (May 10, 1957)

Deterrence, Retaliation, Second Strike
CAPTION: [Adenauer to Strauss]: "Soon you'll get
real bombs."

Frankfurter Rundschau (April 16, 1957)

First Lesson: The Atom
CAPTION: A tutorial for the Göttingen
[18] Professors

Die Debatte (May 1957)

Bad: Tactical Atomic Weapons
Worse: H-Bombs
Worst: My Election Defeat
CAPTION: Nuclear Physicist Dr. Dr. Dr. etc. Konrad
Adenauer Gives a Lecture

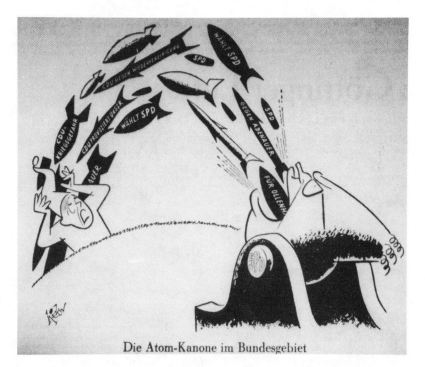

Die Atom-Kanone im Bundesgebiet

Die Zeit (May 9, 1957)

Bundestag Debate, May 1957: Ollenhauer as Cannon
CAPTION: The Atomic Cannons of West Germany

Frankfurter Rundschau (September 17, 1957)

A Citizen Views Adenauer's Election Victories

Ikarus

Zeichnung: Party (Copyright „Rheinischer Merkur").

Ollenhauer: „Können Sie überhaupt meinem Gedankenflug folgen?"

Rheinischer Merkur (January 24, 1958)

Ollenhauer as Icarus
CAPTION: Ollenhauer [to Adenauer]: "Do you catch my drift?"

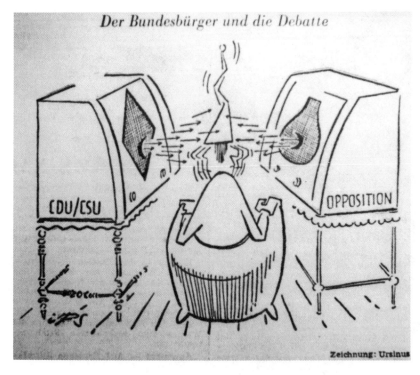

Die Welt (March 24, 1958)

A Citizen Listening to the Debate

Nach dem Kampf . . .

Die Welt (March 27, 1958)

After the Battle: Adenauer as Victor

government's position. "Nuclear weapons are not immoral. A gun in the hand of a murderer is immoral. Effective defense weapons are not immoral. A totalitarian state—which considers the use of force a permissible principle, when its goals can be achieved with little risk—is immoral."[36]

Strauss incited immediate responses. "I sat in my seat and re-flected: today this legislature is struggling over nuclear weapons for the Bundeswehr," Erler commented in a speech that sent the entire CDU/CSU delegation from the chamber in protest. "I was reminded of a frightening time in the past, when a man—whom we all now consider the destroyer of our nation—stood before a huge crowd in our former capital city and said: 'Do you want total war?' "[37] FDP chairman Reinhold Maier (1957–1960) added:

> I would never trust the defense minister even with a field gun. A man who speaks like our defense minister does, such a man will also shoot. That was no longer the speech of a statesman, that was a speech about war. It was nothing but a war-whoop. . . . Today we did not hear the defense minister discussing the arms buildup of the Federal Republic; rather we heard a Reich's war minister. It was a megalomaniacal speech. It was no longer the language of a friendly minded state, it was the language of a highly armed military state.[38]

By the second day, the debate no longer occurred at the podium, as the ordinary rules of plenary session had ceased to function. Deputies exchanged barbs from their seats, interrupted speakers, shouted obscenities, called each other "louts," "headhunters," "Nazis." "As soon as someone has an opinion other than that of the CDU," Wolf-gang Döring of the FDP admonished, "the clamor begins: 'neo-Fas-cist, national Bolshevist, half-Communist, full-Communist, Soviet follower.' We've heard this litany before. . . . But, you see, we at least know something about Communist practitioners. Many of you have only tried to acquaint yourselves with Communism by reading Alfred Rosenberg."[39]

Helmut Schmidt's oratorical excesses had long earned him the unaffectionate nickname, "Schmidt the Loudmouth." On this oc-casion he outdid himself, indulging in ferocious attacks on govern-ment spokesmen. He taunted the CDU/CSU deputies for their blind loyalty to the chancellor: "He thinks for you all; and how logically and how simply and how primitively." He called Strauss a "power-possessed" and "dangerous" man. He told government leaders:

> When you speak of the West, you really mean NATO, nothing but NATO, only NATO. . . . When you speak of NATO unity, you mean nuclear bombs for the Bundeswehr. When you speak of atomic bombs for your Bundeswehr, you really mean military power, nothing but power, and power for its own sake. . . . We say to the German people, in complete and earnest conviction, that the decision to equip both parts of our fatherland with atomic weapons directed against each other will be seen by history as a decision as important and ominous as previously the Enabling Act was for Hitler.[40]

In the end, the government carried the day. CDU/CSU deputies handily passed the March Resolution. Since most FDP deputies abstained, the SPD's defeat appeared even greater. But, in truth, neither side won. Newspapers covered the event in detail, and most speeches could be heard live over radio, but hardly anyone praised the parliamentary pugilists. The Bundestag, wrote Fritz René Allemann of *Die Zeit,* had brought discredit on West Germany. "By your lack of self-control, you have done more damage to democracy in these few days than all the enemies of the constitution from left to right could have accomplished in several years." The whole affair was nothing but the "continuation of the election campaign by cruder means."[41]

The chancellor himself admitted that it had been "a grave mistake" to have called the debate in the first place: it had served no useful purpose in the formation of defense policy, or public opinion.[42]

THE March Resolution ended a five-year parliamentary battle over West Germany's role in NATO's nuclear defense. Perhaps the most striking, and unfortunate, aspect of the debate was its gradual deterioration. The most constructive discussions occurred in the early meetings of the Bundestag Defense Committee. As parliamentarians learned more about military strategy, they seemed increasingly incapable of debating with any degree of detachment or sober reflection. The 1957 election campaign propelled the polemical escalation, but so, paradoxically, did the election results. The CDU/CSU's absolute majority lent an element of irresponsibility to Bundestag affairs. There existed no incentive for the government to seek a political consensus, while the opposition parties, relegated to the sidelines, masked their impotence in angry verbiage.

Still other factors exacerbated the rancor. The West's defense policy underwent continual evolution. Not even the most conscientious Bundestag spokesmen could keep fully abreast of the developments in strategy. The domestic debate, therefore, often digressed to nothing but a struggle over who possessed the most up-to-date information, or who could best interpret the remarks of this or that NATO general. The time lag in implementation bedeviled parliamentarians. For three years, NATO included a nonexistent Bundeswehr in its defense calculus, while waiting for the West Germans to initiate a buildup. The long delay helped create the need for a tactical nuclear alternative. But this solution, by altering the rationale for a Bundeswehr, aggravated the domestic discord and delayed a defense buildup for several more years.

The permutations in strategy all led in one direction: the stockpiling of ever-increasing numbers of nuclear weapons on German soil. The buildup occurred at an astonishing pace, and by the end of the decade, West Germany had become one of the most densely stockpiled nuclear sites in the world. This nuclear top-heaviness reflected the strategic rationale of the New Look, and the triumph of Strauss' priorities over those of Adenauer, Blank, Heusinger, and other military experts. By the time the chancellor reversed himself in late 1956, he had delivered to the opposition all the sound arguments against the New Look. They needed only peruse his remarks on the Radford Plan to gather ammunition against the government. The irony ran deeper. A greater commitment to conventional forces was the best alternative to a top-heavy nuclear deterrent. But the party most opposed to a nuclear defense—the SPD—was also opposed to a conscripted Bundeswehr.

Politically, the chancellor had the upper hand, and he won victory after victory in the Bundestag. The list of parliamentary successes was long: the European Defense Community Treaty (March 1953), the federal elections (September 1953), the Paris Treaties

(February 1955), the Volunteers Bill (June 1955), the Universal Military Conscription Bill (July 1956), the March Resolution (1958). But what eluded the government was a broad consensus, an agreement among the parties over the principles of security policy that would end the discord and divisiveness within the nation. Without it, West Germans could only expect an indefinite cycle of defense debates.

A full two years would elapse before the Bundestag broached matters of foreign and defense policy again, under circumstances more favorable to mutual understanding and cooperation. But it was a circuitous route toward consensus: the opposition parties had no intention of dropping the nuclear issue. Unable to exert influence over NATO policy at the parliamentary level, they explored extraparliamentary channels, giving sustenance and leadership to the burgeoning antinuclear movement. From 1958 to 1960, the nuclear debate took place outside the corridors of government, in the scientific community, in church synods, in trade union congresses, and on the streets.

the politics of peace

INTRODUCTION

WHATEVER the justification—religion, monarchism, free trade, capitalism, nationalism, socialism, imperialism—the Old World has been an arena of battle and slaughter for centuries. Often there was a visible "culprit": Spain's Phillip II, France's Napoleon, Germany's Hitler. Yet the causes of war, rooted deep in human motivation, have defied simple explanation. If most Europeans preferred peace, they nonetheless proved their willingness to die.

Throughout Europe's turbulent history, there have been eloquent protests against the destructiveness and futility of battle. "There is nothing more wicked," the humanist Erasmus said of warfare, "more disastrous, more widely destructive, more deeply tenacious, more loathsome, in a word more unworthy of man, not to say a Christian."[1] But until the past two centuries, such splenetic outbursts were exceptional; peace groups like the English Quakers were rare. Monarchs could count on the nobility's martial spirit, the bishops' blessings, bourgeois pocketbooks, and the blood of commoners.

The Napoleonic wars altered the picture. Peace societies (organized movements for the abolition of war) became a familiar feature of the European political landscape. Twenty-five years of revolution and warfare, conscription and state-of-the-art weaponry, had exposed war's sinews. "It was horrible to see that enormous mass of riddled soldiers," said Barclay de Tolly of the Battle of Borodino.

"French and Russians were cast together, and there were many wounded men who were incapable of moving and lay in that wild chaos intermingled with the bodies of horses and the wreckage of shattered cannon."[2] If governments could mobilize for war, citizens could mobilize for peace.

Germany produced a wide variety of peace ideologues over the centuries: religious conscientious objectors (Mennonites), philosophers of peace (Immanuel Kant), pacifist scientists (Albert Einstein). Germany's middle classes founded grassroots antiwar groups, joined international societies, and spawned some highly esteemed activists (Bertha von Suttner). Most active of all were socialist and trade union leaders: armed with Marxist peace palliatives, a proletariat, and a parliamentary soapbox, they were at the vanguard of the German peace movement by the beginning of the twentieth century.[3]

The antinuclear campaign from 1958 to 1960 was inexorably bound to this antimilitarist tradition, as well as to Germany's recent past. While scientists worked in their laboratories, they recalled how close they had come to producing an A-bomb for Hitler. When churchmen confronted the morality of nuclear war, they remembered the wholesale slaughter of the past two wars. "The training of soldiers today," asserted Hessen-Nassau church president Martin Niemöller, a World War I submarine commander turned militant pacifist, "is nothing but advanced schooling for the professional criminal."[4] As socialists and labor leaders discussed the pros and cons of a conscripted Bundeswehr, they recollected the demise of the Weimar Republic. "We observe with increasing concern and distress," stated the 1954 resolution of the Metalworkers' Union, "that unrepentant neo-Fascists have maneuvered themselves into important posts in the state and economy of the Federal Republic."[5] The government must "halt all attempts by reactionary and nationalistic elements to exploit rearmament for their own political and military goals," stated the 1956 resolution of the DGB, which represented the country's six million organized workers. "It must hinder the creation of a state within a state—similar to the days of the Weimar Republic—by exerting effective parliamentary control over the Bundeswehr."[6]

Despite all the homiletics about the "dawning" of the nuclear age, another issue tormented the popular imagination: who had been responsible for Germany's Götterdämmerung. The credibility of all German political leaders—conservatives, liberals, socialists, and Communists alike—rested on their ability to prove that they had opposed Hitler in the 1920s, that they believed in democracy, and that they could best guarantee peace in Central Europe.

3

THE GÖTTINGEN REPUBLIC:
THE NUCLEAR PHYSICS COMMUNITY

> What for, I ask you, do we *need* the bomb? It only
> gives the military a bad name. The scientists have
> stolen the victory from us—sitting at home
> on their butts—they . . . the winners!
>
> —Rolf Hochhuth,
> *Soldiers: An Obituary for Geneva* (1968)

SHORTLY before Hitler's defeat, a group of German nuclear physicists were strolling down Unter den Linden. This famous Berlin avenue had been nicknamed "Unter den Laternen" ever since
the Fascists replaced the linden trees with lamp-posts. "I have
counted the lamps," one said. "They would just suffice to hang all
of Hitler's regional and district leaders on them." "All right," a col-
league replied, "but after the next war, it is the physicists who will
be hanged."[1]

German scientists, both inside and outside their homeland, felt
keenly responsible for the production of the world's first fission bomb.
Albert Einstein, Werner Heisenberg, Max Born, and others at
Göttingen University had revolutionized modern physics with their
theories of relativity and quantum mechanics. Fission research done

in Berlin under Otto Hahn during the interwar years aided American and British research teams in developing A-bombs. Few scientists doubted Hitler's willingness to exploit nuclear technology; fewer still doubted the capacity of German physicists to unlock the secrets. It was Einstein, a pacifist by conviction, who gave impetus to the American bomb project, not the least because of his concern over political conditions in the Third Reich. "I understand that Germany has actually stopped the sale of uranium from the Czechoslovakian mines which she has taken over," Einstein wrote to President Franklin D. Roosevelt in his famous letter of 1939, urging the creation of the Manhattan Project. "That she should have taken such early action might perhaps be understood on the ground that the son of the German Under-Secretary of State, von Weizsäcker, is attached to the Kaiser Wilhelm Institute in Berlin, where some of the American work on uranium is now being repeated."[2]

The Nazi government was in the A-bomb race, but it is clear in retrospect that emigré scientists and Anglo-American political authorities greatly overestimated the pace. Carl-Friedrich von Weizsäcker, the son referred to in Einstein's letter, made no effort to win over his prominent father, Ernst von Weizsäcker, to the idea of an atomic arsenal. The German scientific community, moreover, had grown sterile since 1933: "Aryan physics" killed the spirit of independent research, and the Gestapo drove many fertile scientists into exile (Einstein, Leo Szilard, Edward Teller, Hans Bethe, among them). Nuclear research continued to 1945, but the Germans lagged far behind the Americans: Heisenberg's group of theoreticians never deduced the feasibility of a chain reaction; Walther Bothe's group of experimentalists incorrectly hypothesized heavy water as the ideal moderator for a uranium pile. Wartime scarcities, budget constraints, and allied bombing raids brought research to a virtual standstill. By war's end, the Germans had yet to build an adequate nuclear reactor, let alone a prototype bomb.[3]

The leaders of Germany's nuclear project—Gerlach, Hahn, Weizsäcker, Heisenberg—first learned that America had dropped an A-bomb on Japan while interned at a British military camp. The news caught them completely by surprise. Gerlach, who had served as the Reich's Plenipotentiary for Nuclear Physics, was crestfallen that German research had fallen so far behind that of the Anglo-

Americans. Hahn, whose fission research had made the bomb possible, felt personally responsible for the deaths at Hiroshima. "I believe the reason why we didn't do it was that all the physicists didn't want to do it, on principle," Weizsäcker asserted. "If we had all *wanted* Germany to win the war, we could have succeeded." Heisenberg, the skeptic, thought the announcement was wartime propaganda.[4] But the truth soon sank in: nuclear weapons had not awaited "the next war."

No German physicists were hanged, on lamp-posts or elsewhere. After a short imprisonment, most of them took up residency in the Western sectors of Germany, where they resumed teaching at universities. For several years, the occupying authorities curtailed all nuclear research; but as West Germany rebuilt its industry and demonstrated its commitment to the Western world, this ban was partially lifted. The 1952 European Defense Community allowed limited research on nuclear reactors, while the 1955 Paris Treaties removed most hindrances to the nonmilitary exploitation of nuclear energy. With the establishment of the Ministry of Atomic Affairs in 1955, full-scale nuclear research began anew.[5] At the same time, the German Physics Society (to which most nuclear physicists belonged) expressed its unanimous support for the "Pugwash movement"—an organization of scientists, begun by Bertrand Russell and Einstein, which lobbied for the abolition of nuclear weapons. "In view of the fact that in any future world war nuclear weapons will certainly be employed," stated the Russell–Einstein Manifesto, "and that such weapons threaten the continued existence of mankind, we urge the Governments of the world to realize, and to acknowledge publicly, that their purpose cannot be furthered by a world war, and we urge them, consequently, to find peaceful means for the settlement of all matters of dispute between them."[6]

The Paris Treaties foreclosed a West German nuclear defense industry, and precluded nuclear defense research. Given Adenauer's nonnuclear pledge, the dearth of research facilities, and the pro-Pugwash sentiment among scientists, there seemed little prospect West Germany would join the nuclear club anytime in the near future. But West Germany's physicists soon came to realize that one prominent government leader—Franz Josef Strauss—wanted to follow the path of Britain and France. Strauss served as Minister of

Atomic Affairs from 1955 to 1956, before becoming Minister of Defense.

Strauss and the Scientists

STRAUSS was a gregarious politician, whose administrative abilities won the admiration of the nuclear scientists: during his one-year tenure as Atomic Minister, Germany began recovering quickly from its decade-long technological lag. But he also awakened the physicists' distrust "through his indiscreet remarks made after an evening glass of wine," in which he divulged his "desire to have nuclear weapons."[7] When Strauss tempted Heisenberg's research team with a joint German–French nuclear defense project, distrust turned to active opposition. "What could we do," Weizsäcker asked his colleagues, "if the Bundeswehr first got possession only of the launching ramps for nuclear warheads and then sometime later the bombs and grenades themselves via foreign production?" How could the scientists thwart the step-by-step process by which their country might acquire and ultimately produce its own warheads?[8]

The physicists all agreed: "once was enough."[9] None of them wanted Germany to play great power politics again, none wished to resume nuclear defense research. They wrote Strauss, asking him to "declare publicly that the federal government was not thinking of producing or stationing atomic warheads" in Germany. If Strauss refused, the group threatened to take its letter to the press.[10] Strauss met with the group in January 1957. To the assurance of the physicists, Strauss "rejected a German atomic armament under national sovereignty." To their dismay, he "considered a massive atomic armament of the European NATO forces a necessity." To their surprise, he unveiled his grand design for defending the continent: "a large supranational Western European atomic defense, in case the Americans withdraw someday from Europe."[11] Central Europe could not be defended with "bow and arrow" technology.[12]

The physicists, who had marshalled all their arguments against a national atomic policy, were caught off guard. They differed among themselves as to whether to support or oppose a supranational European nuclear force. Under these circumstances, Strauss wrested a gentlemen's agreement from the group not to publish its letter.[13] But a number of coinciding events unraveled this agreement in early April 1957: American medium-range missiles arrived for deployment in West Germany; Strauss visited France to win acceptance for a joint German–French nuclear research project; Adenauer delivered his "artillery speech." Weizsäcker contacted his colleagues anew. Were they now willing to go public? He reworked the letter to Strauss and brought it to the German Physics Society meeting in Bad Nauheim on April 11. By next day, he had collected eighteen signatures. It was a *Who's Who* of Germany's famed scientists: Fritz Bopp, Max Born, Rudolf Fleischmann, Walter Gerlach, Otto Hahn, Otto Hazel, Werner Heisenberg, Hans Kopfermann, Max von Laue, Heinz Maier-Leibnitz, Josef Mattauch, Friedrich-Adolf Paneth, Wolfgang Paul, Wolfgang Riezler, Fritz Strassmann, Wilhelm Walcher, Carl-Friedrich von Weizsäcker, and Karl Wirtz (see document 1).[14]

The first part of the Göttingen 18 text addressed Adenauer's intemperate remarks during his "artillery" interview. NATO relied primarily on large-yield weaponry, they noted; the utilization of even a fraction of this arsenal spelled doom for Europe. They also felt the chancellor had underestimated the lethalness of tactical warheads; any bomb with a destructive capability equal to the one dropped on Hiroshima could not be frivolously labeled "artillery." The second half of the manifesto addressed the scientists' role in political matters. They expressed their awareness that they were straying into partisan waters, and voiced their fear that the manifesto might be misused in the coming election campaign. They tried to make clear that they were speaking as concerned scientists, committed to the defense of the West against Communism.

Oddly, the manifesto never addressed Strauss' plans for a European-wide nuclear research project. While the Göttingen scientists pledged "not to participate in the production, testing, or use of atomic weapons in any way," they left the public in the dark as to why the issue was being broached at all. Who was asking West German physicists to research and develop nuclear weapons? Did the group have evidence that the government was planning to violate its nonnuclear pledge? Equally perplexing, the physicists were unaware of the new low-yield weaponry. In making his "artillery" statement, Adenauer was referring to sub-kiloton devices, not the Hiroshima-size weapons (15 kt.) of the past. Had nobody informed German physicists of the new generation of weapons under deployment?[15] Equally surprising was the physicists' claim that they were addressing the public as scientists, not politicians. They gave a political prescription for West Germany's health: "We believe that a small country like the Federal Republic best guarantees its own safety and contributes to world peace by expressly and voluntarily renouncing the possession of nuclear weapons of any sort." Did the scientists naively believe that their pronouncement would not fuel political fires, especially in an election year?[16] The manifesto, moreover, was misconstrued by East German authorities to discomfit the chancellor and make it appear to the world that the Göttingen scientists were rebelling against a resurgence of German militarism. "In view of the lessons of two world wars," a manifesto signed by fourteen East German nuclear physicists stated, "we have been watching with increasing concern over the past several months the developments in West Germany concerning the stationing of atomic warheads and the nuclearization of the Bundeswehr."[17]

The Göttingen Manifesto was a testament to the scientists' sense of ethical responsibility, a distillation of the year's events, a proof that the German scientific community was still not up-to-date on nuclear matters. It did not have the lofty tone of the Russell–Einstein appeal, nor the far-reaching tone of many of the congratulatory letters, manifestos, and declarations of support that the Göttingen scientists received in its wake. The discussion surrounding the controversy (which lasted nearly a year) was emotional, propagandistic, and factually distorted. Contrary to what much of the populace came to believe, the Göttingen Manifesto made no call for the immediate withdrawal of American troops, no wholesale condemnation of nuclear weapons, no demand for Germany's unification and neutralization, and no demand for a nuclear-free zone in Central Europe. The Göttingen Manifesto struck a nerve in the nation's body politic, but one that controlled the heart more than the brain.

Privately, Adenauer bluntly expressed bitterness over the scientists' declaration. He told CDU leaders:

The SPD is agitating against atomic weapons for the Bundeswehr. Whether NATO thereby goes overboard is fully irrelevant to them—they have opposed NATO from the outset. It makes no sense to say that someone should take the first step. The eighteen nuclear physicists have said the same thing: Germany should begin. That is the silliest thing I have ever heard because it changes absolutely nothing. But that will be the SPD tactic and we must adjust to that. Please don't repeat what I have just said to the scientists themselves.[18]

Publicly, the chancellor approached the scientists (to use his phrase) "with flowers."[19] He acknowledged their world-renowned scientific capacities, their civic concern, their ethical considera-

DOCUMENT 1

The Göttingen Manifesto of April 1957

The plans to nuclearize the Bundeswehr have aroused great concern among the undersigned atomic researchers. Many of them already expressed their misgivings several months ago to the responsible ministry. Lately the debate over this question has become widespread. The undersigned therefore feel obliged to highlight publicly several facts which are known to specialists but which seem insufficiently clear to the larger public.

Tactical nuclear weapons have the destructive power of normal nuclear bombs. The term "tactical" designates that they will not solely be used against human settlements but also against troops in ground fighting. Each tactical atomic warhead today has the equivalent effect of the one that destroyed Hiroshima. Since there are presently a larger number of tactical warheads available than earlier, the net destructive effect would be far greater. These bombs are "small" only in comparison to the more recently developed "strategic" bombs, above all the H-bombs.

There is no known natural limit to the genocidal destructive potential of strategic atomic weapons. Today a tactical nuclear weapon can destroy a smaller city, while an H-bomb can make an area the size of the Ruhr temporarily uninhabitable. Through the dispersion of radioactivity from H-bombs, the entire population of the Federal Republic could probably be extirpated. We know of no technical possibility of protecting large population centers from this danger. We know how difficult it is to draw the

tions; he only regretted the "predominantly political character" of the manifesto, and questioned their competence in military strategy.[20] Government leaders met with the Göttingen scientists shortly after the manifesto's publication. The chancellor began the meeting with a plea for the "unanimity of the West." General Heusinger followed with an analysis of world power politics, then General Speidel explained the principles of nuclear deterrence. Finally, Strauss reiterated that the Federal Republic was not striving for direct control over atomic warheads. It became apparent, however, that the two groups were talking at cross-purposes. Adenauer and his advisers were concerned with America's global strategy, Western solidarity, and cold war politics—not to mention the federal election and public opinion polls. The physicists were animated by their ethical sense

political consequences from these facts. Since we are not politicians, our qualifications to do so will be a matter of dispute. But since our activity concerns pure science as well as its application, and since we introduce many young people to our subject, we feel the burden of responsibility for the possible consequences of our activity. Therefore we cannot be silent on all political questions. We profess our allegiance to the freedom that is today safeguarded by the Western world against Communism. We do not deny that the mutual fear of thermonuclear bombs makes an essential contribution both to the maintenance of peace in the whole world and to freedom in a part of the world. But we view this mode of protecting peace and freedom as unreliable in the long run, and we consider the danger in the case of its breakdown to be lethal.

We do not feel competent to make suggestions concerning superpower politics. We believe that a small country like the Federal Republic best guarantees its own safety and contributes to world peace by expressly and voluntarily renouncing the possession of nuclear weapons of any sort. Under no circumstances would the undersigned be willing to participate in the production, testing, or use of atomic weapons in any way.

At the same time we stress that it is of utmost importance to promote in every way the peaceful use of atomic energy, and we intend to continue this task as in the past.

and their concern over Strauss' ultimate intentions; they opposed nuclear proliferation and hoped to keep Germany out of the nuclear maelstrom.[21] Adenauer prepared a joint communique for the press, highlighting the areas of agreement; but the physicists amended it before its release. "The nuclear physicists who took part in the discussion would like to make clear that their primary goal was not just to keep the Federal Republic out of the global calamity," they added to the communique. "They meant to take an initiative that would help protect the world from this threatening catastrophe. They felt that it was imperative to begin in the country of their citizenship."[22]

The Göttingen Manifesto: Three Critiques

THE political fallout from the Göttingen controversy never forced the West German government to reevaluate its defense policy. But since the manifesto was published at the beginning of the federal election campaign, the chancellor wanted to blunt its impact upon the public. He chose Pascual Jordan, Karl Jaspers, and Helmut Thielicke (among others) for an "enlightenment campaign" against the Göttingen scientists.[23]

Pascual Jordan was a theoretical physicist. In the 1930s his writings had a distinct Aryan flavor; after the war he cultivated a love of freedom, democracy, and the CDU.[24] Adenauer selected him because he was one of the few German scientists willing to attack the Göttingen group. He was, however, not an ideal choice for spreading enlightenment. His first rumination on the nuclear age, *Der gescheiterte Aufstand* (1956), combined social Darwinism and science fiction. Jordan felt the chances for disarmament and a world government would remain slim for the next millennium or two, roughly until the year A.D. 4000. Scientists, he felt, ought to quit wasting valuable research time on dire public warnings (like the Russell–Einstein Manifesto) and return instead to their laboratories. To avoid the immediate risk of extinction, Jordan advocated the construction of huge underground cities, where humans could live in the event of war "for five years at a time under the earth without difficulty and inconvenience until the atomic stink outside subsided." Nuclear warfare, he admitted, would leave a mega-trail of corpses in its wake; but he viewed radiation poisoning as nature's latest answer to the "threatening overpopulation of the earth," replacing plague and natural catastrophe as God's curse upon mankind. Jumping a few centuries into the future, Jordan conjured powerful gangs blackmailing innocent countries and threatening vast areas with extinction; he foresaw putsches, revolutions, and civil wars fought with nuclear weaponry. Despite these catastrophes, he asserted, "millions will be living on Mars" by A.D. 3000. By A.D. 3500 galactic overpopulation would again beset our genetically altered species.[25]

Jordan's cloak-and-dagger political hysteria matched his overactive imagination. Jordan's world was peopled with "countless paid agents" commissioned by the Kremlin to "prepare the public with propaganda" for a takeover. These agents had created an "atomic panic" in West Germany, weakening NATO. The unwitting helpers of these agents were "intellectuals and pacifists" whose antinuclear manifestos proclaimed the West's "collective suicide."[26] For all his powers of fantasy, Jordan's own political horizons did not extend much beyond the mundane world of CDU/CSU politics. Communism threatened the free world, the Soviet Union threatened West Germany; the Western world needed NATO, and NATO needed nuclear weapons; tactical atomic weapons were harmless, strategic weapons were necessary as a deterrent. These were the stock phrases of the CDU/CSU, and Jordan as well. But Jordan's proclivity for exaggeration, his hysterical effusions, and his excursions into the fantastic gave his writings the air of self-caricature and psychological projection. He criticized the Göttingen scientists for their dilettantism: "A surgeon, a pianist, or a prominent soccer player has exactly the same factual competence to judge this question as a nuclear physicist, namely none at all."[27] Yet he himself was a scientist with little background in politics; apparently the degree to which he injected his own political venom into the matter never occurred to him. He censured the Göttingen Manifesto as an "extreme, one-sided judgment of the problem brought before the public in sensational form."[28] Ironically, the rebuke captured Jordan's own style in a nutshell.

The critique of the Göttingen physicists by the internationally renowned philosopher Karl Jaspers had a more profound impact on the scientific community. In 1956 Jaspers gave a radio lecture, "The Bomb and the Future of Mankind." When he expanded that lecture into a book, he used the opportunity to appraise the Göttingen Manifesto and its impact on German society.[29] Jaspers combined a democratic-liberal political philosophy with a strong humanist appeal. "The atom bomb, as the problem of mankind's very existence," he wrote, "is equalled by only one other problem: the threat of totalitarian rule (not simply dictatorship, Marxism, or racial theory), with its terroristic structure that obliterates all liberty and human dignity. By one, we lose life; by the other a life worth living."[30]

Jaspers felt that the Western world was forced to live in the shadow of the mushroom cloud or permit the triumph of totalitarianism; to risk the destruction of mankind or abandon the principle of freedom. "Totalitarianism and freedom are conflicting principles," Jaspers noted, "Russia and the West are conflicting historical realities. In the long run, the two conflicts need not coincide. Nations are not principles. The Russians, like the Germans, have potentials other than totalitarianism. Both principles—of political freedom and totalitarianism—undergo changes and can appear as functions of the deeper, enduring substance of great nations. The Russians are not one with totalitarianism."[31] Jaspers saw the creation of a world government as the inevitable long-range solution, but the principle of freedom would first have to triumph over totalitarianism.

Jaspers approved of the Göttingen 18's statement on nuclear deterrence ("we view this mode of protecting peace and freedom as unreliable in the long run, and we consider the danger in the case of its breakdown to be lethal").[32] Jaspers also saw in the manifesto a "nonpartisan spirit of the reflective consciousness," and an intelligent willingness to "renounce great power politics."[33] He felt the scientists had done the West German public a great service by pricking the political conscience and sparking the first widespread discussion of the nuclear peril. Yet he was otherwise critical of the Göttingen Manifesto, arguing that it was neither ethically nor politically defensible. He considered contradictory the scientists' willingness to research atomic energy while refusing to involve themselves in weapons research. Had they refused to perform any atomic research, their standpoint would make sense; but since all nuclear research could be exploited for industrial and defense purposes, the willingness to engage in one aspect of that research meant implicit acceptance of the other. It was ethically irresponsible on the part of the physicists, he noted, to lay the sole responsibility for nuclear weapons on Edward Teller and others who were directly engaged in defense projects. Jaspers considered it frivolous to profess a belief in freedom, yet refuse to participate in the West's defense, to acknowledge the need for nuclear deterrence, yet not be willing to engage in nuclear defense research.[34]

The Göttingen 18 physicists, Jaspers believed, had confused their authority as scientists with their authority as political analysts. All political and military considerations, he stated, must be made with an eye to the worldwide ideological struggle. Western Europe had a choice between the "free hegemonial" power of America, and the "unfree satellite relationship" of the Soviet Union:[35]

> The discussions of German reunification provide an example (hard on us Germans!) of Russian totalitarian policy, both as it is and as the West widely misunderstands it. We hear that Germany could only be reunited if Central Europe were so ordered as to threaten neither Russia nor the West. This is quite true, but also pointless—for there can be no such order, unless the two great powers should cease to appear menacing to each other. While they are in conflict, any change in the confines of power will threaten both. A demilitarized zone, an atom-free zone, a neutral zone, a vacuum—both sides would judge all these only by the dangers and advantages they would entail for each.[36]

The Göttingen Manifesto, Jaspers concluded, had to be judged by its own criteria: would a nonnuclear Bundeswehr promote world peace and the preservation of Western values, or undermine the West's ability to resist Soviet expansionism? Jaspers felt a one-sided renunciation would simply weaken NATO, without bringing the Russians a step closer to the negotiating table. Even the vast destructive power of nuclear warheads was not an argument for unilateral renunciation. A renunciation would not promote a new political ethos based on the principle of freedom, nor permit West Germany to escape the consequences of nuclear war. Furthermore, Jaspers saw in the manifesto an unhealthy dose of the "count me out" nostrum, and a "tendency toward neutralism." Were this attitude confined to the eighteen scientists themselves or their work as atomic physicists, he added, their position would be ethically responsible because it would touch on the inviolability of the conscience. But the scientists had appealed to the public, thereby turning a personal ethical decision into a political decision affecting the lives of millions of fellow citizens. The political direction they chose, Jaspers concluded, promoted neither Germany's security nor world peace.[37]

Unlike Jaspers, Helmut Thielicke was more concerned with the scientists' ethical message than their politics. A Lutheran theologian and popular Hamburg preacher, Thielicke was editor of the *Zeitschrift für Evangelische Ethik*. He was a conservative churchman, who distrusted involvement by political outsiders in state affairs. He seemed an ideal candidate for Adenauer's campaign against the Göttingen scientists. The chancellor asked him to give the keynote address at the 1957 CDU party convention, with the scientists' manifesto as his topic.[38]

Thielicke used this opportunity to go far beyond the Göttingen appeal, conspicuously choosing to address all the major parties, not just the CDU delegates. The starting point for his reflections was the intertwined relationship between politics and ethics. Political outsiders often cultivated the "pathos of the absolute," he noted, only to discover later that political decisions were not made in a vacuum. He found Einstein's dilemma in this regard particularly instructive. As scientist and citizen, Einstein was a lifelong pacifist. In 1939, however, weighed down by a sense of responsibility for the fate of millions, he recommended to Roosevelt the construction of the atomic bomb, it seeming a lesser evil than Nazi victory. Similarly, the scientists who wanted to halt the arms spiral in the years from 1945 to 1949 were gradually confronted (in light of the Soviet Union's nuclear capacity) with a political-ethical dilemma: could they assume the ethical responsibility for the West becoming the "defenseless object of Eastern despotism?"[39] The political situation under which mankind lives today, Thielicke stressed, was the division of the world into two massive power blocs. Given the enormous distrust and fear on both sides, the only guarantee for peace was a matched strength. Under these unstable conditions, any political concession (by Eastern or Western statesmen) which put one side at the mercy of the other would be an ethically unconscionable act. Unlike Jordan and Jaspers, Thielicke did not feel competent to judge whether a renunciation by West Germany would tip the scale in favor of the East; the decision belonged to political authorities.[40]

Yet if Adenauer thought he had found an ideal court theologian and defender of the CDU faith against the Göttingen heresy, he soon discovered otherwise. What appeared as the heart of Thielicke's speech was prelude to a different message. The Göttingen Manifesto, he told the CDU audience "had made a lasting impression" on him. In particular, the scientists' argument that the government ought to make a move in the direction of avoiding a chain-reaction of nuclear proliferation was an eloquent expression of the Christian ethic of "taking the first step." What impressed Thielicke deeply was their claim that diplomatic and military calculations were not the only factors involved in a political decision of such magnitude. Ethical acts contributed to the decision-making process as well: "an act of the conscience spawns new political realities; it sets a spark and thereby alters the existing circumstances."[41]

Not the physicists' political dilettantism, but the political parties' ethical bankruptcy alarmed Thielicke. He told his audience:

It is a very serious symptom of decrepitude and political idolatry when in many quarters—alas even political circles—an appeal of the conscience can no longer be heard or heeded for what it is, but instead is comprehended in political terms or exploited for political purposes. The press of one party writes (in so many words) that the eighteen nuclear physicists are the tools of a dubious political realm. The press of another party apparently has nothing better to do than feed the machine of its election campaign, in other words to transform the gold of conscience into partisan baubles. If that is the case, I can only say how sad it is. It does not serve to legitimate the inner credibility of those politicians.[42]

Thielicke criticized the West German government for ignoring the essential questions: Had the scientists acted in the name of their conscience against the unconscionable? What combination of conscience and expert judgment went into their decision? "Instead of turning up one's nose at the dubious nature of some of their arguments," he stated,

> one ought simply to rejoice that leading scientists left the ghetto of their laboratories and study rooms. That shows how seriously they understand the interwoven nature of their research with social, economic, and political matters, even if they do so with political arguments that are perhaps disputable. Not only have they shown a so-called sense of "scientific responsibility," but they have also proclaimed the responsibility of scientists as a whole, and I therefore consider their appeal as nothing less than an ethical sensation.[43]

Thielicke's speech was easily the most eloquent analysis of the Göttingen Manifesto, the only one to give adequate expression to the diverse political and ethical factors that went into the scientists' decision. At the time it was delivered, however, it was not seen as a middle way between the two fronts, or as a plea for moderation and reflection in the midst of an increasingly emotion-laden debate. Adenauer jumped to his feet after the speech, and reiterated only those aspects of Thielicke's address favorable to the government's politics. The response of Ernst Wolf, one of Thielicke's church colleagues, was not much different; he dismissed Thielicke as an Adenauer lackey.[44] The reactions (which were echoed in the media) proved the aptness of Thielicke's message: it had become increasingly impossible to perceive a moral argument as anything but an adjunct to a particular political cause.

Weizsäcker: Living with the Bomb

JORDAN, Jaspers, and Thielicke all agreed that the Göttingen physicists had exceeded their political competence. Anticipating this rebuke, the scientists had originally pleaded their case through private channels. The majority of them supported the chancellor's politics and voted CDU. Not relishing a head-on confrontation with the defense ministry, they only sought an assurance that the government would continue to adhere to its nonnuclear pledge. But they became convinced that Strauss would exploit loopholes in the Paris Treaties; that he would enlist German scientists in a nuclear defense project; that he would eventually secure nuclear weapons for the Bundeswehr. Only a public manifesto, they concluded, would "create a political atmosphere in which a national nuclear force was unthinkable."[45]

It became a yearly ritual for the Göttingen 18 scientists to proclaim their continued support for the manifesto. In 1959, they founded the Federation of German Scientists (modeled on the Federation of American Scientists) as a forum for political lobbying. Many of them stayed active in the Pugwash movement; a few of them (especially Born) lent their energy to the SPD's burgeoning peace crusade. But the public's fascination with the scientists soon abated, and they gradually disappeared from view.[46]

Carl-Friedrich von Weizsäcker was the exception. Politics came naturally to Weizsäcker: his father had been Under-Secretary of State during the Weimar Republic and Third Reich. So did the burden of responsibility: his family connection had been the inadvertent catalyzer of the Manhattan Project (Einstein's 1939 letter to Roosevelt). The critiques of Jordan, Jaspers, and Thielicke addressed Weizsäcker as scientist, Christian, and philosopher: he was a nuclear physicist, a lifelong Lutheran, and a professor of philosophy at Hamburg University. Sharing his critics' distaste for political dilettantism, he endeavored to master nuclear strategy, devoting the next thirty years of his life to NATO's defense policy.[47]

Weizsäcker was not only the primary author of the Göttingen Manifesto, he also lent the text its political tone. He would have given it an even greater politico-strategic flair had his colleagues allowed. "The maintenance of peace and freedom through these destructive weapons is very problematic," stated a passage deleted by the other seventeen scientists. "The bombs fulfill their goal only if they never fall. But if everyone came to realize that they would never be used, then they would also no longer fulfill their goal."[48] While in North America attending a Pugwash conference in early 1958, Weizsäcker met with Anglo-American strategists to discuss alternative strategies for NATO. His follow-up statement to the Göttingen Manifesto, published as *Mit der Bombe leben,* emerged from this visit.

Mit der Bombe leben handles four themes: disarmament, deterrence, world government, and Germany's place within Europe. Weizsäcker advocated a nonproliferation treaty, a test ban, and a nuclear freeze. He opposed any attempt to strangle the Soviets economically or militarily, arguing that world stability would best be served if the West tied the East as tightly as possible to the international order. He greeted the restriction placed on European national sovereignty since 1945 as a welcome progress toward international cooperation and integration. Weizsäcker saw little immediate hope for general disarmament. He agreed with Leo Szilard's assessment (from which he derived the title of his work): "Our problem is not how to get rid of the bomb, but how to learn to live with it."[49] The existence of the H-bomb arsenal, said Weizsäcker, rendered unlikely a large-scale conflagration in the near future; faced with the prospect of annihilation, each side would conduct its foreign policy cautiously. But H-bombs, he argued, did not inhibit proxy wars or preclude the piecemeal loss of territory; therefore the West had to be capable of fighting limited wars with conventional weaponry. The readiness to engage in a limited retaliatory attack would act as a deterrent to Soviet aggression. Disarmament was the final goal, but that could only be achieved through a long-term political strategy. Until then, a military doctrine was imperative that placed less reliance on the immediate first use of nuclear warheads.[50]

Through Edward Teller, Sir Anthony Buzzard, Henry Kissinger and others, Weizsäcker learned that NATO doctrine was under attack by Anglo-American strategists. "If you in Germany are offered nuclear armaments in connection with the doctrine of massive retaliation," Weizsäcker was told by these critics, "then you can hardly do anything else but reject the offer."[51] Weizsäcker agreed that NATO policy was too inflexible, too geared for an all-or-nothing response. He feared that it would allow the Soviets to "chew up" Western Europe "in such small bites, that none of the world powers would have occasion to begin a suicidal war in its defense. Communism might win the world war by exposing the retaliatory threat of the large weapons as a 'bluff.' "[52] Teller also informed him that the new sub-kiloton and low-kiloton weapons had a battlefield potential left out of account in the Göttingen Manifesto. Weizsäcker became convinced that neither the West German government, nor its political critics, had formulated an adequate defense strategy.

Persuaded by the viewpoint that tactical weaponry was useful for limited strikes against military targets, Weizsäcker introduced the Anglo-American term "graduated deterrence" (abgestufte Abschreckung) into German strategic parlance. This doctrine spelled out different levels of military response, from border dispute to all-out war; though it still relied on a nuclear deterrent, it gave greater credence to a conventional defense of Europe. Weizsäcker's attitude toward the doctrine, however, was ambivalent: while welcoming it as a great improvement over current strategy, he opposed its corollary—limited nuclear war in Europe (advocated by Kissinger and others). Weizsäcker championed a flexible deterrent, not a new war-fighting strategy. His train of thought was much more akin to the doctrine of "flexible response," adopted by NATO in 1967. "The goal is not to make limited wars possible again," he wrote. "It is rather the opposite—to make limited acts of violence hopeless, and thus make limited wars extremely unlikely." A doctrine was needed that "extends the stalemate that exists on the large weapons to the smaller ones." A successful strategy must ensure against war of any kind, conventional or nuclear.[53]

Weizsäcker's main purpose in writing Mit der Bombe leben was to acquaint German readers with the emerging strategic debate in the United States. He suggested a number of routes for the future, which later influenced SPD defense thinking. In his view, the decision to nuclearize NATO was more a political than a military decision—it highlighted the sense of political unity among the Western powers and made clear to the Soviets that an attack on Europe was tantamount to an attack on the U.S. homeland. Because European troops lent credibility to the West's deterrent capability, he cautiously supported NATO's decision to make them nuclear-capable. But Weizsäcker was not convinced that the West had found the proper mix of conventional and nuclear forces. He was suspicious of the sword-shield doctrine, and he felt that the new medium-range missiles (Thor, Jupiter, Matador) served no useful purpose in Europe, except as an interim solution pending the buildup of ICBMs in the United States.

Weizsäcker proposed the creation of a separate nonnuclear NATO force (as advocated by Adenauer, Blank, and Heusinger until mid-1956). For large-scale global conflicts, Weizsäcker saw the virtue of the nuclear deterrent; in light of tactical weaponry, he realized that some NATO troops would have to be equipped for nuclear war. But he opposed the immediate first use of nuclear weapons in the event of conflict. He championed instead a strong, effective nonnuclear army at the front, capable of deterring conventionally a wide range of Soviet options against Western Europe. Nuclearized troops were to be held in reserve and sent to the battlefield only as a last resort. "In terms of global strategy," he concluded, "it might be cheaper and more efficient to make the 'shield,' in so far as it is nuclearized, not permanently stationed in a region, and, in so far as it is permanently stationed, nonnuclear."[54]

Mit der Bombe leben revealed a far better grasp of nuclear strategy and technical questions than was evident in the Göttingen Manifesto. But the tract was imbued with the Göttingen spirit; it was a maturation of Weizsäcker's thinking rather than a departure from previously held views. His cardinal messages—particularly his opposition to proliferation and to the then current NATO strategy—were still evident. Would he have refused to perform nuclear defense research, even on the new sub-kiloton weapons? His comment suggests an ethical ambivalence: "Along with a number of German colleagues I have committed myself not to assist in any way with nuclear weaponry," he wrote. "It is therefore impossible for me as a physicist to assist in the technical preparations for a graduated deterrence. I do not regret this decision. It was made at a time when the doctrine was unknown or barely known to us all. We considered—as I still do today—the doctrine of 'massive retaliation' to be politically absurd and immoral."[55]

Weizsäcker's tract had a long-term effect on the nuclear controversy. Written in part to clarify the Göttingen Manifesto, it lent a scholarly tone to the debate and focused attention on the competing strategic doctrines in America. Many of his ideas were shared by

SPD leaders, most prominent among them Helmut Schmidt, who used Weizsäcker's thoughts as a starting point for his own famous book *Defense or Retaliation* (1962). The short-term effect of Weizsäcker's contribution, however, was less visible. He discovered—as did many others in the public eye—that a factual discussion on the nuclear topic was a rarity. For the remainder of the decade, Weizsäcker battled against an emotional and propaganda-laden debate, which the Göttingen scientists themselves had inadvertently done much to catalyze. Ironically, the most intense debate took place in Weizsäcker's spiritual homeland, the Protestant church.

4

MISSAL DIPLOMACY: THE PROTESTANTS AND NUCLEAR WEAPONS

> What men write about war, saying that it is a great plague, is all true. But they should also consider how great the plague is that war prevents. . . . The small lack of peace called war or the sword must set a limit to this universal, worldwide lack of peace which would destroy everyone.
>
> —Martin Luther (1526)

> What is the church's message to soldiers who hold the means of mass destruction in their hands . . .?
>
> —Martin Niemöller (1957)

WHEN Emperor Constantine declared Christianity the official religion of the Roman Empire in the fourth century, the church abandoned its doctrine of nonviolence. Since a Christian monarch needed Christian armies, a "Christianized" empire required a creed that allowed for the realm's defense. Religious pacifism was no longer practical; the "just war" doctrine took its place.

As formulated by St. Augustine, this new creed combined Roman law and Christian piety. A just war had to be fought by a legitimate government—an emperor, king, or prince—for the preservation of the state (*jus ad bellum*). To ensure that warfare did not kill innocent civilians or wreak havoc on property and territory, the military response had to be proportional to the attack, the battle restricted to enemy combatants (*jus in bello*). Lust for power, love of violence, and pleasure in cruelty were evil, but war itself was not, so long as it was fought in order to obtain a just peace. "Peace should be the object of your desire," St. Augustine wrote. "War should be waged only as a necessity and waged only that through it God may deliver men from that necessity and preserve them in peace. For peace is not to be sought in order to kindle war, but war is to be waged in order to obtain peace."[1]

The Augustinian just war theory guided Christianity from the time of the barbarian invasions of Rome in the fifth century. It was a Christian pact with the secular world, made in the hope of preserving the *pax Romana* until the triumph of the *pax Christi.* The legalistic chicaneries of feuding monarchs and the false pieties of crusading Christians often led to abuse. But the criteria themselves rarely came under attack, except among the ranks of Christian pacifists—from Mennonite to Anabaptist, from George Fox to Leo Tolstoy—who never made the Augustinian compromise.

With the publication of Martin Luther's *Whether Soldiers, Too, Can Be Saved* (1526), the Protestants adopted the main tenets of the Augustinian just war theory. Luther tailored it to his "two kingdom" doctrine: in heaven, God ruled with love; in the world, he ruled with wrath and punishment.

> For God has established two kinds of government among men. The one is spiritual; it has no sword, but it has the word, by means of which men are to become good and righteous, so that with this righteousness they may attain eternal life. . . . The other kind is worldly government, which works through the sword so that those who do not want to be good and righteous to eternal life may be forced to become good and righteous in the eyes of the world. He administers this righteousness through the sword.[2]

The events of the twentieth century—world wars, Fascism, Hiroshima—called both Augustine's just war theory and Luther's two kingdom doctrine into question. Could modern weapons be used in proportion to the attack? Had not modern strategists targeted civilians as well as soldiers? Would nuclear warfare destroy the territory it was supposed to preserve? Could nuclear weapons be used to ensure the triumph of a just peace, or was nuclear pacifism the only route Christians could choose? "War no longer recognizes combatants," wrote Martin Niemöller. "For the past forty years we have been talking of total war."[3]

It would be hard for any Christian—Quaker or Catholic, Protestant or Orthodox—to deny the existence of two incongruous realms. Hate, greed, and violence belonged to one sphere; hope, faith, and charity to another. There was a heavenly kingdom and a mundane one, a beatific vision of a *pax Christi* and a grim reality of a war-torn world. From the viewpoint of Calvinists, however, German Lutherans seemed to make the distinction more emphatically than other Christians. "Render unto Caesar that which is Caesar's" had too easily become a shibboleth for obedience to the kaiser; the two kingdom doctrine offered too convenient an alibi for political passivity. "The German people suffer from the error of the greatest German Christian, Martin Luther," wrote the Swiss theologian, Karl Barth, in explaining why Germans obeyed Hitler. "The distinction between law and gospel, between world and spiritual spheres, rather than limiting and confining man's natural paganism, actually glorified it ideologically, approved it and strengthened it."[4]

After 1945, Protestant assemblies—the World Council of Churches (WCC), the Lutheran World Federation, the German synod—addressed anew the Christian viewpoint on war. Church leaders agreed that the just war doctrine was problematic: "Lofty objectives so often invented to justify war cannot conceal the truth that its violence and destruction are inherently evil."[5] They also agreed that a test ban treaty symbolized a "first step" toward peace: "There is a risk for the sake of peace which Christians, especially in countries projecting tests of nuclear weapons, are justified in advocating, in the hope of breaking through barriers of distrust."[6] They were unable, however, to reach a consensus regarding the proper Christian attitude towards modern warfare. A majority of Christians (especially Lutherans) upheld a modified version of the two kingdom and just war doctrines; they felt that Communist atheism and Soviet expansionism were worse evils than the possession of nuclear weapons. A second group of Protestants championed either absolute pacifism (based on the Sermon on the Mount), or nuclear pacifism.

German clergymen were at the forefront of the worldwide Protestant debate. It seemed only natural that Germany—the homeland of Luther, Marx, and Hitler—should become the main theological battleground.[7]

Rabies Theologica

HELMUT Gollwitzer, in his celebrated antinuclear tract, *Die Christen und die Atomwaffen,* never questioned the legitimacy of the just war theory. Instead, he used these traditional criteria to test whether Christian belief was compatible with nuclear strategy. "Are all wars the same?" he asked. "Is a saber and musket the same as an atomic bomb or chemical and biological means of extermination, which are primarily directed against civilian populations rather than enemy troops? Is that covered by the Augustinian creed?"[8] Modern military doctrine, he argued, did not distinguish between soldiers and civilians. This was especially true of nuclear strategy, which placed a premium on retaliation against civilian populations, but it was also true of biological and chemical warfare. Combatants no longer fought to protect civilians; instead they treated them as "insects deserving of extermination." The Augustinian creed, Gollwitzer noted, only permitted the use of force in order to convince the opponent to "cease and desist from his unjust goals" and to "accommodate himself anew to peaceful coexistence." Modern weaponry deprived the aggressor of the chance to rethink his position, confronting him instead with utter destruction or utter capitulation. Nuclear weapons forced enemy states to treat each other in the same manner that Hitler and Stalin dealt with their domestic opposition: by wholesale slaughter.[9]

The concept of a defensive war—defined as the "protection of the homeland lying behind the front"—was also rendered completely obsolete by the nuclear age. Defense policy only served the self-preservation instincts of the military-state structure, while robbing the populace and its elected representatives of the final decision over their own destiny. Nuclear war would entail the "end of democracy and freedom, in whose name the war is allegedly being fought."[10] Ideological tensions between East and West were so deep-seated that the slogan "better dead than red" was used to justify a defense policy that really meant "better to commit mass suicide while annihilating your opponent than to come under his control." Nuclear deterrence, moreover, did nothing to save the East Germans from their fate. "For the millions of humans who were liberated from Hitler only to be delivered to Stalin, the American nuclear weapons offer no solace or hope of freedom. They must evolve Communism from the inside, and make it bearable by democratizing and humanizing it. The alternative: enslavement or nuclear weapons, says nothing to them; the nuclear threat is for them no longer the way of avoiding or overcoming enslavement."[11]

Christian leaders, Gollwitzer felt, must take an immediate unilateral initiative in the disarmament process, even at the risk of diluting the West's defense. He said:

> We have never demanded a one-sided renunciation by the United States of nuclear weapons as the mechanical consequence of recognizing their reprehensibility. We have always said that this recognition must be translated into responsible steps, the details of which it is not the duty of the church to sketch. But that can only happen if two things are constantly kept in mind: it is a sin before God and a crime against humanity to continue threatening with these weapons; and the temporary retention of nuclear weapons cannot be justified (as was the case with previous weaponry) for use in the event of an emergency. At best they can be justified as a way of reaching the goal of their abolition.[12]

Under the motto: *Si omnes, ego non* (implying "even if everyone else consents, I refuse"), he advised Christians not to be involved in the production, stationing, or use of nuclear warheads.[13] "Today one cannot speak of Holy Communion without taking a stance on nuclear warfare. Today one cannot believe in and evangelize about the atonement of man and God on the cross of Golgotha without labeling nuclear intimidation for what it is, namely a revolt against the reality of atonement."[14] Gollwitzer elevated the nuclear question to that of *status confessionis,* challenging the Protestant church to answer "whether a human involved in the manufacture and use of these modern 'weapons' is accountable before God's commandments, whether in doing so he is in a 'state of grace.' "[15]

Gollwitzer's nuclear pacifism found its most eloquent critic in Helmut Thielicke (*Die Atomwaffe als Frage an die Christliche Ethik*). Thielicke's message combined biblical aphorism and theological reasoning in defense of traditional Lutheranism. He viewed the inclination to violence as fundamental to human nature, rooted in the "fall of man" from a state of grace. "Mankind, in forsaking God, lost the element that bound it together. Humans behave unpredictably, they are fraught with fear and mistrust of one another. This creates a centrifugal force, and it seems to me that this centrifugal force—this veiled and overt mutual mistrust—has a central importance for understanding mankind's posture toward nuclear weapons." Due to the pervasive sense of distrust, mankind can experience only a *pax timoris,* a "peace based on fear." This was no real peace, but rather a "neutralization of the elements of disorder."[16]

Thielicke agreed that nuclear weapons rendered the theological concept of the just war outmoded. Nuclear war was absurd, he noted, as all possessors and nonpossessors of nuclear weapons have admitted; logically, then, these warheads ought to be condemned and nuclear disarmament begun. Why have governments not drawn the logical conclusion? Why have they continued to produce "means" of warfare that bear no relation to the "goal" of protecting the homeland in the event of war? Thielicke attributed this to the fear that the other power (or powers) would secretly continue to produce these weapons despite any disarmament agreements. Neither side was willing to "relinquish the relative security offered by the balance of forces." What had evolved in world politics, Thielicke maintained, was "nothing other than the attempt by the mutually mistrustful nuclear powers to produce a kind of division of power, to create thereby a balance of power, a kind of neutralization of nuclear might and a *pax atomica.*"[17]

Since this peace rested on a readiness to use the means of mass destruction, the question still arose as to whether a Christian could justify the production, stationing, or use of nuclear weaponry.

Thielicke drew a different conclusion than Gollwitzer. "Would not a renunciation of one's defense readiness give unrestricted scope to the arbitrariness of a nuclear-equipped opponent, thereby making the right of the stronger the guiding world principle?" Thielicke asked. "Would it not entail surrendering to the means of mass destruction and to a cynic willing to use these means?"[18] Nuclear pacifists falsely reduced mankind's options to the triumph of Communism or nuclear catastrophe, to a choice between the "'moral' or 'physical' destruction of the world."[19] They failed to perceive that a third choice—nuclear deterrence—might best uphold the power balance and guarantee peace.

"The conditions of a *pax atomica* are more dangerous than every other form of *pax timoris*," Thielicke admitted, but that did not mean "a radical, one-sided renunciation of nuclear weapons is imperative and that no other choice is open to Christians." A Christian could decide that the "readiness to risk destruction" was an acceptable last choice, and thereby "accept the balance of the nuclear potential"; or he could decide that a "readiness to risk destruction" was not acceptable, and join with the nuclear opposition. It was a "choice between two evils." But it was solely a "matter of discretion and in no way a matter of belief, as to which evil one considers greater: whether a nuclear power sits on one side and a power vacuum on the other; or whether an equivalent nuclear potential exists that keeps both sides unwilling to use them in an emergency."[20]

The viewpoints of Gollwitzer and Thielicke invite comparison; they argued from similar theological and ethical premises, and shared a common view of church–state relations. Both felt that a main pillar of the just war doctrine (*jus in bello*) had collapsed in the nuclear era, but they disagreed sharply over whether pacifism was the best Christian response. Gollwitzer believed that any involvement with nuclear weapons was incompatible with Christian belief, regardless of the alleged consequences for the Western world. For Thielicke, the preservation of a legitimate political order was paramount, even at the risk of nuclear devastation. Gollwitzer emphasized how much the world had to lose in a nuclear holocaust, Thielicke how much the world had to preserve against Eastern despotism. Gollwitzer sought to keep Christians from abetting the nuclear spiral; Thielicke felt the nuclear era obligated Christians to devote en-

ergy to a gradual and balanced disarmament, but that nuclear weaponry did not leave Christians with only one ethical choice.

Gollwitzer composed a formidable challenge to traditional Christian doctrine. By aiming at the means of modern warfare, he struck
the Achilles heel of the just war creed. The sword had more in common with the plowshare than with nuclear weapons, and the grisly
wars of the sixteenth century were more akin to peacetime than to
a nuclear catastrophe. The new mode of fighting forced the Christian to commit himself, if not to peace, than at least to nuclear pacifism. But Thielicke turned the argument on its head, asking whether
nuclear pacifism would contribute to the triumph of a "just peace"
or whether it would allow arbitrary power to guide the world. Would
might become right? Would humanity survive, but in chains?

While Gollwitzer and Thielicke debated the Augustinian creed, a
small group within German Protestantism—the Church Brethren—
assaulted the Lutheran two kingdom doctrine. Though Brethren
leaders drew heavily on Gollwitzer's analysis, they did not distinguish between nuclear and absolute pacifism. The Brethren's theology was Christocentric and political: biblical, without being fun-
damentalist; political, without distinguishing between the mundane
and the heavenly spheres.[21] Since nearly all Brethren had belonged
to the dissenting Confessional church during the Nazi era, they tended
to view current church problems through the prism of the 1930s
("Is the church not today challenged by the nuclear question as it
was with the Jewish question during the church strife?" asked Helmut Simon).[22] Most Brethren were Calvinist, their patron saint Karl
Barth, a cofounder of the Confessional church. "The rigid separa-
tion of belief and behavior, especially in the political realm," the
Brethren theologians wrote, "is one of the problems of evangelical
Christendom that has yet to be sufficiently overcome."[23] The church
must "replace a theological metaphysics of the state with an evangelical doctrine based on political virtues," which would "simply
transform what it means to be a Christian into the political realm."[24]

The Brethren championed a return to the pre-Constantine doctrine of nonviolence. They condemned the just war theory, rejected
the concept of two kingdoms, sought to politicize the German clergy,
and demanded that the Protestant church take a definitive stance
against a nuclearized Bundeswehr. "In the name of Christ, we pledge

not to go one step farther on the path toward nuclear armaments,"
the Rhineland Brethren stated at its Easter 1957 meeting in Wermelskirchen. "We will sharpen the conscience of all persons en-
trusted to us, in the recognition that no goal can justify production
or use of the means of mass destruction. We bear witness to all
mankind that Christ is the only salvation of the world."[25]

Walter Künneth and Hans Asmussen led the battle against the
Brethren, forming a rival organization, the Rhine Convent, in 1958.
The Convent set out to act as a bulwark against the "lordship of
organizations" who sought "the intervention of the church and its
functionaries in political decisions that do not belong to their authority."[26] Both Künneth and Asmussen anchored their theological
positions in the traditional Lutheran two kingdom doctrine; unlike
Thielicke, they saw no reason to question the just war doctrine in
light of nuclear weapons. "From a theological perspective," Künneth
wrote, "it is too seldom noted that the dreadful nuclear destructive
potential represents in concentrated form the entanglement of the
world with the diabolic spirit of destruction. In the nuclear age, a
final satanic-human potentiality manifests itself in a universal and
intensive dimension, a potentiality which was nonetheless always
latent and which has often enough in partial eruptions illuminated
the human situation in a flash."[27]

Künneth considered the Brethren's political activism a "perver-
sion" of the church's role. Not every citizen, he claimed, had a political responsibility equal to that of the chancellor, or the competence to make government policy. The church should "sharpen the
conscience," not "make politics." He foresaw a Calvinist putsch to
displace the Lutheran two kingdom doctrine in favor of a "Chris-
tocracy," in which every political act would be performed "in the
name of God, in the name of the gospel, in the name of the Sermon
on the Mount."[28] The Brethren represented a dangerous symptom
of "ethical pacifism," more akin to Tolstoy than Luther: "if I as a
Christian say 'yes' to participating in defense tasks in the nuclear
age, then I do not believe that Christ has risen."[29]

Politically, Künneth held, the Brethren's position endangered the
survival of the West. "Without doubt, this kind of political-military
self-surrender and capitulation to the threats from the East would
certainly get Moscow's approval. . . . It is the most certain means

of endangering the peace. Advocating unilateral disarmament actually provokes catastrophe."[30] He saw the spread of Communism, not nuclear proliferation, as the peril of the modern age. "It is the responsibility of all statesmen before God and man to take all timely measures to avert this threatening calamity, to deter the overpowerful opponent, and to protect against a 'mass murder' of soul and body by Communist atheism."[31] He posed the question in hyperbole: "Cannot the possession of nuclear armaments in a highly paradoxical way constitute a political mode of loving thy neighbor?"[32]

Like Künneth, Asmussen's conception of how the state maintained order worked like a dike: it dammed the flood of Communism from the East. He also shared another of Künneth's concerns —damming (not to mention damning) the flow of ideas coming down the Rhine River from the headwaters of Barth's Basel. Nuclear weapons were the "disciplining rods of God," the means by which the heavenly father chastised his flock. "That we are in this situation thirteen years after the horrible second world war should be accepted as God's punishment," he wrote. "It would be a good thing if the synod—instead of yielding to the political decision demanded of it—would make evangelical Christians more aware that God is powerfully at work. Whoever has no other goal than to stay alive, perhaps as a dead soul, will not endure God's judgment."[33]

The Convent stoked the flames with hellfire and brimstone. Its members followed—to use Max Weber's terminology—an "ethics of responsibility." The consequence was paramount, not the individual's moral behavior. How would a particular ethical decision affect the future? What might transpire as a result of any given choice? Convent leaders were unswerving in their defense of the Western world; they believed nuclear pacifism served Moscow's interests, not God's. But the group's political intransigence tended to subvert its ethics. While Convent leaders spoke often on the evils of Communism, they reflected little on the consequences of a nuclear exchange. Was that not ethically irresponsible by their own standards? Was there no avenue for an arms control accord with the East, no possibility of a Christian "first step" toward reconciliation?

Brethren members—to use Weber's terminology again—adhered to an "ethics of conviction." Kant's dictum, "Do what is right even though the world shall perish," was their moral guide. They considered it better to live under Communism than to threaten with ungodly weapons, better to yield than show strength. But many churchmen viewed the Brethren's pacifism not as a lofty expression of ethical purity, but rather as a symptom of spiritual cowardliness, an ethics of no conviction. "Are we really prepared to place a reverence for our naked physical existence above something as valuable as our freedom?" asked a Brethren member in tendering his resignation.[34]

As Lutherans debated with the Brethren over the merits of Barthianism, the East German government insinuated its own brand of theology into the debate. With Marx as their messiah and dialectical materialism as their creed, the Communists adhered to a "single kingdom" doctrine, a secular heaven on earth in which religion would wither away. The East German government was especially hostile to the Protestant church: as the only remaining all-German institution, it was the only force capable of effective resistance to Communist control. Since over 80 percent of East Germans were practicing Lutherans, overt suppression of the church was politically risky. The Communist authorities implanted socialism indirectly: they censored sermons, closed missions, arrested pastors; devout Christians were kept out of the teaching profession and were denied civil service jobs. All Eastern pastors were forced to take an oath of allegiance to the East German state. For every religious ritual, an official state-sponsored ceremony was created, from secular confirmation to civil marriage. "When in the next few years the last of the old women has died off," the Communist propagandist, Alfred Norden, predicted, "the pastors will have to weep their tears alone on the lifeless walls of their empty churches."[35]

East German clergymen prepared their churches spiritually for a long war of attrition. With the two kingdom doctrine as their shield, they resisted a Communist assault on the spiritual realm. Most pastors served the church first, even if they pledged allegiance to the state; most continued to deliver an essentially Christian message, even if they sprinkled their sermons with socialist rhetoric; most continued to administer religious rituals, while accepting the secular ones as unavoidable evils. The East German government had little success locating pastors who shared the Communists' "progressive" ideas on religion. "One must look for them with lanterns," Norden admitted, "and they are mostly old men who are looking for a quiet and comfortable eve of life."[36]

An alliance of Communists and Brethren came into being against East German and West German Lutherans. Brethren leaders were pacifistic, the Communists atheistic; the Brethren aspired to live in heaven, the Communists to create a heaven on earth. What cemented the alliance was a common perception that Lutherans were "religious Fascists." At each stage of West German rearmament, the East German government tightened its grip over Protestantism, threatening to sever contact between the Eastern and Western churches. Each time the Bundestag debated defense legislation, Brethren leaders introduced a new antirearmament resolution at the German synod, threatening a religious schism if their advice went unheeded. The Lutheran majority, caught in a two-front war, struggled to uphold the principle of unity against theological diversity and East–West tensions.

There were three major synodal battles: in 1956, over the Conscription Law; in 1957, over the Military Chaplain Treaty; and in 1958, over the Brethren's Ten Theses. By the decade's end, theological barbed wire ran the length of German Protestantism, from Basel to Berlin.[37]

Furor Politicus

IN 1956, the Bundestag approved the Conscription Law, making every West German adult male liable for military service. Since Article 4 of the constitution guaranteed the right of conscientious objection, the new law established a draft board along the Anglo-American model. "Whoever opposes *all* use of weapons for reasons of conscience in state relations and therefore objects to compulsory military service," the law stated, "must perform a compulsory civilian service outside the Bundeswehr."[38]

Whereas the Conscription Law satisfied the Catholic church, many Protestant leaders felt the conscientious objectors clause gave secular authorities excessive control over the Christian conscience. They sought a different wording: "whoever resists taking up arms for religious or moral reasons of conscience in conflicts between states can refuse conscription in the armed forces."[39] They also felt that some consideration had to be given to nuclear pacifists. "We are of the opinion that in the atomic age a young man cannot simply present himself for compulsory service with the same sense of inner certainty as perhaps was the case in 1910," testified the Protestant church's emissary, Hermann Kunst, before the Bundestag's Defense Committee.[40]

The Protestant Council (a five-member board that oversaw church affairs) was not inclined to challenge the Bundestag's decision; the law was not ideal, but at least it protected conscientious objectors (the East German government had refused to consider a similar clause in its defense legislation). Brethren spokesmen, however, lobbied for the Conscription Law's annulment. Each individual, they felt, should function as his own priest, foreign minister, and military general. Their proposal defined a conscientious objector as anyone who "in accordance with a conscientious and responsible examination of all the conditions—including the political situation, the state of weapons technology, and the relevance of the state community—decided against compulsory service."[41]

Brethren leaders demanded a special synod devoted to the Conscription Law. West Germany's admission to NATO, they argued, had prompted a crackdown by East German authorities against the Eastern churches; unless reunification came soon, the church would be cleaved in two. The council, however, refused to convoke a special synod to discuss defense issues, pointing out that East German Communists, not NATO leaders, were harassing the church. "The real problem is not the division of Germany into two parts," the council noted, "but rather the fact that one part of Germany is now suffering from political pressure."[42]

Brethren leaders eventually got their way, making rearmament the hidden agenda of the regular 1956 synod.[43] Their resolution called on both German governments to "avoid conscription" and "keep their military forces to a minimum pending unification."[44] They ultimately failed, however, to garner a majority. The synod sent only a mild admonishment to both German governments expressing its concern over West German conscription and East Germany's "forced entrance" into service (the Communists coerced all males into volunteering).[45] Unwilling to acknowledge defeat, the Brethren started a signature drive: "The undersigned agree with the reservations expressed by the synod against compulsory service and against the methods of forced service in the army. These reservations will be presented to the governments in Bonn and East Berlin by a church delegation." Without informing the Protestant Council (or anyone who might oppose their methods), Brethren leaders secured signatures from exactly 51 percent of the attending delegates, then sent the results to the East Germans. The Communist press deciphered its contents: "Majority in Protestant Church Opposes West German Conscription Law."[46]

Conscription was not the only issue to challenge the church's unity; equally divisive was the Military Chaplain Treaty. Since the seventeenth century, Lutherans had regulated army–church relations by special treaties, which defined the rights and responsibilities of the church within the armed forces. With each new government, a new treaty was necessary. Negotiations were conducted by Defense Minister Blank and Hermann Kunst (whom the Protestant Council designated as its Military Bishop). Since the East German government refused to negotiate, only the Bundeswehr was considered. The West German government offered generous terms: the treaty provided for one army chaplain per fifteen hundred Protestant soldiers; chaplains would be "civil servants in the service of the state," but the church was to select the chaplains, who would remain under the church's control and jurisdiction. The chancellor left the chaplain's duties largely unregulated, explaining that "the government sought a formulation, by which all influence by the state over church affairs would be impossible."[47]

The treaty became, Kunst complained, "the whipping boy for all the ills of the church."[48] For Brethren leaders, the text was less controversial than the mere existence of a treaty. "Is it even possible to care for souls in a nuclear-equipped army?" they asked at the 1957 synod where the treaty was under discussion. "What is the church's message to soldiers who hold the means of mass destruction in their hands and who will be trained in their use? Can we really create an organization to handle the care of souls, and can we ratify a treaty without knowing what a military chaplain is supposed to say or advise in this crucial and decisive question of modern warfare?"[49]

Brethren leaders had their own prescription. They introduced a resolution calling for a clear-cut synodal "no" to nuclear warfare. They advocated active opposition to the stationing of nuclear warheads on German soil, calling on churchmen to preach to their congregations that "absolutely no purpose can justify the production or use of the means of destruction."[50] The Brethren lost on both fronts. The Military Chaplain Treaty passed by a large majority (ninety-one to nine, including forty-three votes from East German churchmen). The synod then rejected the Brethren's resolution in favor of a generally worded call for a test ban treaty, which admonished churchmen "not to make themselves coresponsible for starting a new war by their indifference."[51]

Brethren leaders continued their battle against the treaty for the next several years. At first they tried to block ratification by the regional churches; they failed to sway even the state synods in their Rhine homeland. Next, they sought the treaty's annulment on the grounds that it interfered with church–state relations in East Germany. This failed to sway church leaders, since the treaty's provisions did not apply to the East. Finally, they sought a synodal reversal on the grounds that the treaty had been negotiated before the Bundestag decided to nuclearize its armed forces. But the Protestant Council rejected this plea also. The treaty had been ratified "in full recognition of the possibility of a nuclearized armed forces," the council noted, and "especially in this case, soldiers would be in need of pastoral care." With that pronouncement, resistance to the Military Chaplain Treaty came to an end.[52]

"Last year, passions were running so high that an intensification seemed hardly imaginable," wrote the editors of the *Church Yearbook* in summation of 1957:

> But even the previous outbreak of *furor politicus* and *rabies theologica,* of hard colliding opinions and pungent discussion, of mutual recrimination, unreasonableness, misunderstanding, and mistrust was outstripped by what the nuclear debate brought in the year 1958. . . . The defenders of the divergent conceptions on the question of nuclearizing the Bundeswehr no longer stood

side-by-side as fellow citizens and fellow Christians. They stood as united fronts of bitter intransigence, mutual irritation, induration, and heretical branding.[53]

At the Berlin synod of April 1958, tensions came to a head over a new Brethren resolution, the Ten Theses (see document 2).[54] The Protestant Council considered postponing the synod until later in the year, or even cancelling it altogether, rather than face another politicized meeting. But they reached, instead, a compromise: the synod devoted the first four days to regular church affairs, reserving the final day for the nuclear question.[55]

While the synod met, a special committee under the chairmanship of Ludwig Raiser discussed the Brethren's Ten Theses. At the core of the committee was the Evangelical Study Group, established by Military Bishop Kunst shortly after the 1957 synod. The proceedings were dominated by outspoken Brethren members—Gollwitzer, Heinemann, Heinrich Vogel—and their foes from several camps—Thielicke, Weizsäcker, Künneth, Asmussen.

There were four distinguishable theological positions. Thielicke's deterrence theory and the Convent's anti-Communist platform both originated in Lutheran two kingdom doctrine. Gollwitzer's nuclear pacifism was rooted in Augustinian just war theory, while the Brethren's absolute pacifism derived from a rejection of both Augustine and Luther.[56] Politically, the committee divided into two camps. Künneth, speaking for one side, argued that the church had a moral duty to "build a dam against inhumanity," and that it was a "sin to renounce nuclear weapons." Vogel, speaking for the Brethren, called nuclear weapons a "covenant with nihilism," against which the church must take a stance: "One cannot counter sin with a deterrent when that deterrent itself serves the cause of sin. The vicious circle of fear—which today has a greater destructive effect than imperialism—must be short-circuited, and it is the duty of the Christian community to do so."[57]

It was, however, Weizsäcker who caused the greatest stir with his political-military critique of the Ten Theses on the basis of graduated deterrence doctrine. He argued that the new small-scale nuclear weapons, designed for precise military assignments, did not come under the Brethren's rubric of "means of mass destruction."

In formulating its stance, the Brethren had assumed all modern warfare entailed the use of large-yield H-bombs directed against civilian populations. The group did not take into account the deterrent value of nuclear weaponry, the geographic problems involved in a defense of Europe, or the implications of new defense strategies. Weizsäcker accused Brethren leaders of evolving an "awe-inspiring theology," while "blinding themselves to the realities that exist around them"; they had neglected the political consequences of their actions, and overstepped their range of competence. To put his argument simply, the Protestant church was "intellectually unqualified" for the task of saying "yes" or "no" to the nuclear arsenal.[58]

DOCUMENT 2

The Brethren's Ten Theses (1958)

1. War in all its manifestation is the most dubious means of political conflict between peoples and states.
2. Up to today, churches everywhere have viewed the use of these means as a possibility, on the basis of both good and bad reasons.
3. In light of the prospects of a future war in which modern means of destruction would be used, the church cannot remain neutral.
4. Nuclear war entails the mutual destruction of the populations involved, as well as countless other uninvolved peoples.
5. Because nuclear warfare requires illegitimate methods, it is unsuitable for political conflict.
6. The church and the individual Christian must say "no" in advance to a war that will be fought as a nuclear war.
7. The preparation for such a war is under all conditions a sin against God and your neighbor, for which no church and no Christian ought to make himself culpable.
8. We demand in the name of the gospel that the preparations for this war in the realm of our land end immediately, without taking into account any other considerations.
9. We call on all who earnestly want to be Christians to refuse unreservedly and unconditionally to prepare for a nuclear war.
10. An opposing position or neutrality on this question is indefensible for a Christian. Either of these positions signifies the disavowal of all three articles of Christian belief.

After exchanging theological barbs for several days, the members of Raiser's commission recommended the rejection of the Ten Theses. As an alternative, they spliced together a resolution that was, in the words of the participants themselves, a "formula of impotence" (see document 3).[59]

The 1958 Resolution only reflected the acute divisions within the church over the correct political and theological path. "We have suffered, and we continue to suffer, from the fact that neither of the two factions that formed during our discussion has been successful in convincing the other of the correctness of its position," Raiser told the synod, in explaining the compromise wording. "We discovered to our mutual dismay that we faced two horrendous alternatives: the one led to defenselessness, the other necessitated the acceptance of two nuclear power blocs with the vague hope that a balance of power would be maintained."[60] He concluded on a note of pessimism:

We were forced to realize that a middle way—which we and our populace seek—between the two awful consequences of these alternatives will possibly (indeed, most likely) prove elusive, because it cannot put our consciences to rest. But we demand emphatically of those governments responsible for this matter not to let it come down to these two radical alternatives, but rather to spare humanity and our divided countrymen this decision. In

---

DOCUMENT 3

Excerpt from the 1958 Synodal Resolution

The antagonism among us over our judgment of nuclear weaponry is very deep. Some believe that the manufacture and deployment of all tools of mass destruction are a sin against God. Others believe that situations are thinkable in which, as part of a defense duty, resistance with equivalent weaponry is justifiable before God.

We remain together under the roof of the gospel and strive to overcome the opposing views. We ask God to lead us to a common understanding and decision through His words.

this sense, we are united in expressing our urgent request to the government to do their utmost to avoid the nuclearizing of German forces in East and West.[61]

Synodal debate over the 1958 Resolution took several hours, climaxing in a sharp exchange between Vogel and Eugen Gerstenmaier, the Bundestag president, over the role of the church in state affairs. As it began to appear that the Protestant church might shatter over the nuclear question, Martin Niemöller appeared as a deus ex machina with an eloquent plea for unity. "Where do we stand on the nuclear question?" he asked. "Not next to one another, but apart from one another!" The time had come to "take a step toward one another," he said. "Accept the text as it is written! Then we will know what has to be done in the future, what is still incumbent upon us to do, and what is still demanded of us to do together."[62] Thereafter, the commission's resolution passed unanimously.

The debate, however, was far from over. Hardly had the synod ended when controversy erupted over the actual intent of the 1958 Resolution. One sentence proved troublesome: "We remain together under the roof of the gospel and strive to overcome opposing views." The majority laid emphasis on the first half of the sentence, with its implicit pluralism: the church had refused to pretend that consensus had been reached; the church had also preserved its unity despite those theological cleavages and cold war tensions.[63] The Brethren, however, emphasized the latter half of the sentence. A question of such importance, they argued, rendered "mutually incompatible opinions within one church" impossible.[64] The 1958 Resolution was a temporary measure, pending the achievement of synodal unity. "The opposing convictions expressed at the synod cannot remain as they are. We demand from those of an opposing view that they ground their belief in the gospel."[65]

Since the synod had rejected, but not disproven, the Ten Theses, Brethren spokesmen enjoyed full freedom to propagate their ideas to other Protestants. They feverishly went about this task for the next several months, collating and analyzing the arguments presented by their theological opponents, altering the Ten Theses in response to synodal objections. The amended version, the "Theological Declaration," was less provocative than its predecessor (more subdued in tone and less overtly directed at the Lutheran two king-dom doctrine) but it was primarily a restatement of the group's po-sition. The new declaration, therefore, met with the same stiff op-position from other church leaders. As long as the Brethren would not yield on the question of *status confessionis,* it had little chance of winning over the synod. The Theological Declaration only preached to the converted.[66]

Raiser's committee reconvened in November 1958 as the Atom Commission. The Protestant Council assigned it the task of "trying to overcome the intellectual dissonance" within the church, pre-paring the groundwork for accord at the next synod, scheduled for 1960.[67] The commission met three times in 1959. It analyzed in turn the theological arguments of Thielicke, Gollwitzer, the Brethren, and the Convent. But, once again, the Protestants found no common the-ology or political ethic upon which to formulate a united stance. Disagreement occurred over "whether the maintenance of a politi-cal-military balance of power can be viewed as an ethical neces-sity." A second area of controversy concerned the role of the church in politics: should the Christian resign himself to political "inev-itabilities," or follow "the dictates of religion" without considera-tion of the political context? Finally, there was no agreement on the "legitimacy of these weapons as instruments of power in the hand of the state."[68]

Unable to resolve the theological divisions, the commission turned its attention to the Heidelberg Theses. These theses (prepared by members of the Evangelical Study Group) sought to spotlight the common concerns of Christians in the pursuit of peace. The first five theses caused little disagreement within the Atom Commission. But the latter six theses did. Especially troublesome was the con-cept of "complementarity," which the Heidelberg authors had bor-rowed from physics. The basic idea was that the church could allow two complementary ethical viewpoints to coexist. Depending on perspective, one path or the other might appear more secure, but both led to the goal of peace. It allowed the Protestant church to "live with the bomb" and tolerate conscientious objectors within its ranks (see document 4).[69]

The pluralism intrinsic to the concept of "complementarity" had an allure, especially to Thielicke, Künneth, and Asmussen. But, as even its staunchest supporters admitted, complementarity abandoned the ethical ideal of a "timeless truth" in favor of a "confession of the historicity of God's revelation and our human experi-

---

DOCUMENT 4

A Summation of the Heidelberg Theses (1959)

1. The nuclear era has made peace a prerequisite for living. But mankind has not achieved a Christian peace.

2. Christians must make a special contribution to the preservation of peace. The Christian consoles himself with the message of Christ: "In the world you are afraid, but take heart; I have overcome the world."

3. War is like a thousand-year illness. Today's balance of terror relies on the continued readiness for war; it is like a dangerous vaccination with the serum of the illness itself.

4. The Christian's foremost duty is the pursuit of peace. The underestimation of the small step is fatal to the great aim.

5. In the past, the "just war" doctrine has guided Christians. But this principle cannot be applied to nuclear war. It destroys what it claims to preserve.

6. The common aim is the establishment of world peace. The different paths taken by Christians in pursuit of that goal are complementary. It may be that one person can only follow his path because someone else is following another.

7. Pacifism is a Christian way of behaving. The church must recognize the right of conscientious objecting.

8. A Christian can believe that nuclear weapons safeguard peace and freedom. Any realistic political proposal must foresee the provisional retention of these armaments.

9. If a person says "A," he must say "B." A soldier in a nuclear-equipped army cannot put on his uniform if he intends from the beginning not to obey orders in the event of nuclear war.

10. When the church speaks on world politics, it should advise those without nuclear weapons not to try to acquire them. It would seem pointless to persuade the world powers to renounce nuclear weapons.

11. Not everyone must do the same thing, but each must know what he is doing. Today, two attitudes undergird each other. Nuclear weapons preserve a realm of freedom in which conscientious objectors enjoy civic liberties. And objectors help keep a spiritual realm open within which new decisions may become possible.

ence."[70] Brethren leaders had two further objections. First, the Heidelberg Theses upheld the 1958 decision with the "bland assurance that the opposing perspectives are not so bad after all and can coexist as equals."[71] Second, complementarity legitimized the pronuclear position. Since nuclear weapons were an integral part of modern politics, only a radical condemnation by the church could reverse the course of history. The toleration of diverse ethical perspectives rendered pacifists powerless to halt the nuclear arms race. "A concept drawn from epistemology cannot be used to reconcile divergent ethical positions," argued Brethren spokesmen.[72] Complementarity was a "magic formula" that "seduced" the Christian into a "lazy peace."[73]

When Raiser addressed the 1960 synod, he admitted that "a significant rapprochement of the different viewpoints has yet to become visible." All commission members agreed, he noted, that the Christian had a special task in the promotion of peace, but unity broke down whenever discussion turned to the best path to peace. All attempts to build a consensus failed due to "comprehensive differences in systematic theology." The commission was not able even to agree in principle on the meaning of the 1958 Resolution. Some felt its strength lay in the pluralism it evinced; others saw it as a milestone on the way to unity. For the same reason, the concept of "complementarity" had not proven "a solid bridge in overcoming the differences of opinion." The Protestant church stood no more united than in 1958.[74]

Raiser tried to adjourn the commission in 1960, but met with resistance from Brethren leaders and the Protestant Council. Not until 1962 did he convince the council that consensus was unattainable. "We Christians must acknowledge that we have many contradictory sketches, but no unified and ready-made answers as to the proper way to act in this new and untested situation," he noted in his final report.[75]

"IF all men were to do the same as you," complained a third-century Roman to a Christian pacifist, "there would be nothing to prevent the king from being left in utter solitude and desertion, and the forces of the empire would fall into the hands of the wildest and most lawless barbarians." The Christian responded: "We do our ruler better service than do those who bear the sword. . . . Truly, we do not go with him into the battlefield, not even if he commands it, but we fight for him in our camp, a camp of holiness wherein we pray to God."[76]

The Rhine Convent played the Roman role: how would a particular ethical decision affect the future? The Brethren (like the pacifist) wanted to live in a camp of holiness. The East German authorities, cast in the role of the "wildest and most lawless barbarians," performed beyond expectation. They were always visible—calling the Protestants CIA lackeys, berating the church as a pro-Western institution, labeling Church President Otto Dibelius as "NATO's Pope." East German youth who refused military service landed in jail. No ecclesiastical influence over East German defense matters was tolerated; no Military Chaplain Treaty existed in the East. Once it became clear that Protestants would not become politically active in the antinuclear effort, the East German government forced a de facto split. Since 1960, East and West German synods have met separately.

Given the theological and political tensions, it was not surprising that the Protestants never reached consensus. The Heidelberg Theses came to serve as the unofficial majority opinion, the amended Ten Theses as the minority opinion. Though Brethren leaders never galvanized the church into an opposition force, neither did their foes convert them to the two kingdom doctrine or convince them to adopt just war theory. The Protestants remained more divided than unified, more discordant than harmonized, more paralyzed than activized. If the principle of plurality and tolerance triumphed, it was a Pyrrhic victory.

The Brethren found itself isolated on ethical, theological, and political grounds. Its leaders championed a pure morality, an absolute pacifism; they rejected just war doctrine and disregarded the political consequences of their convictions. On theological matters, the Brethren preached Calvinism; but most Protestants, schooled in the Lutheran two kingdom doctrine, felt that nuclear politics was beyond the church's competence. On political matters, the Brethren appeared to many churchmen as the witting or unwitting tools of East German authorities. Most churchmen, in East and West, preferred West Germany, where they could enjoy religious freedom;

they were simply unwilling to jeopardize Western values in the vague hope of placating the Communists. As a result, the Brethren leaders never won a synodal victory, or swayed the churchmen to their cause. They lost on the issue of conscientious objection to nuclear warfare; they failed to halt the Military Chaplain Treaty; they converted few to the Ten Theses.

The 1958 Resolution has remained, to this day, the last word on nuclear weapons for German Protestants. Given the diversity of opinion within the church, the "formula of impotence" was the only possible solution if unity was to be preserved. In practice, the synodal declaration has come to approximate the intent of "complementarity": the Protestant church tolerates the bomb, but protects those who oppose it. The church has eschewed direct intervention in politics, but has nonetheless become a haven for all the Protestant groups seeking to halt the arms spiral.

This pluralism, however, did not signal the complete defeat of the Brethren. One of its most politically active members, Gustav Heinemann, became president of the Federal Republic during the chancellorship of Willy Brandt (1969–1974). The Dutch Calvinists, who were instrumental in catalyzing the peace movement in the late 1970s, were directly influenced by Barthian theology and the Brethren's Ten Theses. Two of the largest West German groups that sponsored the massive peace rally in Bonn in October 1981 (the Action Committee for Reconciliation/Peace Service and the Action Committee in the Service of Peace) were founded by Protestants in 1958, in the wake of the synodal debates. If Brethren spokesmen failed to sway the church, they at least guaranteed that their ideas would continue to influence succeeding generations.

All in all, the 1958 Resolution was a disappointing denouement to a hard-fought battle. "We leave as perplexed as we came!" exclaimed one delegate at the synod.[77] No dictum was offered, no steps outlined. The Protestant church's statement was far short of a solution, and far less than a comfort to the soul. It did not ensure the triumph of the *pax Christi*. It signaled only continued tolerance of the fragile balance of terror: the *pax atomica*.

5

THE COLD PEACE: IDEOLOGY AND CONFRONTATION IN THE ANTINUCLEAR CAMPAIGN

The peace-at-any-price party would leave
an unarmed Europe a prey to Russia.

—Karl Marx (1867)

FASCISM was defeated by two powerful forces: parliamentary democracy and Bolshevik Communism. It was, therefore, no surprise that the peace movement after World War II divided into warring camps along the lines of the burgeoning East–West ideological struggle. There were two antinuclear campaigns—one led by Communists, the other by non-Communists—and each confronted the other with the same undisguised hostility as the cold warriors of Washington and Moscow.

The World Peace Council spearheaded the Communist peace offensive. Its membership lay mostly in the East bloc, but its offshoots extended throughout the world. A creation of the Kremlin, it was called into existence (as the Soviets undertook their first nuclear testing in 1949) to spread the message that the Soviet Union's nuclear arsenal maintained world peace against American capitalists,

NATO imperialists, and German "revanchists." The Soviet peace warriors in West Germany were assembled in the Standing Congress of All Opponents of the Nuclearization of the Federal Republic, with three activists as chiefs: Renate Riemeck, cofounder of the Standing Congress and chancellor-candidate of the Deutsche Friedens-Union (DFU, or German Peace Union) in 1961; her protégée, Ulrike Meinhof, a student activist (who in the 1970s lent her name and energy to a terrorist organization, the Baader–Meinhof Red Brigade); and Klaus Rainer Röhl, editor of *konkret,* a student journal financed by the East German government.[1]

The non-Communist campaign, democratic and decentralized, was not the plaything of any government. The British philosopher Bertrand Russell was its shining light; its members—socialists, churchmen, professors, scientists, and labor—were generally pro-Western, despite their misgivings about NATO. The two largest organizations were the Campaign for Nuclear Disarmament (CND) in Britain, and its imitator, the SPD-backed German Campaign against Nuclear Death (GCND). Comparable groups existed in Austria, Switzerland, France, Norway, Sweden, Belgium, and Holland. All nine of the non-Communist organizations were affiliated with the European Federation against Nuclear Armaments, headed by Russell and the German novelist Hans Werner Richter.[2]

A bitter struggle ensued between the Communist and non-Communist peace forces in West Germany. The ambitions of the Standing Congress far exceeded its tiny popular support. Not content to lie in the shadow of the GCND, Standing Congress leaders plotted to infiltrate its ranks, seize control of the movement, and harness it to the goals of East Germany's foreign policy. An examination of West German antinuclear activism is a study of cold war ideology. This in turn offers insight into why the peace movement failed so miserably to attain its goals.

GCND: The Limits of Agitation

THE lessons of history were not lost on SPD leaders as they contemplated a British-style antinuclear campaign. Parliamentary life was old and hearty in England, young and fragile in Germany. Extraparliamentary activism slipped easily into antiparliamentary agitation, then tumbled into an antidemocratic movement. SPD leaders had experienced enough right-wing and left-wing terrorism, witnessed enough Fascist and Communist subversion, seen enough of putsches and prison walls, to make them wary of toying with the floodgate of democracy. On the other hand, the tide of extraparliamentary agitation might carry the SPD to the chancellorship: the polls indicated that antinuclearism was a "vote-getter"; the Rapacki Plan seemed a reasonable solution for Central Europe; and the public viewed Defense Minister Strauss as an old Prussian warmonger. And anyway, the socialists had run out of other options. Why nurse blisters on the opposition bench? Why not run with the GCND?[3]

The Social Democrats approved the GCND in early 1958, placing Walter Menzel and Alexander Maass in charge. Menzel, North Rhine-Westphalia's former Minister of Internal Affairs, was a socialist stalwart with a passionate dislike for Communist peace ideologues. Under him the Bonn Central Committee kept tight control of the GCND. Socialist and trade union leaders secured key positions within the state and city committees. There was no room for local initiatives inconsistent with directives from Bonn. "Keep a rein on the whole organization," Menzel advised. "But it's a good idea to give the public the impression that the matter is in the hands of the universities, novelists, actors, and scientists."[4]

The GCND's rigid hierarchy—consistent with a German proclivity for organizing "from above"—eased Menzel's task of weeding out Communists. But it also stifled grassroots activism, alienated the "prominent personalities" allegedly at the avant-garde of the movement, and diminished the campaign's appeal to the broader public. By and large, Germans perceived the GCND as a creation of the SPD, and viewed the demonstrations as belated electioneering. Those who became members of the GCND, and spoke at its rallies, were either SPD partisans or long-time opponents of Adenauer's security policies. Among the scientists, Max Born was active (but not the Göttingen 18 or German Physics Society). Brethren leaders joined (but not the Protestant church). Dehler and Döring joined (but not the FDP). A handful of writers, artists, and professors also lent their names to the Bonn Central Committee's manifesto (see document 5).[5]

The GCND's aims—a nonnuclear Bundeswehr, a test ban treaty, a nuclear-free Central Europe, and general disarmament—came directly from the SPD's party platform. The GCND explored three avenues for getting its message across. The first (peaceful demonstrations) was legal; the second (a political strike) was semi-legal; the third (referenda) was unconstitutional—the SPD called the referenda "public opinion polls" in an attempt to dodge this issue. The crucial test of all this agitation came during the July state elections in North Rhine-Westphalia. If the SPD could turn extraparliamentary agitation into a parliamentary majority without undue strain on the constitution, the campaign was well worth the risk.[6]

The state and local GCND committees founded by the Bonn Central Committee in the summer of 1958 comprised the real heart of the campaign. The first, largest, and best-funded was organized in North

---

DOCUMENT 5

The GCND Manifesto of March 1958

In the event of war between East and West, the German people on both sides of the border zones will be the certain victims of nuclear death. There is no protection against it.

Participation in the nuclear arms race and the utilization of German territory as a launching pad for nuclear weapons can only heighten this threat.

The goal of German politics must be the relaxation of tensions between East and West. Only such a policy serves the security of the German people and the national existence of a free and democratic Germany.

We demand of the Bundestag and federal government not to participate in the nuclear arms race, and instead to support an atomic-weapon-free zone in Europe as a contribution to the relaxation of tensions.

We call on all German people regardless of differences of social rank, confession or politics to resist a defense policy that is life-threatening, and to promote instead a policy of peaceful cooperation. We will not halt, as long as nuclear death threatens our people.

Rhine-Westphalia, in conjunction with the state election campaign. It had twenty-seven local wings, and a sizable membership in the larger cities (Bielefeld, Cologne, Dortmund, Düsseldorf, Essen, Münster, and Bonn).[7] State committees were established in Bremen, Hamburg, West Berlin, Hessen, Rhineland-Pfalz, and Bavaria in April; Lower Saxony and Schleswig-Holstein in June; Baden-Württemberg in September (though local affiliates had sprung up earlier). By summer's end, the GCND had spread into nearly every large and middle-sized city of West Germany, as well as many towns and villages. With rare exception, the most active committees were in SPD strongholds (Hamburg, Bremen, and Hessen), and areas where labor unions were strong (North Rhine-Westphalia and Lower Saxony). Antinuclear agitation was minimal in conservative strongholds (Rhineland-Pfalz and Schleswig-Holstein).[8]

Bavarian particularism infused the campaign in southern Germany. A GCND committee was established by the SPD, but no one paid much attention to it. Instead, Hans Werner Richter created an alternative organization, the Komitee gegen Atomrüstung (Committee against Nuclear Armaments or CNA) in April. Richter, leader of the "Gruppe 47" literary circle and president of the European Federation, gave the Bavarian campaign a more intellectual and internationalist flavor. Its manifesto, titled "Appeal from Personalities of Cultural Life," highlighted the need for a spiritual climate in Europe, if detente and disarmament were to flourish. Though financially tied to the GCND, the Bavarians rarely followed the directives of the Bonn Central Committee.[9]

The West Berlin GCND also gained semi-autonomy. The city, though socialist, evinced little enthusiasm for the antinuclear campaign. Its citizens felt vulnerable, fully dependent on America's willingness to defend it; most, including West Berlin's dynamic new mayor, Willy Brandt, saw wisdom in the chancellor's national security policy.[10] Brandt was wholly at odds with the national SPD's defense policy; if possible, he would have declared West Berlin a nuclear-rhetoric-free zone. But Brandt's chief rival within the local SPD, Franz Neumann, repeatedly tried to use the antinuclear campaign to discredit the young mayor. Brandt took the path of least resistance and supported the GCND; but he placed his own men in charge of the local committee, giving it a different accent from that of the national campaign. No referendum motion was introduced into the Berlin Senate; and the local May Day parade—which since 1945 had been held to celebrate the city's freedom from the East— was not turned into an antinuclear demonstration. Furthermore, the party convention passed a strong anti-Communist resolution. "The Communists have up to this very day greeted with jubilation every Soviet nuclear test and every missile experiment. They lack any moral justification for meddling in these matters which are of such concern to us."[11] Brandt was able to dominate the local GCND, but not without alienating the intellectuals, theologians, students, and Neumann supporters who made up the campaign's ranks.[12]

The eleven state and city-state GCND committees held nearly a hundred demonstrations throughout the country during the summer of 1958. The greatest number, twenty-six, occurred in North Rhine-Westphalia, as part of the election campaign. Eighteen demonstrations were held in Bavaria (five in Munich alone). Fourteen took place in Baden-Württemberg, nine in Lower Saxony and Hessen, five in Rhineland-Pfalz. In West Berlin, four demonstrations occurred, while Bremen and Hamburg each held two. In Schleswig-Holstein, only one major demonstration took place. Most of the demonstrations attracted 1,000 to 2,000 sympathizers, though in smaller cities crowds of 500 were typical. Eight demonstrations brought ten thousand or more to the streets: Hamburg (150,000), Bielefeld (25,000), Munich (10,000), Bremen (25,000), Karlsruhe (20,000), Frankfurt (30,000), Ulm (15,000), and Hanover (40,000).[13] Student antinuclear groups synchronized demonstrations on May 20 and 21 at fifteen major universities; taken together, they drew crowds of 20,000.[14]

The wave of demonstrations in North Rhine-Westphalia and Bavaria best illustrates the course of the GCND campaign. In North Rhine-Westphalia, demonstrations commenced in mid-April in Cologne and continued until the election in early July. The April demonstrations, insofar as attendance figures are available, showed a modicum of success for the organizers: Dortmund (2,500), Bielefeld (25,000), Wuppertal (4,000), Münster (1,400), and Bonn (700). Fewer demonstrations were held in May, but attendance was still noteworthy: Münster (1,200) and Essen (2,000). By June, however, attendance had dwindled to less than a thousand (no records were even kept for some of the later events); the exception was an 11,000-strong demonstration in Dortmund.[15]

In Bavaria, the CNA forces implemented a different strategy. They planned a series of small demonstrations for April. As the populace became more enlightened, they reasoned, larger events would be generated until the whole nation became activized. Instead, a skewed bell curve emerged. The first Munich demonstration attracted 2,000. The second one drew 10,000, a record-breaking crowd in postwar Bavaria. Follow-up demonstrations in May and June, however, never attracted more than 5,000. Some demonstrations were also held in other cities, Nuremberg (3,000), Augsburg (2,000), and Erlangen (1,200); but in the heart of "Strauss country" (the farms and villages) the CNA never even got organized.[16]

The pattern repeated itself in all eleven states. The best-attended events were in April and May; by June, interest had ebbed to such a degree that subsequent demonstrations became painful reminders of a colossal failure.[17] All together, perhaps a half million persons joined the official GCND demonstrations. At best, a full million were drawn peripherally into the cause, if the DGB-sponsored May Day celebrations and the numerous local antinuclear initiatives are included in the tally. The totals, while not in themselves minuscule, were insignificant within a larger framework. The Metalworkers Union alone had nearly two million members; the other fifteen unions had another four million members. In the last federal elections, over nine million had voted for the SPD. The GCND leaders were unable to mobilize even a significant fraction of their own forces, let alone the fifty-five million citizens across the land.[18]

Were socialists rushing in where liberals feared to tread? From the outset, the FDP's participation in the GCND was downright hesitant. They sent a representative to the first meeting, but he refused to commit his party to the campaign. When elected to the Bonn Central Committee, he declined the honor, leaving the spot vacant.[19]

It was the arrows in the GCND's quiver—demonstrations, strikes, referenda—that made FDP leaders fear that democracy (not nuclear policy) would fall victim to SPD agitation. The liberals, parliamentarians to the core, savored election campaigns, not protest rallies; Bundestag debates, not extraparliamentary agitation; political consensus, not street demagogy. How could the FDP support a political strike when the party's strength lay among middle-class business-men, professionals, and industrialists? How could they support the SPD's unconstitutional referenda initiatives, when the FDP's own founding father, Theodor Heuss, had written the West German constitution in the first place?[20]

The FDP's dilatoriness also reflected a six-week impasse among liberal leaders over the future political direction of the party. Chairman Reinhold Maier, Erich Mende, and Wolfgang Mischnick felt that "SPD" was indelibly stamped on the antinuclear banner; if the liberals joined the GCND, the FDP would appear redundant to some voters, too radical for others. They wanted the party to withhold its blessing to the GCND campaign unless "more groups from the political middle became involved." The FDP's former chairman, Thomas Dehler, and the "Young Turks" of North Rhine-Westphalia, felt otherwise. The FDP *was* the political middle! They planned to participate in GCND rallies, and urged the party to join them.[21] In the end, both factions found a mutually acceptable solution: the FDP would not lend institutional support to the GCND, but FDP members could speak at the rallies and campaign against nuclear weapons (see document 6). While condemning the "radical-Communist" and "radical-pacifist" elements within the antinuclear campaign, the FDP advised its members to "support all appropriate efforts to enlighten the populace on the dangers of nuclear armaments."[22]

As with the GCND, so with the referendum motions. There was never a possibility the FDP would give its blessing to the SPD's national, state, and local referendum initiatives. The constitution prohibited national referenda except for the purpose of settling boundary disputes; and it invested the federal government (not the states and cities) with full authority over defense and foreign policy. The issue was so clear-cut, the outcome so predictable, that virtually all national and state parliamentary factions chose to side with the CDU/CSU against the SPD in the upcoming Bundestag and Landtag debates.[23] But a few state and local factions—Bremen, Hamburg, Frankfurt am Main, and North Rhine-Westphalia—had either already committed themselves to the referendum initiatives, or were inclined to do so in the interest of an FDP–SPD alliance. As a result, no one in the country seemed to know "what the FDP actually intended to do."[24] Was the FDP supposed to tell voters that referenda were demagogic in most instances, but lofty expressions of democracy in Hamburg and Bremen? That they were unconstitutional in Mainz, but not in Frankfurt? The FDP national leaders' final decision on referenda (made in mid-April) combined principle with pragmatism. State leaders were told to eschew further referenda; the next seven state elections were to function as "substitute" referenda in which the will of the people would find expression. Since it was too late to reverse the decisions already made in Bremen, Hamburg, and Frankfurt, the liberals sanctioned these only on the grounds that no elections were scheduled in the immediate future.[25]

The FDP's decision doomed the referenda almost everywhere, but the socialists decided to hold the debates anyway for their agitational value. Their Bundestag motion called for a direct vote by the electorate on two questions: "Do you agree that the German armed forces should be equipped with nuclear explosives?" "Are you agreed that launching pads for nuclear explosives should be placed in Germany?" The SPD introduced similar parliamentary motions in Bavaria, Schleswig-Holstein, Lower Saxony, Baden-Württemberg, Hessen, Bremen, and Hamburg.[26] The national debate occurred in

---

DOCUMENT 6

The FDP Executive Board's Official Election Platform for North Rhine-Westphalia

1. The FDP supports West Germany's adherence to NATO and a German defense contribution composed of modern, conventionally equipped air, naval, and army units.
2. Membership in NATO does not obligate West Germany to nuclearize its Bundeswehr.
3. Nuclearizing the Bundeswehr does not increase West Germany's security; instead it greatly increases the danger of nuclear war.
4. Nuclear weapons in both Germanies inhibits detente in Central Europe, and thereby thwarts the reunification of Germany.
5. By nuclearizing West German troops, the federal government is undermining its own efforts at securing a general, controlled disarmament worldwide.

late April. The gravity of the nuclear issue necessitated a direct vote, the SPD argued; the results would be morally if not legally binding on the Bundestag. The CDU/CSU responded that West Germany was a parliamentary democracy and the Bundestag had the final word on all foreign policy issues. The outcome was predictable: the SPD's motion lost by a vote of 215 to 123.[27] The state debates (simultaneous with the national debate) offered the public the exotic spectacle of foreign policy being discussed in state chambers. The best display took place in Bavaria. State SPD leaders, reiterating the viewpoint of the national party, argued that nuclear weaponry was not the proper defense for a divided country. The CSU Minister-President responded that referenda were "instruments of demagogy" that undermined parliamentary politics. "The populace is not like a parliament or government which can meet every day in order to assess the changing world situation and reevaluate the opinion-building process in light of these changes."[28] The debate ended in a defeat for the Bavarian SPD, an outcome that was replicated in Schleswig-Holstein, Baden-Württemberg, and Hessen.[29]

In Bremen, Hamburg, and Frankfurt, where the local SPD and FDP voted in favor of referenda, the chancellor threatened court action. "The referendum signifies an attempt to exert influence on the Bundestag and federal government in an unauthorized manner," he noted in a letter to these municipalities. "Both defense and foreign policy belong to the exclusive jurisdiction of the federal government."[30] The three city governments postponed their referenda, but a few tiny villages on the outskirts of Frankfurt—Odersbach, Niedershausen, and Blessenbach—failed to oblige. They were all workers' towns, their residents predominantly SPD. The local mayors drafted referenda that "prohibited the deployment or stationing" of nuclear warheads within their town limits. Citizens needed only go to the local Rathaus and sign their names to a prepared list. When only ten percent made use of their voting privilege, volunteers took the lists door-to-door. By the next day, over 90 percent had "voted" in favor of nuclear-free villages. "Even most of the farmers gave their signature," explained the Odersbach mayor to *Der Spiegel* in an interview. "They have been grumbling for a long time about the weather: 'if they'd knock off all that nuclear rubbish, the weather would get better.' "[31]

The chancellor took the issue directly to the German Supreme Court. When the Court adjudicated the case two months later, it decided in the chancellor's favor on all counts. "Matters of defense and foreign policy belong exclusively to the legal, governmental, and administrative competence of the federal government as stated in Articles 65, 73, and 87 of the Basic Laws." The Court declared the Bremen and Hamburg referendum laws unconstitutional, and held the state of Hessen legally responsible for tolerating the referenda in the three villages. The Court's decision put an end to all plans for a direct vote by the populace.[32]

As the GCND held rallies and the SPD pursued referenda, the trade unions wrestled with another means of agitation—the strike. Two types of strikes were possible (though the distinction was frequently blurred): a short-term "warning strike" to demonstrate the unions' political clout; and a "general strike" with the goal of toppling the chancellor and his government. The general strike was the greatest weapon in the DGB's arsenal; but, like any superweapon, it carried with it enormous political, financial, technical, and legal fallout.

Pressure in the direction of a political strike mounted on the DGB from above, from below, and from the left. SPD and GCND personnel wanted a one- to three-day work stoppage if the referenda failed. Renate Riemeck penned the "Appeal of the 44 Professors," which called for a nuclear-free zone. Thirteen of the DGB's sixteen unions pushed for greater labor activism; small "wildcat" strikes broke out at some twenty factories.[33] Opinion polls suggested that over 50 percent of the populace found it "appropriate to engage in a strike in order to hinder the nuclearization of the Bundeswehr."[34]

From the Soviet zone came the demand for a general strike. (While hardly surprising, their demand was rich in irony: the East German government itself had survived a general strike only through Soviet military intervention in 1953.) Thousands of letters arrived at DGB headquarters from East Germany, signed by Communist party functionaries, World Peace Council members, union shop stewards, professors, teachers, students, and even schoolchildren, who wrote letters to the DGB as part of their homework assignments. "The Adenauer clique is accelerating with a mad fury the resurgence of Fascist militarism," one such letter stated. "The reactionary majority in Bonn's parliament have voted in favor of nuclear weapons against the unanimous will of the German populace. They have thereby increased the chances for annihilation through nuclear war."[35] Meanwhile, counterfeit circulars arrived at local DGB offices. Their message: "DGB members! Prepare your colleagues for extraparliamentary action against the threatening nuclear danger! Total resistance to the total war!"[36]

At DGB headquarters, the "wildcat" strikes were condemned, the East German letters left unread, the political pressures unwelcomed. It was one thing for outsiders to cry for action, quite another for those responsible to examine the legal, technical, and financial consequences. DGB leaders had weighed all their options—strikes, demonstrations, antinuclear May Day parades, work stoppages at nuclear sites, internal DGB referenda, financial contributions to SPD candidates—long before the letters and manifestos began to pour in. If anything, the pressure made DGB leaders resistant to taking action, so as not to seem to be kowtowing to pressure from East Germans, labor radicals, or the SPD.[37]

"What can and what should we do in the present situation?" DGB chairman Willi Richter asked the executive board when it met to discuss strike policy in late March. "What goal should a general strike have? Should the government's resignation and new Bundestag elections be demanded?"[38] Hermann Grote, the DGB's legal expert (and a GCND activist), easily convinced the executive board that neither a general strike nor a large-scale work stoppage was in the unions' best interests. West German law, he noted, permitted strikes over "working conditions" and "industrial relations agreements"; political strikes were permissible only during a "state emergency," as had occurred during the Kapp putsch of 1920. If the unions went on strike for a political cause, the DGB would have to pay compensation and workers' wages would be docked. "A political general strike cannot be used against a legitimate government that respects the fundamental rights of the constitution. This holds true even if the trade unions consider it necessary to fight with all legal means this freely elected government because of its politics."[39]

The question of a short-term work stoppage was less easily resolved; on this issue, all the political fissures within the DGB became exposed. Otto Brenner (of the Metalworkers' Union) and a handful of board members demanded a one-day strike; others wanted an hour-long strike in connection with a GCND demonstration. Still others felt it sufficed to march under the antinuclear banner at the approaching May Day parades. The Christian-Socialist Collegiate, a CDU-inclined labor faction, opposed any antinuclear activism.[40]

Eventually, the executive board selected Hamburg as the ideal testing ground for a work stoppage. Hamburg was a large city, controlled by an SPD government. (As one board member put it, the citizens there "expected a large demonstration" and would be disappointed if the DGB failed to oblige them.)[41] The local unions, instead of proclaiming a work stoppage, simply instructed workers to leave work an hour early, thereby generating a de facto strike while sidestepping the legal and financial problems. To augment attendance, the local Transportation Union brought mass transit to a standstill, trapping commuters in the downtown area where the demonstration was to be held.[42] The good organization and timing worked. The demonstration—at which Hamburg mayor Max Bauer and FDP leader Wolfgang Döring spoke—attracted 150,000 persons, a record-breaking crowd in postwar Germany (not topped until the antinuclear demonstrations of 1981 and 1982). And two weeks later, at the Hamburg May Day parade, nearly 200,000 took to the streets in what was the most highly charged May Day celebration since the 1920s.[43]

The Hamburg demonstration reopened discussion over a larger strike initiative. As before, the executive board opposed a long-term or general strike. ("The populace is not ready for that," Reuter told GCND leaders in late April. "Our populace is still slumbering, the boiling point of indignation has not been reached.") But labor leaders were divided on the question of sponsoring another warning strike. Some felt it would serve as a "means of consciousness-raising," others that it would lead to costly litigation. There was also the question of effectiveness: would a warning strike alter the government's stance?[44]

The DGB's executive board finally hit upon a possible way out of its impasse. As an alternative to a work stoppage in West Germany, it tried to interest its European colleagues in a short, European-wide warning strike in conjunction with the upcoming NATO Foreign Ministers Conference or the next superpower summit meeting. This would call attention to international labor solidarity and focus pressure on the chancellor. But the plan backfired when the International Confederation of Free Trade Unions (ICFTU) met in Brussels in May. ICFTU delegates told the DGB leaders that they "wanted nothing to do with such actions." They suggested that—in the interest of labor solidarity!—the DGB drop the strike issue.[45] Hamburg remained the sole site of a political strike.

On July 6, 1958, North Rhine-Westphalians went to the polls. While it was merely a state election, everyone knew that each vote counted as an unofficial plebiscite for or against nuclear weapons, for or against an SPD–FDP alliance, for or against the CDU's defense policy. It was the optimal site for the SPD to test the effectiveness of its antinuclear effort. Lying along the Ruhr valley, North Rhine-Westphalia was highly industrialized and densely populated (over one-fourth of West Germans resided there), a power base for unionism and socialism. Since 1956, an SPD–FDP coalition governed under an SPD Minister-President.

While the SPD looked at the elections with hope and optimism, the liberals were full of apprehension and dread. The FDP had a troubled past in North Rhine-Westphalia; in the early postwar era, its leaders tended to be more nationalist than liberal, more Fascist than democratic. Though the so-called "Young Turks" purged this element in 1956, they did not proceed in an artful manner. They had first withdrawn the FDP from the state government coalition, forcing the resignation of a popular Minister-President, Karl Arnold; they then established a socialist–liberal coalition, in defiance of the FDP's election promises. North Rhine-Westphalia's voters responded by giving the liberals only 7 percent of the vote in the 1957 federal election, a drop of 5 percent from four years earlier. When Karl Arnold died in the midst of the July 1958 election campaign, the FDP's prospects for a reconciliation with voters grew even dimmer.[46]

The SPD–FDP coalition had another liability. The two parties were united mostly over the matter of national security policy. Defense politics, as "Young Turk" Wolfgang Döring pointed out, cemented the coalition; it was the nuclear issue "around which the election campaign would revolve." But domestic issues, not national defense policy, tended to be decisive in state elections, and the coalition partners were at odds over socioeconomic policy. While the SPD was eager to implement a planned economy, the FDP demanded "no socialist experiments on the Rhine and Ruhr." The coalition partners had to convince voters that the nation's foreign policy hinged on a state election; and they had to mask their divergences in domestic policy in the interest of a smooth election campaign.[47]

For the CDU, the state election was a critical test of the chancellor's nuclear policy. In the previous federal elections, CDU/CSU had highlighted the nation's domestic prosperity, while relegating defense policy to a secondary place. But since that time, a number of events—the recent Bundestag debates, the 1958 Protestant synod, and GCND demonstrations—had made nuclear politics the leading issue of the day. For the only time during his tenure in office, Adenauer allowed defense matters to dominate the CDU/CSU's election strategy.[48]

The conservatives reminded voters of Central Europe's vulnerability to Soviet military might, and stressed the Federal Republic's dual commitment to a Western alliance and a balanced arms control agreement. "What about the Campaign against Nuclear Death?" the chancellor asked at a Krefeld rally in June:

> I want to tell you the following tale, which some of you may have already read in the newspapers. Two months ago I was in London, and in front of the German embassy where I was staying, a 36-hour or 48-hour demonstration was taking place. Men and women were taking turns carrying signs in front of the embassy. The first sign read: "No nuclear bombs for Khrushchev." I wish our GCND movement would carry a sign like that for once! The next sign read: "No nuclear bombs for Eisenhower"; the next read: "No nuclear bombs for Macmillan"; and the last read: "No nuclear bombs for Adenauer." Now, my friends, since that so completely dovetailed with my own politics, I invited them into the German embassy to drink tea with me. Some of them accepted. They gave their signs to others and came to visit with me. One thing I can tell you. We were completely unanimous in our political views.[49]

The voters listened to the chancellor, not the GCND forces. In a microcosm of the federal election, the CDU won an absolute majority (50.5 percent), the first in North Rhine-Westphalia's history. The SPD gained slightly from previous elections (39 percent, which meant five more mandates). The FDP (with 7 percent of the vote) lost ten of its twenty-five mandates.[50]

The North Rhine-Westphalian election robbed the GCND of its momentum. The whole offensive ended in a rout. Nowhere had West Germans expressed their support for the antinuclear campaign— not in the polling booths, not in the streets. The referendum motions had been defeated everywhere except the SPD-controlled regions of Hamburg, Bremen, and Frankfurt. Even in these cities, it never came to a vote, for the German Supreme Court had declared the referenda unconstitutional. Legal concerns also hobbled the effort to organize a politically inspired work stoppage. Trade union leaders shrank from the prospect of declaring a general strike. While toppling the chancellor, they might have undermined the efficacy of parliamentary democracy—a consequence none of them welcomed. A warning strike posed the reverse problem. Largely a symbolic gesture, at best its effects were indirect—if the strike found resonance within the populace, it might swell the ranks of the GCND, tip the state elections, and force the government to rethink its position. But these "ifs" and "mights" had to be measured against more immediate consequences for the DGB. Warning strikes were opposed by the Christian labor faction and the DGB's international organization. The DGB would be fined, the strikers' wages docked. Prudence dictated that the DGB use the strike sparingly—in Hamburg, for instance, where they need not fear repercussions.

Had the city-by-city demonstrations achieved momentum, the DGB executive board might well have reconsidered its position (the Metalworkers lobbied diligently all summer for a strike). But the GCND demonstrations did not mobilize citizens against the government; instead, the rally wave swelled and ebbed within a few short months without becoming a mass movement. "Unfortunately, things did not develop along the lines that would allow us to engage in larger actions now, as the most recent poorly attended demonstrations prove," the DGB chairman, Willi Richter, admitted at summer's end. "The populace has spoken in favor of a Bundeswehr in the elections."[51] The amount of financial assistance that the DGB gave the GCND exceeded that of any previous cause they had supported. But it all came to nought. "The public hardly pays any attention to the nuclear question anymore," the Transportation Union's president told his colleagues when they discussed the future of the GCND. A strike? "We wouldn't get anyone to take to the streets."[52]

The demonstrations forced the DGB (not the government) to rethink its position. Labor leaders did not want to abandon the GCND; but neither did they wish to throw good money after bad. So the funds dried up (except for those secretly channeled to the GCND by the Metalworkers) and the DGB awaited further developments.[53] All this passivity had a depressing effect on GCND rank-and-file. By November, North Rhine-Westphalian leaders reported that their committee was "at a complete standstill." The Hessen committee was set to dissolve within a month. Other committees had planned some local events, but subsequently cancelled them due to lack of funds and public interest. Antinuclear leaders had retired from public view, the media had ceased covering the campaign, state and local committees were falling apart.[54]

The most visible consequence of the North Rhine-Westphalian election was the FDP's retreat from antinuclear politics. The liberals, having suffered three consecutive electoral defeats since leaving the government coalition in April 1956, could now only conclude that they were on the brink of political extinction. "The CDU-backed Bundestag decision of March 25 to nuclearize the Bundeswehr only aroused the emotions of the populace at the beginning," noted the FDP's postmortem election reports. "The excitation could not be maintained over the long run because the opposition could not keep it alive sufficiently." The chancellor had taken advantage of the dwindling enthusiasm. He turned the public's attention back to overall strategic questions, reminded voters of West Germany's affinity with the Western world, and turned the nuclear scare into a "Bolshevik panic." By stressing West Germany's commitment to global disarmament, the chancellor successfully co-opted the GCND's own slogan and amended it to read: "Campaign against Nuclear Death *in the Whole World*."[55]

SPD leaders were more optimistic than trade unionists and liberals. Unlike the FDP, the SPD had not suffered a resounding defeat in North Rhine-Westphalia. Socialists had picked up 700,000 new voters since the last 1954 state elections, a gain of five percent; these were the best election results for the socialists in the Rhine-Ruhr area in the postwar era. Interpreting this as a sign of burgeoning opposition to the chancellor's defense policy, the SPD decided to run the next several state elections under the antinuclear banner.[56] Two events, however, forced the SPD to rethink its position: the Berlin crisis of November 1958, and the Berlin Student Congress held in January 1959, in which the Communist-led Standing Congress and socialist-led GCND forces struggled for control of the peace movement.

Berlin: A Pax Bolshevika?

WEST Berlin's role in postwar European affairs was unique. Situated deep within the Soviet zone, the city was a major battleground of the cold war. For the Western allies, it was a store window, with democracy and freedom on display; for the Soviets, it was a conduit through which Western ideas poured in and East German citizens poured out. In 1948, Stalin blockaded West Berlin, unsuccessfully trying to turn military proximity into political control without risking a larger confrontation. A decade later, in the midst of the GCND campaign, Khrushchev convinced himself that the "balance of forces" had changed, and that his "missile diplomacy" would succeed where Stalin's blockade had failed.

In November 1958, Khrushchev demanded that West Berlin be turned into a "demilitarized free city" and gave the Western powers six months to negotiate an acceptable settlement. "The Soviet government holds to its position that the Federal Republic renounce nuclear weapons," the Soviet foreign minister, Andrei Gromyko, wrote in a private letter to Hans Kroll, the West German ambassador in Moscow. "It will not make the Federal Republic stronger since the utilization of these weapons is for all practical purposes impossible. In the event of war, the Federal Republic would be annihilated. Moreover, nuclearizing the Bundeswehr will necessarily trigger a nuclear arms race that will enormously increase international tensions and the danger of war."[57] The blustering went on for months. Berlin was likely to become a Sarajevo, Gromyko warned, if no agreement was reached. Khrushchev told West German journalists that their country would be "rubbed off the face of the map" in the event of nuclear war with the East.[58]

While Western leaders entered into protracted negotiations with the Soviets, Mayor Brandt turned the local Berlin elections of December into a virtual referendum against the Khrushchev ultimatum. He distanced himself from the SPD's national party plank, kept GCND leaders out of the campaign, and avoided the socialists' traditional policy slogans. Adopting the chancellor's campaign style and message, he promised Berlin voters "no experiments," and highlighted the SPD's affinity to the West.[59]

Through Brandt's eloquence, the Berlin SPD received an absolute majority—its second-best election victory in postwar history. Nearly 53 percent voted SPD, 38 percent CDU, and less than 4 percent FDP. The SPD received 78 mandates, the CDU 55; since the FDP failed to jump the 5 percent hurdle, they were not represented.[60] The ironic twist was that Brandt secured for the SPD its long-sought victory against the CDU under circumstances that caused the SPD's national leadership great embarrassment. Brandt attained what Ollenhauer could not, in the name of diametrically opposite politics to the GCND. Having achieved his goal, Brandt magnanimously formed a "Great Coalition" with local CDU leaders, setting a precedent that would launch his drive for the chancellorship. "We are not being confronted with an Adenauer ultimatum, but with a Russian ultimatum," Brandt noted at the local party convention in late December. "We and the world are being threatened by Russian nuclear bombs."[61]

Khrushchev's ultimatum and the Berlin elections put a kink in the GCND's agenda. A Student Congress was scheduled for West Berlin on January 3, 1959, with the purpose of breathing new life into the peace movement. Originally conceived as a closed-door meeting of three hundred West German student activists, it was now most certainly going to be held amidst political crisis, sensation-seeking reporters, and a hostile citizenry.

The Berlin Congress was the brainchild of university students under the aegis of Frankfurt University's Central Coordinating Committee. Like other antinuclear groups, it consisted primarily of socialists, liberals, and Protestants, with leaders of the SPD's Socialist Student Federation at the helm. But the student movement was unique, for it viewed itself as a "united front" with Communists and Communist sympathizers in its ranks: World Peace Council members, Standing Congress students, and the editorial staff of *konkret*. Klaus Rainer Röhl and Ulrike Meinhof led this faction.[62]

The socialist–Communist alliance caused the GCND's Bonn Central Committee grave concern. For months they pressured the students to select a site other than Berlin for the Student Congress, twice cutting off funds to forestall the event. But the students—delighting in the opportunity to harass Brandt—refused to budge. The SPD also tried to force a break with the *konkret* faction, on the grounds that it would be prelude to a takeover. "There exists a concrete [*konkret*] danger that the planned congress will be sabotaged by antidemocratic forces," student leaders were warned confidentially.[63] But this only made the student Coordinating Committee more intransigent (for a while they even considered making Renate Riemeck the host speaker), and the *konkret* faction was able to maintain a student majority in favor of a united front. "Only one fact can govern our judgment about the various groups and personalities: their opposition to nuclear armaments," Meinhof argued at the decisive meeting.[64]

Were GCND and SPD leaders overreacting? Were the Communists interested in "peaceful coexistence" within the peace movement? Not at all. *Konkret* leaders invited hundreds of East German students to attend the West Berlin Congress in early January. When barred admission, they staged a parallel "Friendship Congress" at East Berlin's Humboldt University. Robert Havemann, East Berlin's World Peace Council chairman, exhorted the students of West Berlin to "unite the peace forces of the entire nation against the nuclearization of West Germany. . . . Whoever wants the Germans to do something about the problem, cannot but promote a neutralization status for West Berlin."[65]

As the East Germans worked from the outside, the *konkret* faction seized control of the West Berlin Congress from the inside. With the GCND campaign at a virtual standstill, the trade unions inactive, and the SPD unsure how to react to the Khrushchev ultimatum, the time had come to channel the students' frustration into radical activism. ("We wanted, to put it simply, a victory, although we did not possess a majority," Röhl later admitted).[66] The events that unfolded had all the elements of a romanticized Bolshevik takeover. Röhl's memoirs are bombastic (and his account of Meinhof's role overdramatized) but they offer a psychologically revealing glimpse into the Communist-backed side of the antinuclear campaign:[67]

> There were five working groups. We didn't send anybody to two of them. One I set aside to tie up potential opponents. There remained two working groups, one that handled the "All-German" theme, the other the "International" theme. We made it look like we were concentrating our best forces in the International working group. There we shadowboxed with the best speakers of the opposition. Ulrike [Meinhof], Erika [Runge], and I were there, with Ulrike as discussion leader. Helmut Schmidt—the star speaker for the SPD—dissipated his energies in long discussions with Ulrike. Meanwhile, the decision fell in the other working group, the All-German one. We had more good people. Opitz and Stern, with the help of Erich Kuby, pushed through a resolution that was sensational for its day.

The "sensational" resolution reiterated in mild form the long-standing demands of the East German government and the Khrushchev ultimatum. Claiming that Adenauer had followed a policy of "No negotiation with Pankow [the provisional capital of East Germany]," it demanded that West Germany sign a peace treaty with East Germany and "seek an interim confederation."[68] The *konkret* forces then introduced the resolution to the full plenum, where it received a majority before the GCND could muster enough voices against it. The vote was a major symbolic victory for the *konkret* forces, highly touted by the East German press as proof that students had grown tired of the socialists, trade unionists, and bourgeois pacifists who had led the antinuclear campaign in the past.[69] "On the morning of our complete victory," Röhl rhapsodized, "I ran from lecture hall to lecture hall, and assembled our people. I distributed vitamin tablets and glucose, and showed them the morning newspapers with the headlines: 'Castro Takes Havana!' "[70]

The headlines in West German newspapers read differently: "Gravediggers of Freedom," "Duped," "Sabotaged"—West Berlin, not Cuba.[71] "The terminology of the resolution and the one-sided accent on a confederation, not to mention the circumstances under which it was sanctioned yesterday after the psychological ground-work was laid elsewhere, has created an enormous fissure," the SPD's representative, Helmut Schmidt, told the delegates before abandoning antinuclear activism for good. "The sanctioning of such a one-sided resolution does nothing to serve the German movement against the nuclearization of the Bundeswehr. Instead, it undermines its credibility."[72]

The original GCND–SPD student organizers of the congress, now cast in the role of Mensheviks, confronted the *konkret* group at a private meeting in late January. They threatened to withdraw their support if the controversial Berlin resolution was not immediately rescinded.[73] At the Coordinating Committee meeting a month later, they requested the antinuclear committees to commit themselves to "the battle for the maintenance of the legally sanctioned democracy and the basic freedoms of citizens" and demanded that the committees eschew cooperation with "unmistakably anti-democratic forces—be they demonstrably Communist or demonstrably Fascist."[74]

Konkret leaders, however, were not interested in yielding to these demands, so obviously directed at them. "The guiding principle of further activity," they argued, "is the campaign against the acquisition of nuclear weapons by West Germany, and—in keeping with the spirit of the Berlin resolution—the pursuit of democracy, detente, a nuclear-free zone and new steps toward reunification."[75] Nor were they interested in reconciliation. Sensing that they could still ride the wave of student frustration, they convinced the Coordinating Committee to select a new five-member governing board, monopolized by the *konkret* forces. The GCND–SPD faction promptly withdrew its support. "The distinguishing characteristic of the student movement against nuclear weapons has always been the number of socialists, liberals, Protestants, and Catholics, where young people of diverse origins and opinions work together," its leaders noted in resignation. "The committees we represent are not willing to become a platform for the one-sided propagation of negotiations between Bonn and Pankow, especially when the objective of these negotiations is to be limited to the confederation and peace treaty questions."[76]

The *konkret* faction—now virtually the only active extraparliamentary force—set out to breathe life back into the peace movement. But was it "peace" they offered, a *pax bolshevika?* And was there still a "movement"? Storming a congress was not the same as taking Havana, and forging an offensive was not as easy as sabotaging the opposition. They were, in fact, the proud victors of an utterly discredited movement. Aside from a few radicalized students, the tiny *konkret* faction found support only among East German youth and West German Communists. For the next several months, *konkret* sponsored congresses, distributed leaflets, wrote articles, staged demonstrations. But they soon came to realize that the antinuclear forces now had more chiefs than Indians; the other peace warriors had migrated away. "We were victorious at the congresses that we ourselves convoked," Röhl admitted, "but in reality we were completely isolated."[77]

In the minds of West Germans, the Berlin Student Congress had irreversibly cast the GCND as an organization of well-meaning Social Democrats, university professors, and students easily duped by a tightly knit organization of Communist saboteurs. The Khrushchev ultimatum, Brandt's electoral victory, paralysis within the DGB, the dissolution of state committees—the tales of woe were long. "It's all very distressing," wrote the GCND's general manager, Alexander Maass, about the course of recent events. "The New Year is beginning with little to rejoice about."[78]

THE catchy message of the 1960s war protestors—"What if they held a war and no one came?"—must have seemed ironic to the GCND veterans of the 1950s. They had mobilized for peace, and no one marched with them; they had held demonstrations and no one had come. The GCND had striven to activize the populace, solidify an SPD–FDP alliance, and win electoral victories against the conservatives. By 1959, it was clear that the GCND could not attain any of its goals. The demonstrations had not kindled the fire of opposition to the chancellor's nuclear policies. The FDP, far from embracing the socialists, had only loosely associated itself with the

GCND; when the North Rhine-Westphalian elections resulted in a conservative victory, the FDP simply dropped out of antinuclear politics, allowing it to become the exclusive province of socialist and labor leaders.

The DGB backed the GCND vigorously, supplying it with personnel and financial assistance. But DGB leaders were at odds over policy. Brenner had wanted to use the strike as the DGB's main weapon, despite the legal and financial difficulties involved. Others wanted to proceed more cautiously, following rather than leading public opinion. The DGB could therefore satisfy no one. Labor's left wing found the executive board too timid, its right wing found it too bold. The SPD wanted labor to get more involved in the parliamentary and election process, but this brought the DGB into conflict with everyone from the chancellor to the FDP, from Christian labor leaders to the DGB's own international affiliate. Unable to resolve the tensions within its organization, or influence public opinion on the nuclear issue, the DGB eventually took a passive stance, leaving only the SPD at the forefront of the campaign.

It is not difficult to trace, step-by-step, the SPD's disillusionment with antinuclear politics. First, the North Rhine-Westphalian election (and subsequent state elections over the next year) made clear that an antinuclear platform was not a "vote-getter," despite the highly touted opinion polls showing nearly 80 percent of West Germans as opposing nuclear weapons. The only region where the SPD actually increased its rolls was in West Berlin, where Brandt was pursuing a policy diametrically opposed to that of the national leadership.

A second cause of disillusionment was the Berlin crisis. There was no doubt in the minds of West German voters that the Soviet Union was pursuing an expansionist policy against the West. The chancellor's popularity rose, as it had during all previous East–West crises, leaving the opposition parties little room to maneuver. After Khrushchev's ultimatum, any Western leader championing nuclear-free zones in Central Europe was courting political suicide.

The third stage of disillusionment followed from the second: the SPD could never free the GCND from the stigma of Communist infiltration. Despite repeated attempts by Menzel to purge Communists from the GCND's ranks, there was simply too much visible sabotage, too many camouflage organizations, too many parallel demonstrations. When the *konkret* faction undermined the Berlin Student Congress, they only confirmed what most West Germans suspected all along.

The demise of the GCND campaign completed a pattern of defeat that had begun several years earlier. Antinuclear advocates had failed to mobilize the scientific community against the chancellor's defense policies; they had failed even to prod the Göttingen 18 scientists or the German Physics Society into the forefront of the antinuclear movement. Similarly, the Brethren had failed to convince the Protestants to take a stance against nuclear weapons. Brethren leaders found themselves isolated within the religious community, and unable to spread their message beyond their own constituencies. Trade union and socialist leaders learned the same lesson from the GCND campaign: it was easier to preach to the faithful than to win new converts.

Without doubt, the chancellor played a major role in the defeat of the extraparliamentary forces. He was an effective communicator, with a well-deserved reputation for explaining complex issues to the public in simple terms. He had the party press at his side, and more access to the media than his opponents. He enlisted support for his policies among a wide range of intellectuals from Helmut Thielicke to Karl Jaspers; and occasionally, as during the critical North Rhine-Westphalian elections, he entered the fray himself, exploiting his enormous popularity in order to tip the scales in favor of conservative candidates.

The responsibility for the demise of the antinuclear movement, however, did not reside in the chancellor's prestige, or the manipulation of public opinion by conservatives. Nuclear annihilation was an abstract threat to Germans, whereas the spread of Communism in Central Europe was not. Every disturbance in the Soviet bloc— from the Czech coup of 1948 to the Hungarian revolt of 1956, from the Berlin blockade of 1948 to the Khrushchev ultimatum a decade later—gave the aging chancellor a new lease on his political life. Given the alternatives, voters preferred the relative security of NATO to the iron hand of Soviet power. Weighing the risk of nuclear war against the risk of a conventional Soviet invasion, voters handed the chancellor victory after victory.

The nuclear opposition in West Germany was deeply divided internally, particularly between its Communist and socialist wings. This alone should have offered sufficient warning to both sides that their hopes would come to nought. Rather than presenting a united front against nuclear weapons, the competing groups mirrored the cold war divisions. They stood in opposing camps, and they represented different political and economic values. The Social Democrats of the GCND were devoted to parliamentary life and democratic politics. Though they kept their distance from the Communist factions, they were nonetheless slow to realize that their democratic values were threatened as much by Communist peace ideologues as by Warsaw Pact troops. The Standing Congress and its affiliates had no intention of basing a lasting peace on compromise and accommodation. They were proponents of the East German political system, and their solutions to East–West tensions were fully consistent with those of Khrushchev. The Communists added a new twist to Clausewitz's dictum: peace, like war, was the continuation of policies by other means.

If the two rival peace groups differed in their goals, they nonetheless shared a common weakness: they consistently misinterpreted the climate of opinion in West Germany. The Communists tended to view the hatred of the Soviet Union as a reverberation from the Nazi period. They hoped to convince the populace of a simple line of continuity from the policies of Hitler to those of Adenauer; in time, they felt, voters would come to view a nuclear-capable German army as the first step toward World War III. It is hard to imagine a viewpoint more incompatible with the actual public mood. As the decade passed, West Germans came to see the virtues of a Bundeswehr. The steady stream of refugees from the Iron Curtain, Soviet military intervention in Eastern Europe, the Berlin crises, daily disturbances along the inter-German border—all testified to an atmosphere of oppression in the Soviet zone. Renate Riemeck, Ulrike Meinhof, and the dozens of other prominent members of the Standing Congress failed to win support because their message was inconsistent with the experience of West German voters. Nothing demonstrated this incongruence better than the ludicrous attempt by the *konkret* group to assume control of the peace movement in the wake of Khrushchev's ultimatum.

THE POLITICS OF PEACE

The socialists had a far keener sense of the West German temper than the Communists; but they, too, consistently misread the public mood over defense matters. They viewed European security almost entirely through the prism of Germany's past, and failed to understand that the post-1945 period had irreversibly altered the global and regional power balance. Because they did not think in terms of West Germany's security needs, but always in terms of a reunified Germany, they failed to devise a workable alternative to the chancellor's defense policies. Harnessing the youthful "count me out" sentiment to the party's platform did not constitute a defense policy. Playing on the populace's fears with such ominous slogans as "The Campaign against Nuclear Death" did not constitute a strategic alternative for NATO. The socialists had merely made foreign policy the pawn of domestic politics. "The Germans never seem to learn," NATO commanders at SHAPE headquarters told the SPD leader, Fritz Beermann, in regard to the GCND campaign. "They are playing politics with pure emotion, just as they did during the Hitler era."[79]

As the decade progressed, it became embarrassingly apparent that the SPD's defense conceptions were based on an illusory vision of the East–West power relations. Reunification was not feasible, a European-wide security pact not imminent. As long as there were global tensions between the Soviet Union and the United States, as long as regional tensions plagued the European nations, the West Germans would have to seek security within the Western alliance. SPD and FDP leaders only gradually came to realize that the chancellor's foreign and defense policies were based on a more realistic evaluation of world affairs than their own. This realization put an end to their attempts to influence public opinion through extraparliamentary channels, and forced them to accept West Germany's obligations to NATO.

The domestic nuclear debate, however, did not come to an end in 1960. Rather, it returned to the parliamentary level, and to the ongoing Anglo-American strategic debate. This offered the socialists (and to a lesser extent, the liberals) the promise of a belated victory in the years after 1960, as the new Kennedy administration reevaluated NATO's defense posture along lines they had advocated since

1953. Once the opposition parties finally accepted the basic premise upon which the chancellor's foreign policy rested, they were in a position to build flexibly upon his foundation, promoting a defense alternative for NATO that promised greater protection to Central Europe.

toward a tripartisan defense policy

INTRODUCTION

We intend to have a wider choice than
humiliation or all-out nuclear war.

—President John F. Kennedy
Inaugural Address (1961)

MORE ink has been spilled on the New Look than any NATO doctrine before or since. Critics considered it ill-suited for a forward defense of Central Europe, and warned of its obsolescence as Soviet missile technology advanced. The Eisenhower administration continued to preach the virtues of massive retaliation, sending one awe-inspiring weapon after the next to Europe—Thors, Jupiters, Nike-Ajax, Nike-Hercules. But faith in these nuclear gods declined. American and Western European leaders shared a common enemy, but they did not share the same continent; there was no guarantee that the United States would risk New York or Chicago in order to defend London, Paris, or Bonn. Massive retaliation, Dean Acheson wrote, conjured images of the "monstrous giants" guarding the temples at Nikko; in deterring evil spirits from entering the "sacred precincts," they scared the daylights out of the faithful as well.[1]

SACEUR General Norstad sought to reduce the insecurities of Western Europeans, socialists and conservatives alike. He wanted to give the European governments greater access to NATO's stockpile and more control over targeting doctrine. He demanded the restructuring of NATO's ground forces so that they could withstand the first onslaught with conventional weapons, allowing the Americans and Soviets a "pause" before crossing the nuclear threshold. "There is a real danger that inability to deal decisively with limited or local attacks could lead to our piecemeal defeat or bring on a general war," he said in November 1957. "If, on the other hand, we have means to meet less-than-ultimate threats with a decisive, but less-than-ultimate response, the very possession of this ability would discourage the threat, and would thereby provide us with essential political and military maneuverability."[2] Norstad championed the deployment of mobile, medium-range ballistic missiles in Central Europe. Since they would not be placed in silos, they would be less vulnerable to a preemptive attack than other missiles. They would also give NATO a new degree of flexibility in their deployment and use: if necessary, the missiles could be withdrawn from the battlefield area, thereby allowing the West to fight conventional wars without fear of having its nuclear arsenal overrun.[3]

Though none of Norstad's goals was implemented during his tenure as SACEUR, the U.S. government introduced two similar proposals to allay European fears. The first, the Multilateral Force (MLF), was introduced during the last months of the Eisenhower administration. The MLF foresaw a sea-based deterrent force manned by multinational crews. It gave the Europeans more control over NATO's deterrent force, and a greater voice in questions of targeting and tactics. The MLF, however, had one major weakness: because the United States retained a veto power over a nuclear launch, the president could still choose to abandon Europe if he judged it to be in America's best national interest. De Gaulle expressed the sentiments of many Western Europeans when he called the MLF an expression of American political-military hegemony over the continent. Only the West German government, with Defense Minister Strauss at the forefront, gave its unequivocal blessing to MLF. This, in turn, made it even less attractive to the other European powers, who suspected the Germans of coveting an ersatz national nuclear deterrent.[4]

A second American proposal—flexible response doctrine—fared

better. Introduced by President Kennedy (1961–1963), this proposal envisaged a conventional buildup by America and its allies. Secretary of Defense Robert McNamara believed that NATO had become too dependent on tactical nuclear warheads, the United States too reliant on its strategic nuclear arsenal. In the densely settled region of Central Europe, NATO commanders would have to decide whether to utilize their supply of nuclear warheads or risk their capture by invading forces. A limited nuclear war, he concluded, would spell doom for Central Europe. Western leaders would have to bolster their conventional deterrence in order to ensure that NATO did not have to resort to the early first use of nuclear weapons. Victory would still belong to the side with the largest conventional forces at the end of the conflict.[5]

McNamara's case for a nonnuclear defense was buttressed by Maxwell Taylor, Paul Nitze, Cyrus Vance, Edward Rowny, Alain Enthoven, K. Wayne Smith, and others, all of whom undertook a thorough reevaluation of the Soviet Union's conventional strength. They argued that the United States had greatly overestimated Soviet power in Central Europe. The Soviet army's divisions were smaller than U.S. divisions; instead of enjoying a ten-to-one advantage over NATO troops, the Soviet Union and its allies held a three-to-one edge. Conventional parity was within NATO's reach.[6] "For the kinds of conflicts we think most likely to arise in the NATO area," McNamara told Western leaders at the NATO Council meeting in May 1962, "non-nuclear capabilities appear to be clearly the sort the Alliance would wish to use at the outset. The purpose of our common effort is the defense of the populations and territories of NATO. To achieve this, at least initially, with non-nuclear means requires that our non-nuclear defense begin where the populations and territories begin. A truly forward deployment, along the lines General Norstad has advocated, we consider an urgent need of the Alliance."[7]

McNamara recommended the immediate buildup of the West's conventional forces in Central Europe:

We believe that NATO and its military commanders should undertake as a high priority the implementation of the forward strategy in the Central Region. Specifically, that the ground forces needed to defend at the frontier, on the order of 30 divisions, be provided; that ground and air forces be appropriately deployed and supplied with required combat and service support elements; that adequate equipment and stocks to make these forces effective be made available, and that the air forces, in particular, be protected so as to be able to function effectively in non-nuclear combat.[8]

The McNamara doctrine gave the SPD an opportunity to recoup from its recent defeats and challenge NATO's nuclear strategy anew. But first, the socialists had to put their affairs in order by revising their position on reunification and a conscripted Bundeswehr.

6

THE YOUNG ADENAUERIANS

If you haven't realized that the maintenance of
democracy and the [Weimar] Republic is the single
most important interest of the party, then you haven't
mastered the ABCs of political thinking.

—Rudolf Hilferding,
SPD party convention, Kiel (1927)

Anyone who clashes with Adenauer will get a black
eye just as they would have earlier against
Fieldmarshall Hindenburg or Finland's Mannerheim!
Unfortunately, Adenauer's image has attained nearly
mythical proportions among our citizens.

—Erich Mende,
FDP executive board meeting
(March 21, 1959)

THE Social Democratic Party was revolutionary in rhetoric, but
reformist in deed; strong in numbers, but politically impotent;
progressive in spirit, but traditional in practice. Convinced that it
was the sole legitimate child of German democracy, the SPD expected one day to fall heir to power. But this inheritance was successfully challenged for nearly a century—by Bismarck, Wilhelm
II, Stresemann, Hitler. After reemerging from the rubble of World

War II as West Germany's most potent political force, the SPD lost the 1949 chancellorship to a conservative–liberal coalition by one Bundestag mandate (Adenauer himself cast the decisive vote). The federal presidency went first to the FDP's elder statesman, Theodor Heuss, then to the CDU/CSU leader, Heinrich Lübke. While the SPD's voter strength barely rose above 30 percent, the CDU/CSU's surged from 30 percent to 50 percent. Of the eleven state and city-state governments, the SPD controlled only West Berlin, Hamburg, and Bremen. Elsewhere, the CDU/CSU and FDP kept the SPD on the opposition bench, or tempered socialist programs through coalition government.[1]

The 1957 federal election defeat prodded the SPD into revising its economic and defense platforms at the next three party conventions: Stuttgart (May 1958), Bad Godesberg (November 1959), and Hanover (November 1960). Only the most ardent Marxist traditionalists resisted an overhaul of the party's economic philosophy. West Germany's swift postwar recovery brought full employment and uninterrupted growth; it was political suicide for the SPD to continue its opposition path. The defense plank, however, was a different matter. Most socialists were willing to make their peace with capitalism, but not with NATO; to adopt the chancellor's popular domestic platform, but not his outlook on West German security.

The SPD's antinuclear stance remained essentially unchanged, even after the North Rhine-Westphalian election and the Berlin crisis. But a group of defense and foreign policy experts—Fritz Beermann, Fritz Erler, Herbert Wehner, Helmut Schmidt—pushed for reform. They prepared the groundwork for a reorientation in the years 1960 and 1961 under the SPD's new candidate for chancellor, Willy Brandt.

Beermann and Erler: In Defense of the Bundeswehr

NO SPD leader was more at odds with his party than Fritz Beermann.[2] In February 1958, he prepared a memorandum, "The Consequence of the SPD's Current Defense Conception," for the SPD Defense Committee. Written as the socialists embarked on the GCND, it was his last-ditch attempt to forestall the party's disastrous political course. "With 12,500 East bloc tanks positioned along the demarcation line," he predicted, "no party with pacifist tendencies has a prayer to win Bundestag elections." He accused SPD leaders of inadvertently reviving the catchwords of the past: conservative equals "supporter" of the state, socialist equals "enemy" of the state. "The SPD is the second-largest democratic party in the country. Without its allegiance to a home defense, the Bundeswehr can hardly be expected to become inwardly democratic."[3]

"Our Western allies," Beermann warned, "would regard a Social Democratic government as an uncertain factor with pro-Communist tendencies. By contrast, the chancellor enjoys the support of world opinion (especially in the United States), despite all of his authoritarian characteristics." Though Beermann shared his party's preference for the Rapacki Plan, he realized that a nuclear-free zone was impractical. Modern weaponry, he noted, was in a state of flux: "There are a host of problems, and the technical advances in this sector cannot be predicted. Perhaps in two or three years nuclear armaments will be perceived as normal equipment for an army. Then the SPD will be criticized anew in the 1961 elections for siding with the East because it wants to equip German troops with outmoded weapons against a superior foe."[4] Beermann supported West Germany's pro-Western policies, and championed a revision of the SPD's stance. "Naturally, this conforms to Adenauer's viewpoint," Beermann told the editor of the *Westfälische Rundschau,* when he leaked his memorandum, "but in the last analysis we cannot close our eyes to reality."[5]

Beermann lost his war against the SPD's nuclear stance; but he won the battle for SPD–Bundeswehr reconciliation. Fritz Erler convinced a majority on the SPD Defense Committee that the socialists would achieve nothing through their intransigence; not only had the Bundeswehr won the acceptance of most West Germans, but the CDU/CSU had garnered all the credit for its creation. At the May 1958 Stuttgart party convention, Erler secured passage of a "Home Defense" platform;[6] in October, the SPD's Bundestag faction (again at Erler's behest) urged socialist youth to join the Bundeswehr and encouraged party leaders to establish professional contacts with Bundeswehr officers.[7] The final step toward reconciliation was taken at the 1959 Godesberg party convention: "The Social Democratic Party declares its allegiance to the defense of a free and democratic order. It approves the home defense."[8]

The subtle shift in socialist–Bundeswehr relations went virtually unnoticed amidst the antinuclear fanfare. But once the Berlin fiasco brought GCND festivities to a halt, the SPD's left wing took a more sober look at the changes wrought by Beermann and Erler. Led by Arno Behrisch, these critics charged that the SPD Bundestag faction had overstepped the guidelines laid down at Stuttgart. "The battle against nuclear armaments is the centerpiece of Social Democratic politics," Behrisch reminded the party's Defense Committee. If SPD members joined the Bundeswehr, "they should lead the campaign against nuclear weapons there as well."[9] Once the SPD accepted the Bundeswehr as an institution, argued these critics, it would have to accept conscription, NATO, and nuclear weapons: "He who says 'A' must also say 'B'. Whether we want it or not, we are indirectly approving nuclear armaments for Germany."[10]

To alleviate his colleagues' concerns, Erler oversaw the formulation of a comprehensive policy statement in July 1959, "The SPD and Nuclearization of the Bundeswehr" (see document 7).[11] But he steadfastly refused to backtrack on SPD–Bundeswehr reconciliation: "By 1961 there will be 350,000 soldiers. If we don't do something, they will be schooled in only one direction. . . . We are provoking the Bundeswehr against us, we are prodding it in Strauss' direction."[12] Opposition to the Bundeswehr, Erler argued, played into the hands of the CDU/CSU: "Strauss is trying to force the SPD into a corner from which there are only two escapes. Either we accept nuclear weapons, or we reject in toto the Bundeswehr and thereby eliminate Social Democratic influence over the army. Either choice connotes capitulation to Strauss' politics."[13]

The SPD's majority followed Erler, not Behrisch. Only minor revisions were made in the Godesberg Program's defense plank, which read in its final version: "West Germany must not produce or use nuclear and other means of mass destruction. The Social Democratic Party seeks the inclusion of all Germany in a European zone of relaxed tensions and arms limitations. In the process of restoring Germany's unity in freedom, foreign troops will depart, and no nuclear weapons and other means of mass destruction may be produced, stored, or used."[14] No conscription clause was added to the Godesberg Program, thus nominally leaving the SPD's anticonscription stance intact, while giving the party leadership leeway in the future.

Schmidt and Wehner: From German Plan to Bipartisanship

AS reconciliation with the Bundeswehr proceeded, the SPD published its Plan for Germany (March 1959), the party's final effort to achieve German unification. The SPD sent it to the Geneva Conference (May 1959), a meeting of the foreign ministers of the United States, Soviet Union, Britain, and France. Though ostensibly a new initiative, the plan largely recapitulated the party's demands for a European-wide security pact and nuclear-free zone. A four-power

---

DOCUMENT 7

Fritz Erler's Memorandum, "The SPD and Nuclearization of the Bundeswehr" (July 1959)

1. The SPD will continue the battle against a nuclearized Bundeswehr. Nuclear weapons do not heighten West Germany's security.

2. Success in the battle against nuclear weapons presupposes the possession of political power. We must get a Bundestag majority elected that will pursue detente and reunification, and not a nuclear arms race.

3. The CDU will be strengthened if it succeeds in turning the army into its propaganda school. The SPD must not force the Bundeswehr into the hands of the conservatives. The army must not become a power factor in political controversies.

4. The government's decision to give the Bundeswehr nuclear-capable weapons must be reversed through democratic means. The task ahead is a fundamental restructuring of defense policy. But the burden does not rest on individual soldiers. The Social Democratic soldier must have the support of his party.

agreement would regulate the withdrawal of NATO and Warsaw troops, allowing Germany's reunification to occur in four stages. First, an all-German conference would iron out political differences between the two German states. An elected provisional parliament (with equal representation from both East and West Germany) would then handle fiscal matters (taxation, currency, tariffs). Thereafter, an elected national assembly would draft an all-German constitution. Finally, free elections would be held throughout Germany.[15]

The plan had limited salability in West Germany: it foresaw no automatic progression from one stage to the next; it failed to link unification to a four-power agreement over a nuclear-free zone; it gave East Germany (with a population of twenty million) equal representation with West Germany (population fifty-five million) in the formulation of constitutional and economic policy. The fatal flaw in the SPD's proposal, however, lay in its misreading of East bloc politics. When German socialists delivered their plan to Moscow, they learned that the Soviets were not the least bit interested in a reunified, non-Communist Germany. Khrushchev demanded that the West Germans recognize the sovereignty of East Germany, turn West Berlin into a free city, and withdraw from NATO. He supported a nuclear-free zone, but refused to sign any peace treaty that linked German unification to four-power disengagement. Free elections? The ballot, Khrushchev asserted, guaranteed only that "the majority would win, not the truth."[16] The West Germans, he argued, were the last defenders of reunification; no other power in East or West would support them. "The Soviet leaders stand fully behind East Germany," Erler admitted when he returned from Moscow. "In the last analysis, it is their creation. They showed no willingness to bring pressure on the East Germans so that a step-by-step reunification process could begin."[17]

By the time the Bundestag debated the SPD's initiative in November 1959, the plan was already defunct. But Helmut Schmidt used the opportunity to break the Bundestag's eighteen-month silence on defense matters. While not departing from the Rapacki Plan, his speech nonetheless presaged a new SPD defense policy: for the first time, an SPD Bundestag member focused on *West* Germany's strategic needs, relegated reunification to a minor role, and assumed the permanence of the Bundeswehr.[18] Schmidt advocated a "zone of arms limitations and control" in the two Germanies, Poland, Czechoslovakia, and Hungary. A 300,000-strong West German Bundeswehr, he felt, was ideal: it would not appear provocative to the Soviets, but still be capable of withstanding an assault from the combined half-million-strong Polish, Czech, Hungarian, and East German troops. The superpowers were to install radar stations on the periphery of Central Europe, withdraw their troops from this region, and allow these five countries to dissolve their ties with Warsaw and NATO.[19]

Western military strategists, Schmidt admitted, raised several objections to a disengagement zone: the United States needed European bases for its strategic weaponry; NATO's tactical nuclear warheads compensated for its manpower shortage; West German territory was indefensible without troop strength concentrated along the Iron Curtain; France would refuse to become NATO's forward base; the Soviets would still target Western Europe with long-range missiles. But Schmidt thought that the advantages of a nuclear-free zone outweighed the risks: America's strategic arsenal was more secure if deployed outside continental Europe, and Soviet troop withdrawals from Central Europe would eliminate NATO's need for a nuclear-capable Bundeswehr. West Germany's army would handle small conflagrations along its borders, while NATO would prepare for a conventional defense of the continent. Tactical warheads could still be stored outside Central Europe, available if necessary to thwart a Soviet blitzkrieg.[20]

Several months after Schmidt's speech, one of the SPD's most prominent reformers, Herbert Wehner, called for a bipartisan foreign policy. A Weimar-era Communist turned Social Democrat, Wehner had been highly critical of the GCND. Once the campaign failed, he used his leverage with left- and right-wing socialists to forge a new path: "Foreign policy must not become the punching bag for domestic politics, or be used in the future for such purposes. Domestic politics ought to be governed by the recognition that Germany's division is a situation determined by international affairs. Under the conditions that prevail today, domestic politics must not become the dumping grounds for the rubble of foreign policy."[21]

On June 30, 1960, shortly after the collapse of the Paris summit between Khrushchev and Eisenhower, the Bundestag discussed the possibility of a bipartisan foreign policy. Wehner spoke on behalf of the SPD. He was a volatile orator, more provocative than conciliatory; but on this occasion, he was modest and reserved. The superpowers, Wehner argued, had proven themselves unwilling to make Central Europe the focal point of their discussions; West Germany needed a bipartisan foreign policy to ensure that the German question remained on the agenda of future international conferences. The SPD, Wehner asserted, recognized NATO as the guarantor of peace in Europe; the socialists had always shared common foreign policy goals with the conservatives, despite their difference over European security. The SPD's Plan for Germany had been scuttled, he claimed; henceforth, the socialists would accept the government's position that free elections were the first (rather than the last) step toward reunification.[22]

The Bundestag debate of June 30 was a milestone in West German history. It brought eleven years of acrimony over reunification to an end, and guaranteed the continuation of the government's foreign policy after the chancellor's death. Its immediate effect, however, was less tangible than the SPD had hoped. CDU/CSU leaders showed little interest in bipartisanship: "The federal government does not consider it necessary to take stock of its foreign policy," Foreign Minister Brentano said. CDU/CSU diplomacy was based on a "correct" policy, not a "bipartisan" one; the SPD's desire to revise its stance "proved that its own conception of international affairs was illusory." The government had nothing to reexamine: "It is more than ever convinced that its foreign policy decisions and conceptions were correct."[23]

The government's two defense spokesmen, Strauss and Freiherr zu Guttenberg, insisted that a bipartisan defense policy was more imperative than a common foreign policy. The SPD's affirmative stance toward NATO, Strauss warned, was theoretical; once in office, the socialists might revert to their original position. He reminded the Bundestag that the socialists still championed a 300,000-strong volunteer army, in defiance of NATO's directive that West Germany put 500,000 men in service; he also emphasized the SPD's ambivalence toward compulsory military service. "Whoever opposes conscription in Germany," he argued, "cannot at the same time be in favor of continuing the buildup of the Bundeswehr. It is impossible; it is a contradiction in terms."[24] Zu Guttenberg, moreover, found fault with the SPD's nuclear politics. The socialists, he argued, mistakenly assumed that the U.S. strategic arsenal would keep the peace in Europe indefinitely. They neglected to take into account the problem of extended deterrence in an age of intercontinental missiles: "Whoever wants the [NATO] alliance cannot demand that our soldiers be ill-equipped in comparison to our partners and our potential enemy."[25]

In responding to Strauss and zu Guttenberg, SPD leaders argued that there was no inherent reason why they had to adopt the government's defense policy. Even U.S. policymakers, who had prided themselves on their bipartisanship since 1945, often diverged widely on defense matters (at the very moment, in fact, that the SPD buried its differences with the CDU/CSU, the American Democrats under the leadership of Senator John Kennedy had begun a relentless attack on President Eisenhower's national security policy). The SPD and CDU/CSU, Erler argued, shared three common political objectives: upholding the territorial integrity of West Berlin; keeping alive the hope of German unity; using NATO as a forum for promoting U.S. and Soviet disarmament. "None of these three goals has the slightest thing to do with nuclear weapons," he concluded.[26]

Although the SPD's bid for bipartisanship did not settle the nuclear issue, it nonetheless altered the context of the defense debate. Once the socialists accepted West Germany's membership in NATO, they could not continue their path of pure opposition; once they committed themselves to a common foreign policy, they could no longer support extraparliamentary agitation. Only one route remained open: to formulate a defense alternative for the West, and find support in American and Western European capitals to ensure that SPD proposals were on the agenda at future NATO meetings.

In July 1960, Erler prepared a memorandum for party leaders on the military-technical aspects of NATO doctrine (see document 8).[27] Western Europe's security, Erler argued, rested on the two pillars of deterrence and defense. "Deterrence" was a global strategy, designed to reduce the likelihood of war by threatening the Soviet Union with overwhelming nuclear retaliation. "Defense" was a regional strategy; it connoted an ability to thwart aggression around the periphery of the Soviet bloc without immediately resorting to nuclear weapons. Soviet advances in intercontinental rocketry, Erler argued, had called into question America's ability to extend its nuclear shield to Europe. In order to buttress its credibility, the United States had stationed medium-range missiles in Europe; but while these missiles alleviated the global imbalance, they left the problem of regional security almost wholly unresolved. Given America's vulnerability, the Europeans could never be certain that the president

DOCUMENT 8

Excerpts from Erler's 34-Point Memorandum (July 1960)

1. Until the East and West reach a balanced arms control agreement, the West needs two strategic conceptions: deterrence *and* an effective defense in case deterrence fails.

4. The more vulnerable the United States becomes to a Soviet attack, the less credible America's deterrent capability becomes for any conflict that does not directly threaten America's vital interests.

7. A defense against local aggression (that is, those that do not touch the United States' vital nerve center) must be constructed so that even without nuclear weapons it presents unacceptable risks to an aggressor.

19. NATO units must be equipped so that they are not dependent on nuclear weapons. The more dependent military leaders become on the utilization of nuclear weapons, the less capable NATO will be to withstand an assault without resorting to America's deterrent system.

21. Even Strauss does not adhere to his own slogan: "one's own troops must be equipped exactly like the enemy's." If he followed this dictum, he would have to demand H-bombs and the whole gamut of strategic weapons.

24. A dangerous threshold was crossed when the Bundeswehr was equipped with dual-purpose rockets with up to 1,000-kilometer range (Polaris, Mace, Matador). They are too inaccurate to have military value at the conventional level; they therefore invite an early resort to nuclear warheads in a conflict.

27. If the Bundeswehr is equipped with weapon systems that are militarily useless without atomic warheads, then it can only be concluded that these atomic warheads are going to be used in a conflict. Otherwise, you have given troops a revolver with no ammunition.

would risk the use of nuclear weapons except in response to a direct Soviet attack on North America. Regardless of how many strategic missiles the United States stationed in the vicinity of the Soviet Union, the security of Western Europe would not be improved. Massive retaliation doctrine, Erler claimed, locked the Western leaders into an all-or-nothing response: "NATO possesses a deterrent doctrine, but not a defense conception in the event that deterrence fails."[28]

Erler championed substantial revision of the West's strategy. First, NATO should create a *strategic*-weapon-free zone around the periphery of the Soviet Union (to a depth of 1,000 kilometers, or 650 miles); by withdrawing its missiles from the front line, NATO would gain war-fighting flexibility without diminishing America's deterrent capability. Second, NATO troops had to be trained and outfitted so that they were "not dependent on nuclear weapons"; more attention had to be given to war-fighting strategies that repelled aggression without activating the West's nuclear forces. Third, Erler demanded that NATO's dual-purpose weapons (with the exception of Nike) be removed from Europe; these weapons were ineffective for a conventional defense, and their presence in Europe unduly complicated strategic doctrine. American leaders, Erler concluded, should continue to maintain their exclusive control over the West's strategic deterrent; but no medium-range missiles should be stationed on West German territory. NATO should be nuclear-capable, but the Bundeswehr would become a conventional fighting force. West Germany would play a unique role: its territory would act as a nuclear-free buffer zone in Central Europe, its troops functioning as a firebreak to nuclear escalation.[29]

Erler's memorandum was meant as a starting point for internal party discussion, not as a polished pronouncement of the SPD's nuclear policy. Since it was written as an answer to the government's charges in the June 30 debate, Erler wanted above all to highlight the elements of continuity between the party's past rhetoric and its new defense posture. He did not want to give the appearance that the SPD was retreating on the nuclear issue as it had on foreign policy; nor did he want to link defense and foreign policy in the ongoing effort at bipartisanship.[30] His memorandum had some striking similarities with Beermann's recommendations eighteen months before, as well as with Schmidt's speech of the previous November. Only the fig leaf of a nuclear-free zone remained; although he expressed his misgivings anew about tactical nuclear warheads, there was no clear-cut demand for their removal from Central Europe. But he left a central question unanswered: would the SPD now support a 500,000-strong nonnuclear Bundeswehr, or would it continue to support a smaller volunteer army?

It was Schmidt, rather than Erler, who fleshed out a comprehensive defense alternative for the party. In his book *Defense or Retaliation*,[31] Schmidt argued that America's global deterrent no longer sufficed to stop a local aggression against Western Europe; before launching a retaliatory attack, the American president would have to decide whether to risk the destruction of his homeland in West Germany's defense. It seemed likely to Schmidt that the United States would hesitate before pulling the nuclear trigger, leaving Europe more vulnerable than in the past to Soviet blackmail. The SPD, he argued, must push for a conventional buildup of the Bundeswehr in order to eliminate the rationale for tactical nuclear warheads. His goal was to reverse the sword-shield strategy: instead of a nuclear sword and a conventional shield, NATO's conventional forces would function as a sword, while the nuclear forces would function as a shield.

Schmidt recommended to NATO the doctrine of "flexible response": a defense-deterrent system ranging from conventional weaponry to strategic missiles. Troops along the Iron Curtain would consist primarily of highly mobile, conventionally equipped West German units; they would assist in a home defense and absorb the first wave of attack. Reinforcement troops behind the front line would be capable of launching a tactical nuclear counterattack if the level of violence escalated beyond the conventional level; and medium-range and intercontinental missiles would also be available for use in Europe. "NATO's nuclear weapons must be deployed and organized so that they cannot be drawn into battle except at the express order of the Supreme Allied Commander. The Supreme Allied Commander must operate from the assumption that the so-called tactical nuclear weapons are his 'penultimate resort' (Liddell Hart), while the strategic nuclear weapons are his last resort."[32]

Schmidt opposed the permanent stationing of medium-range missiles in Central Europe; their deployment was, he hoped, a transitory solution to the so-called missile gap. The Soviet Union, he argued, had responded with restraint to NATO's 1957 decision. He did not, however, expect its military leaders to tolerate land-based missiles around its periphery in the long run:

> It appears that the USSR, due to its rapid progress in the field of missile technology, overcame the sense of additional threat which this [1957 NATO Council] resolution instilled. . . . Nevertheless, everyone capable of objective reasoning must acknowledge that the stationing of enemy medium-range missiles on its very doorstep (Turkey), must appear psychologically provocative to any great power. One need only imagine how the Americans would react were the Soviets to station medium-range missiles in Cuba.[33]

Schmidt discouraged the United States from deploying land-based missiles in densely populated regions; in an emergency, NATO leaders would have to resort to an early first use of these weapons. A safer alternative, he suggested, would be a NATO fleet of Polaris-equipped vessels. If deployed in the seas around Western Europe, they would be relatively invulnerable from attack; their presence would buttress the West's deterrent capability without complicating NATO's defense strategy. NATO's edifice must appear unassailable both militarily and politically, so that no Western European nation would feel vulnerable to blackmail or attack. "The strategies devised by NATO to defend Europe must extend continuously without gap from cold war to total and general war. NATO must present a potential aggressor with intolerable risks at both the lowest and highest level of warfare, and also at every conceivable intermediate level."[34]

Defense or Retaliation was widely acclaimed as the first significant German contribution to the debate over nuclear strategy. Schmidt became Europe's foremost champion of flexible response doctrine; his influence was especially visible at the NATO Council meeting of 1967, when the West officially abandoned the doctrine of massive retaliation. He did not, however, intend that his book be read merely as a German primer on military strategy; it was also meant to catalyze a rethinking process within the SPD. He hoped to ease the party into a pronuclear stance, without giving the appearance that the SPD had abandoned its opposition to the chancellor's nuclear politics. He sought, further, to convince the SPD to abandon its opposition to conscription. A 300,000-strong volunteer army, he concluded, was inadequate for a conventional defense of German territory; the SPD would have to support an eighteen-month conscription term, instead of the twelve-month term passed in 1956.[35]

Brandt: Hanover 1960

AS the party's defense experts overhauled the defense platform, SPD leaders chose Brandt as their candidate for chancellor in the 1961 elections. Ollenhauer remained chairman, but he was quickly overshadowed by the dynamism of West Berlin's young mayor. Brandt had a far more realistic understanding of West Germany's international constraints than Ollenhauer, and he took a pragmatic approach to defense questions. In an interview with *Der Spiegel* prior to the Hanover party convention in November 1960, Brandt made clear that he would support the SPD's defense reformers against the traditionalists; future policy would not be inspired by the slogans of the GCND campaign, but rather by a sober evaluation of NATO's strategic requirements. Brandt saw no reason to challenge the basic contours of Adenauer's defense and foreign policies; the West German government had amply demonstrated its commitment to global arms control. The problem was Strauss, not Adenauer: the defense minister's effusive rhetoric, Brandt argued, had awakened the suspicion that West Germany was eager to become a nuclear power. Brandt intimated that he would not seek reversal of the March 1958 Bundestag decision. If elected chancellor, however, he would stress anew West Germany's interest in arms control and nonproliferation; he would also push for a new NATO doctrine that gave more credence to a conventional defense of Europe.[36]

Brandt introduced a platform proposal that sought to defuse the GCND without provoking a confrontation with the party's left wing; to promote a new NATO doctrine without lambasting the current one; and to alter the SPD's stance without allowing defense politics to dominate the next federal election (see document 9).[37] At the Hanover convention, however, Ollenhauer and Schmidt locked horns over future policy. "The Social Democratic Party adheres to the resolution included in the Godesberg Program," Ollenhauer declared in his opening address. "West Germany must not produce or use nuclear and other means of destruction." Recent international events, he added, had not convinced the party to abandon its opposition to the chancellor's policy: "We oppose the nuclearization of the Bundeswehr. Neither geography, technology, strategy, or tactics makes nuclearization necessary. They are not the most suitable weapons for German units. They are also politically dangerous in light of Germany's dividedness and in light of the geographic and political position of Germany in Europe."[38]

"Ollenhauer has disqualified himself as a politician," Schmidt retorted:[39] the SPD would get nowhere by "repeating the naiveté of 1957 to 1958."[40] He urged socialists to abandon their blanket opposition to nuclear weapons, and focus their attention instead on strategic alternatives for NATO: "We must create an element of flexibility in the manner in which we are armed, so that we are not forced to be the first to use these [nuclear] weapons."[41] Since any nonnuclear doctrine would require a conventional troop buildup,

---

DOCUMENT 9

Excerpt from the Defense Resolution at the Hanover Party Convention (November 1960)

West Germany needs the protection of NATO, to which it will loyally fulfill its obligations. The Western alliance must not be weakened unilaterally. A controlled and balanced disarmament must proceed equally on both sides.

A meaningful division of labor adds strength to the alliance and makes it possible to limit the number of nuclear-capable armies. The Bundeswehr must be effectively equipped and armed. West Germany should not exert its influence to bring about an increase in the number of nuclear powers; it should therefore not push for the nuclearization of the Bundeswehr.

he recommended that the SPD support conscription. He tried (unsuccessfully) to convince SPD leaders to strike the final two sentences from the executive board's resolution, and replace it with his own:[42]

> West Germany should help curb the increase in the number of nuclear powers within the NATO alliance. It has to be made clear to NATO that it must possess weaponry in the future that allows Europe to defend itself without resort to nuclear weapons. But it must possess nuclear weapons so long as the Warsaw Pact does. The armaments, training, and size of the Bundeswehr must correspond to the necessities of NATO. For that purpose it needs the assistance of all citizens.

As a result of the tensions between Ollenhauer and Schmidt, Erler emerged as the voice of moderation, both at Hanover and during the 1961 election campaign. Sensitive to the antinuclear current still running through the party, Erler tried to link the Hanover resolution with previous platform resolutions. The SPD, he alleged, was not abandoning its quest; as in the past, the new plank highlighted the party's opposition to nuclear proliferation and a nuclear-capable Bundeswehr.[43] The SPD was not modernizing its platform in conformity with the wishes of the defense ministry; rather, the socialists were fulfilling the true spirit of the March 1958 two-track decision. "In practice, the federal government's politics never corresponded to the text [of the Bundestag resolution]," Erler commented. The CDU "had concentrated solely on the fulfillment of the military angle of this resolution."[44]

Erler secured passage of the executive board's defense plank without amendment. It was a good compromise, given the divergent perspectives within the party. Ollenhauer's supporters could point to the continuity with the party's antinuclear position, while clinging to the hope for a return to a more vociferous antinuclear stance after the election was over. Schmidt's supporters, meanwhile, looked forward to a continued transformation of the party's position in the years to come.[45]

Left-wing critics lambasted the SPD for its reconciliation with the Bundeswehr, its bipartisan foreign policy, its abandonment of the GCND, its choice of Brandt as candidate for chancellor. They claimed that the party's innate conservatism rendered it ineffective as an oppositional political force. The SPD failed to stop Adenauer in 1958 (just it had failed to stop the Kaiser in 1914 and Hitler in 1933) because it was too timid in its methods, too traditional in its outlook, too modest in its goals. According to these critics, SPD leaders did not grasp the ultimate purpose of the antinuclear movement: to topple the chancellor, withdraw West Germany from NATO, and deprive the United States of its bases in Central Europe. The SPD's fixation on parliamentary democracy made it overly distrustful of extraparliamentary agitation. Critics assailed the SPD leadership for sending confusing signals to the West German public: while rank-and-file socialists marched in the streets, their leaders undertook a reconciliation with the army; after the North Rhine-Westphalian election, the party engaged in a step-by-step retreat, while allegedly continuing to support the GCND.[46]

There was a kernel of truth in the charges. The SPD—Germany's oldest parliamentary party—took an ambivalent attitude toward extraparliamentary politics. Its leaders had been slow to mobilize a campaign against the chancellor's defense policy: after a nominal attempt in 1955 (the Paulskirche movement), another three years elapsed before the GCND got underway. Even then, the SPD made certain that the GCND did not overstep the purpose which the SPD executive board defined for it. There was, however, a disingenuous side to the critics' charges: blaming the GCND's failure on the SPD's alleged conservatism allowed left-wing nuclear foes to mask their own political impotence. In 1960, Standing Congress leaders, disgruntled SPD members, and Brethren spokesmen founded a new political party—the German Peace Union—to carry on the antinuclear crusade. Led by Renate Riemeck, the Peace Union received only 610,000 votes in the 1961 federal election, 1.9 percent of the total votes cast. When the Peace Union's share of the vote fell to 1.3 percent in 1965, it virtually disappeared. The party never came close to jumping the 5 percent hurdle, so it never had a Bundestag spokesman or exerted influence in federal politics. The Peace Union was as unpopular at the ballot box as the Standing Congress had been on the streets.[47]

Not only did the SPD's left-wing critics misjudge popular opinion in West Germany, they misperceived the purpose of the SPD's antinuclear campaign. The GCND served Social Democrats, not the tiny fraction of Communists, pacifists, theologians, scientists, and others who mobilized with them. The SPD's foremost goal was not the overthrow of the West German government, but rather the attainment of power through constitutional means. Its leaders did not allow the campaign to become radicalized (as advocated by the rival Standing Congress) because they knew it would bring them no additional popular support. Since the SPD was the only political force in West Germany capable of mobilizing citizens into a large-scale antinuclear effort, the GCND was affected by the movement of the party. There was bound to be consternation when Beermann leaked his pronuclear memorandum to the press, as when Erler pushed for SPD–Bundeswehr reconciliation and Schmidt championed a conscription army; it was also public knowledge that neither Wehner nor Brandt approved of the party's extraparliamentary agitation. But Beermann was a maverick defense expert, who exerted virtually no influence over policy; when he publicly spoke out against the GCND, he was ousted from the SPD Defense Committee. Schmidt spent months on the GCND lecture circuit, stubbornly championing the Rapacki Plan; his alienation from peace politics dated from the Berlin Student Congress. Not only did Brandt wield no power in the SPD executive board, he had a tenuous hold over the West Berlin SPD until the city election of December 1958. Though Wehner was a powerful reforming force in the SPD, he was unable to thwart Ollenhauer. Without doubt, Erler was the key figure in the party's transformation; but he never publicly or privately welcomed a reversal of the party's antinuclear position. Only *after* the GCND failed did these reformers unite and triumph over the traditionalists.

A single motivating force was always at work, regardless of whether the socialists were discussing defense policy in parliament, on the streets, or at their yearly conventions; whether they were pumping money into the GCND or distancing themselves from it; whether they were supporting Ollenhauer or Brandt. "The battle *against* nuclear weapons," Erler liked to remind his colleagues, "is a battle *for* political power."[48] When viewed from this perspective, it is not surprising that SPD leaders abandoned their antinuclear campaign. More surprising is the tenacity with which they clung to antinuclear slogans, their tardiness in coming to terms with the realities of postwar

From GCND to Bipartisanship

Was heißt hier Volksbefragung? Das Volk bin ich.

Vorwärts (April 4, 1957)

CAPTION: [Adenauer]: "Why bother with referenda?
I *am* the people."

Frankfurter Allgemeine Zeitung (April 24, 1958)

Ollenhauer: "Are you against nuclear death?"
"Are you against conventional death?"
"Are you against death in general?"
"Are you for me as chancellor?"

Sprung über den Schatten

Ollenhauer: „Es geht einfach nicht!"

Rheinischer Merkur (July 29, 1960)

Nuclear "Count Me Out" Politics versus a Bipartisan
Defense Policy: Ollenhauer Tries to Jump Over His
Own Shadow
CAPTION: [Ollenhauer]: "I can't do it."

Vorwärts (July 29, 1960)

Adenauer: "Make yourself comfortable, Mr. Ollenhauer."

Ein Mann geht seinen Weg

Frankfurter Rundschau (October 5, 1961)

First Door: Concessions on the Chancellorship
Second Door: Concessions on Foreign Policy
Third Door: Concessions on Ministerial Posts
Mallet: Coalition Government
CAPTION: A Man [Mende] Chooses His Path

„So, meine Herren, dat Kabinett is wieder arbeitsfähig"

Vorwärts (November 15, 1961)

CAPTION: [Adenauer]: "So, gentlemen, the cabinet is once again in tip-top shape."

German politics. It took scores of election defeats to convince the SPD leadership that antinuclear politics was not a "vote-getter." It took months of poorly attended demonstrations, a Berlin crisis, a Student Congress fiasco before socialists contemplated laying the GCND to rest. Even then, the SPD spent a long time mourning the GCND's demise before revitalizing itself (eighteen months elapsed between the Stuttgart and Hanover conventions). As in the Weimar era, socialist leaders celebrated every parliamentary defeat as a moral triumph, interpreted every election loss as proof that their policies were correct, wrung their hands over Germany's predicament without taking charge of affairs themselves.

Brandt's emergence as the SPD's candidate for chancellor symbolized the end of the antinuclear effort. After exploring every route to defeat, the SPD finally found a leader who knew the route to power. He was not wedded to traditional socialist rhetoric, nor tied to the Ollenhauer legacy. As mayor of West Berlin, moreover, he was not only politically experienced, but also acutely aware of the West's geographic vulnerability. As the conservative Social Democrat who had formed a Great Coalition with the Berlin CDU, he was the ideal person to ease the SPD into the seat of government. Erler and Schmidt became the primary architects of the SPD's new defense policy, while Brandt and Wehner handled foreign affairs. But party leaders took pains to win over the pacifist wing of the party. In an exchange of letters between Ollenhauer and Gustav Heinemann, the SPD agreed not to purge the nuclear opposition from its ranks. The two party wings could coexist, since they both opposed nuclear proliferation, supported arms control initiatives, and championed a defense conception that took into account Germany's special status as a divided nation. Heinemann had to acknowledge, however, that the party's defense experts, not the nuclear pacifists, would formulate policy: "The group which opposes nuclear weapons on moral grounds," he wrote to Ollenhauer, "cannot expect or demand that a political party pledge itself to this attitude."[49]

The SPD entered the 1961 elections virtually free of the stigma that beset it in the past. The socialists had bidden farewell to Marx, committed themselves to NATO, accepted the Bundeswehr, and tailored a defense policy to resemble that of the Kennedy administration. For the first time, the SPD looked like a modern, Western-style party, capable of leading its country into a new era. The rewards were immediate. In the 1961 elections, the socialists made their best showing in their ninety-year history: 36.2 percent.

The FDP: From Young Turks to Young Mende

THE liberals were also destined to make a political comeback in 1961, with 12.8 percent of the vote (67 Bundestag seats). But such a fortunate turn of events seemed a pipedream to FDP leaders as they assessed the party's prospects for survival in mid-1958. Ever since the liberals withdrew from the federal coalition in April 1956, their popularity had plummeted; the North Rhine-Westphalian election had left them (in the words of FDP chairman, Reinhold Maier) on the "threshold of political extinction."[50]

The "nationalists"—led by Wolfgang Döring and Thomas Dehler—successfully opposed any major revision of the party's foreign policy plank: "I prefer every Social Democratic worker," said Döring, "who fights with us for the restoration of German unity a thousand-fold over a middle-class separatist."[51] This faction kept detente and reunification at the forefront of liberal politics—in the FDP's Plan for Germany (March 1959), in Bundestag addresses (November 1959 and June 1960), at the party conventions (May 1959, January 1960, March 1961).[52] On defense issues, the "nationalists" were content to revert back to the party's pre-1956 position. "Our emphasis must be on the strengthening and improvement of conventional armaments," said Döring. "Weaponry only makes sense if you have enough options to meet aggression at the level dictated by the enemy's action. We should leave the improvement and buildup of NATO's nuclear weapons to the Americans."[53]

In actuality, however, the "nationalists" took a back seat for the next decade, while the "conservatives" steered the FDP toward a new coalition with the CDU/CSU. This faction was led by Maier, the FDP's aged chairman from Baden-Württemberg, and Erich Mende, who succeeded Maier as chairman in January 1960. Dubbed "Mende the Beautiful" by the press, he was young and dynamic, the FDP's mirror image of Brandt. Like Brandt, Mende came to the forefront not as a compromise candidate, but rather as a product of the party's rightward shift. He refused even to feign a courtship of the socialists during his entire tenure as chairman; in 1970, he switched to the CDU rather than participate in an SPD–FDP coalition.

In March 1959, Maier and Mende reoriented the FDP. "The effect of the January and March [1958 Bundestag] debates," Mende pointed out, "was brought home in five state elections. The result—when viewed from the angle of achievement—was a rather bad election return in North Rhine-Westphalia. But that was the best one of all! Thereafter came the total disaster of the Berlin elections."[54] The FDP had little to gain from pursuing its past causes, especially once the SPD made its bid for bipartisanship with the CDU/CSU. "Keep foreign policy in the background," Mende recommended. "There are no votes to be won on that front."[55] The liberals had either to ally with the conservatives, or face a Great Coalition headed by Adenauer and Brandt. "There is no longer any chance for politicking on the matters of Berlin and a united Germany," said Mende. "Foreign policy is not easily altered. And the cold warriors within the context of the 'policy of strength' are no longer called Adenauer and Brentano, but Brandt and Wehner."[56]

As Mende took over the FDP's helm, a group of party experts, led by Fritz-Rudolf Schultz and Hans-Dietrich Genscher, tinkered with the party's defense platform. Schultz was Dehler's replacement as chair of the FDP's Committee on Defense Questions; Genscher was a key figure in the 1961 coalition talks with the CDU/CSU. Schultz's Defense Policy Draft (March 1961) took cognizance of flexible response doctrine (see document 10).[57] "The question of how to deploy nuclear weapons within the NATO alliance is purely a question of suitability," he told delegates at the FDP party convention in March 1961. "We are not satisfied with the current arrangement; it gives us no security, it only increases our insecurity. . . . Everything hinges on the creation of a deterrence ladder whose upper rung is nuclear weapons. These will be used to localize or stop a war, once all other means have failed. This is why nuclear forces must be removed from normally equipped troops and be brought together as separate units." He added: "It goes without saying that soldiers from our Bundeswehr would participate in these units, just as the soldiers of all other NATO partners."[58]

The Coalition Talks of 1961

SINCE the political positions of the CDU/CSU, SPD, and FDP had converged on many critical issues, the September 1961 federal election was a popularity contest, not a political showdown. The East Germans, in fact, added the only touch of real drama when they constructed the Berlin Wall shortly before the election date. The CDU campaigned with Adenauer at the helm, amidst press speculation that conservative leaders would select Bundestag President Eugen Gerstenmaier to succeed him. The CDU's Bavarian sister party, the CSU, officially endorsed Adenauer, while inching Strauss toward the chancellorship. The SPD expressed its willingness to par-

---

DOCUMENT 10

Excerpt from Schultz's Defense Policy Draft (March 1961)

2. The FDP continues to believe that West Germany's membership in NATO must form the basis of Germany's security policy, as long as a European-wide security system cannot be attained. In accordance with treaty obligations, the party will do everything within its powers to continue the purposeful buildup of the Bundeswehr. The army's strength and its armaments must be such that it is capable of repelling a purely conventional attack without resort to any type of nuclear weapon.

3. The structure and armaments of NATO troops must be altered in order to fulfill the demand that NATO be capable of responding [flexibly] to conventional and nuclear attacks. Nuclear weapons must be removed from the arsenal of all normal contingents. Nuclear troops should be brought together under separate command. Political leaders would reserve the right to use them as a last resort.

ticipate in any government coalition. The FDP told voters to endorse a liberal–conservative coalition under the government's
economics minister, Ludwig Erhard; while Mende did not remove
himself from the chancellor race, he declared his unwillingness to
serve in a cabinet headed by Adenauer.[59]

The election tally left the CDU/CSU by far the most powerful
party; it won 45.3 percent of the vote and 242 Bundestag mandates,
down 5 percent from 1957. The SPD won 36.2 percent of the vote
and 190 mandates, the FDP 12.8 percent of the vote and 67 seats.[60]
Not only were conservatives deprived of their absolute majority, no
splinter parties received enough mandates to make up the difference; for the first time in eight years, coalition government was a
necessity. The possibilities for intrigue were great: Would the CDU/
CSU kill the goose that laid the golden egg, as demanded by the
FDP? Would Adenauer relinquish control over the foreign ministry
either to the SPD or FDP in order to save his own neck? If a Great
Coalition loomed on the horizon, which campaign pledge would
the FDP renege on: its promise not to reelect Adenauer, or its promise not to form a coalition with the SPD?

CDU/CSU and FDP leaders negotiated a joint coalition plank in
a mere three days, beginning October 2. Strauss prepared the government's draft:

> The weapons-technical side of the integrated NATO forces per-
> mits no differentiation. Therefore, the Bundeswehr must be
> equipped with the same weapons as a potential enemy. So long
> as American law does not permit its allies direct control over
> these nuclear weapons, the Bundeswehr must possess at least the
> equipment for launching tactical nuclear warheads and Bundes-
> wehr contingents must obtain the necessary training. Within
> NATO, a guarantee must be secured that the United States would
> make nuclear warheads available in an emergency.[61]

Karl-Hermann Flach and Genscher formulated the FDP's negotiating position. The Genscher–Flach memorandum demanded greater
political consultation among the NATO partners, an enlargement of
NATO's forces, separate nuclear and nonnuclear units, an eighteen-
month Bundeswehr conscription term, and access to "*all* modern
weapons systems" by the NATO partners. "West Germany would

not oppose a decision by NATO concerning control sharing over nuclear warheads with the partners of the NATO alliance. The best solution for an extension of control would be the creation of special integrated NATO troops, under a centralized NATO command system."[62]

Strauss accepted the Genscher–Flach memorandum, with only a minor alteration (the phrase *would not oppose* was replaced with *would accept*).[63] Though he objected to the concept of separate nuclear and nonnuclear NATO units, he saw no reason to let it interfere with an accord. The Coalition Agreement thus sidestepped the issue of a national deterrent force, while bolstering the government's commitment to nuclear control-sharing. "The NATO alliance must be strengthened through the integration of weapons technology among NATO forces," it stated. "This includes equipping the troops of all NATO partners with *all* modern weapons, including systems that fire modern warheads. In the question of nuclear sharing, a solution is to be sought that would give the European parties a right of codetermination within the realm laid down by a NATO formula. The same is true for specially equipped NATO units."[64]

While Strauss reached an accord on defense policy, Brentano and Adenauer negotiated with the FDP over foreign policy. The government accepted with only minor changes the goals outlined in the Genscher–Flach memorandum: "The new government must try to gain the initiative for itself and the West on the matter of German politics. It must strive for a solution to the German and Berlin questions through negotiations for all Germany." The memorandum opposed any solution that recognized East Germany as a separate state, weakened the ties to West Berlin, or accepted the permanency of the Berlin Wall. Flach and Genscher also linked foreign policy and security issues, using a euphemism for the word "disengagement." "Plans for European zones with a special military status can only be discussed in connection with a reunified Germany. Considerations over the creation of wide-reaching control zones against surprise attacks are well suited for creating a basis of trust for a reunified Germany in connection with a European zone with a special military status. Reunification in peace and freedom is not attainable on the basis of a neutralized Germany."[65]

The Coalition Agreement was easily attained; but a six-week "war of nerves" ensued, as the liberals lay siege to the Adenauer–Strauss–Brentano triumvirate. At first, the FDP targeted Adenauer; but conservative leaders threatened to form a Great Coalition with the SPD unless the liberals accepted Adenauer for a two-year interim.[66] By intervening on behalf of the liberals against a Great Coalition, Strauss made himself indispensable to the FDP. In the end, it was Brentano who lost his post. Since Mende had vowed not to join a cabinet under Adenauer, he could not become the next foreign minister; but FDP leaders secured the position of Foreign Office Undersecretary, chairmanship of the Bundestag Foreign Affairs Committee, and access to all confidential documents regarding the conduct of foreign affairs.[67]

On November 7, Adenauer was elected to a fourth term of office by a Bundestag vote of 258 to 206. By the secret terms of the accord, he agreed to resign in October 1963 and allow Erhard to become chancellor.

ALL three of West Germany's major parties had cause to rejoice in 1961. Though the SPD had lost its bid for a coalition, it had broken the 35 percent barrier for the first time in its history. The reformers had not only made the party more attractive to middle-class voters, they had worked out a party platform compatible with those of both the FDP and CDU/CSU. Under Brandt, the SPD's popularity would continue to skyrocket: 39.3 percent (1965), 42.7 percent (1969), 45.8 percent (1972). In 1966, Brandt became foreign minister, in 1969, chancellor. Heinemann served a term as federal president (1969–1974); Schmidt headed the chancellory from 1974 to 1982. The SPD's left-wing critics had been right after all—in their diagnoses, if not their prescriptions. Until the Brandt–Schmidt era, Social Democracy was ineffective, timid, parochial: ineffective in its defense of democracy, timid in its bid for power, parochial in its political philosophy.

The 1961 elections reversed the FDP's four-year slide into oblivion; it remains, to this day, the party's best electoral showing. The liberals achieved this remarkable turnabout at the price of flexibility: they committed themselves in advance to a CDU/CSU coalition. This promise, in turn, greatly circumscribed their ability to topple

Adenauer, leaving them little leverage during the coalition talks, especially on defense issues. (The FDP, Dehler complained, had locked itself into one of three choices: "to capitulate, to be excluded, or to be bamboozled.")[68] But the liberals triumphed in the end: not only did they obtain verbal assurances from Adenauer to pursue a more vigorous reunification policy, they eventually broke the CDU/CSU's control over foreign affairs. The FDP has participated in every federal coalition since 1961 (except one, 1966–69) and has monopolized the post of foreign minister since 1969 (Walter Scheel until 1974, Genscher thereafter).

Despite the loss of Brentano, conservatives had reason to be satisfied with the 1961 election results. The gains by the two opposition parties were a backhanded tribute to the chancellor: the SPD and FDP had brought their young "Adenauerians" to the forefront. The plans of yesteryear—from Bonin to Rapacki, from Pfleiderer to Mende—landed in the dustbins; the rhetoric of the past—"nuclear-free zones," "European-wide security pact," "non-nuclear Bundeswehr"—disappeared. The SPD's experience with the GCND campaign made it unwilling to experiment further with extraparliamentary endeavors; the FDP's abysmal record during the years 1956 to 1961 made it wary of the opposition benches.

The 1961 election foreshadowed the political battles of the next decade. Party alignments were so fluid, and the power balance so delicate, that every shift resulted in a new chancellor, defense minister, or foreign minister.[69] The country's leaders tried every coalition except an all-party government. The 1960s thus contrasted vividly with the time when the Adenauer–Brentano–Strauss triumvirate dominated federal politics. But the frequent coalition breaks did not result in a political stalemate or vacillation in the country's defense and foreign affairs. During the Great Coalition (1966–69), the CDU/CSU and SPD cooperated in the formulation of NATO's flexible response doctrine. Thereafter, an SPD–FDP coalition under Chancellor Brandt (1969–1974) initiated the era of *Ostpolitik.*

Though most SPD and FDP leaders still felt NATO was overreliant on nuclear weapons, they had no intention of continuing the discussion outside governmental corridors. Nothing illustrates this transformation better than the "*Spiegel* affair," the last major controversy of the Adenauer era.[70] In October 1962, *Der Spiegel* published an analysis of NATO's autumn maneuver, "Fallex 62," drawing on classified information obtained from a disgruntled member of Strauss' defense ministry. Like the Carte blanche exercise seven years earlier, Fallex 62 tested NATO's ability to survive a surprise attack from the East bloc. The "war" began with a Soviet nuclear strike at military targets in Western Europe, followed by a blitzkrieg tank invasion of northern Germany. By the time NATO retaliated, the Soviets had overrolled the Bundeswehr's front-line divisions; before German generals had a chance to mobilize their reserve units, many cities were incinerated. At war's end, West Germany's "death toll" was estimated at ten to fifteen million. "After nearly seven years of rearmament, and after six years of Strauss' leadership," *Der Spiegel* claimed, "today's German army still gets the lowest note on NATO's report card: it is only 'conditionally prepared for defense.' "[71]

The *Spiegel* article cost Strauss the post of defense minister, forcing him to withdraw from federal politics for nearly a decade. But he did not come under fire for mishandling West Germany's defenses. Rather, he was dismissed from government service for sidestepping the constitution: he had ordered an illegal search of the magazine's main offices and arrested editor Rudolf Augstein on charges of treason. When political activists took to the streets, they protested the antidemocratic nature of Strauss' actions, not the defense issues raised by the Fallex 62. FDP leaders threatened to withdraw from the federal coalition, but they asked only for Strauss' dismissal, not a reassessment of the country's defense preparations. In the past, Ollenhauer's SPD would have seized such an opportunity to attack the government; this time, Brandt and Wehner contacted Adenauer and secretly renewed their offer to form a Great Coalition.[72] "Oddly enough, no one seemed concerned over the substance of *Der Spiegel*'s expose," noted the *New York Times,* "that despite all the money spent on defense, the armed forces were in bad shape and would crumble quickly under a Communist attack. No official even bothered to deny this."[73]

NATO strategy was no longer a focal point of discontent, the Bundeswehr no longer the scapegoat for domestic ills. West Germans had learned to live in the shadow of the mushroom cloud: the nuclear debate of the Adenauer era had come to an end.

EPILOGUE

What is impressive is the cyclical character of the
debates. Much of what is offered today as a
profound and new insight was said yesterday; and
usually in a more concise and literate manner.

—Lawrence Freedman
The Evolution of Nuclear Strategy (1981)

P RESIDENT Johnson flew to Bonn to meet Chancellor Kiesinger
and Foreign Minister Brandt on the occasion of Adenauer's funeral in April 1967. For the previous several years, the Americans
had been striving to reduce NATO's dependency on nuclear weapons. The Soviets had reached a level of near-parity with the United
States. The Bundeswehr—now almost at full strength—had emerged
as the largest standing army in Western Europe. In the wake of the
1962 Cuban missile crisis, the superpowers had begun to negotiate
a series of arms control agreements and explore the possibilities of
detente. The significance of the encounter at Adenauer's funeral thus
resonated well beyond diplomatic formality: the time had come to
lay massive retaliation doctrine to rest.

At its December 1967 meeting, NATO adopted MC-14/3, a European version of flexible response doctrine. MC-14/3 sought a
middle ground between those European leaders who argued for large

185

conventional forces, and those who argued for primary reliance on a nuclear deterrent. NATO decided to strengthen its nonnuclear capabilities, in accordance with McNamara's 1962 Athens speech and the preferences of West German socialists. The West's front-line forces would ensure that NATO did not necessarily have to resort to the immediate use of nuclear warheads. "It is imperative," Schmidt told SPD delegates in 1966, "that the West strengthen its conventional forces in order to restore the balance of power."[1] But in contrast to McNamara's original proposal, NATO decided against the enunciation of a firebreak between a conventional and a nuclear response. Many European conservatives felt that only the threat of escalation would deter the Soviet army: without the link between America's strategic arsenal and Western Europe's forces, the Soviet Union might entertain the hope of gaining territory through limited excursions without triggering NATO's nuclear response. Defense Minister von Hassel wrote in 1965:

> Since any war would be a catastrophe not only for Europe but for all the nations of the alliance, it is of the highest importance to see that the risk for the potential aggressor remains incalculable and that deterrence remains credible. . . . The concept of flexible response in Europe—both political and military—must not be interpreted to mean that the so-called atomic threshold can be raised unduly high, without reference to political considerations. Apart from the fact that this would lead the potential aggressor to think that he could calculate his risk, it would create a situation in which he could seize pawns for future negotiations.[2]

Responding to European desires for more control over NATO policy, McNamara also established the Nuclear Planning Group (NPG), composed of the United States, West Germany, England, Italy, and two rotating members from among the smaller NATO allies. The NPG offered the United States a forum in which to explain its nuclear policies and gave the Europeans an avenue for expressing their defense concerns. American leaders adopted the European version of flexible response doctrine partly on military grounds, partly on political grounds. They came to realize that the American strategic arsenal offered little solace to the Europeans without a visible link to NATO's ground forces in Central Europe. Nor could the Europeans be assuaged if they had no control over NATO's nuclear stockpile in the event of a war with the Soviet Union.[3]

Flexible response was the first track of NATO doctrine, detente the second. "The Atlantic Alliance has two main functions," stated the Harmel Report, appended to NATO's 1967 communique:

> Its first function is to maintain adequate military strength and political solidarity to deter aggression and other forms of pressure and to defend the territory of member countries if aggression should occur. . . . In this climate the Alliance can carry out its second function, to pursue the search for progress towards a more stable relationship in which the underlying political issues can be solved. Military security and a policy of detente are not contradictory but complementary. . . . Each Ally should play its full part in promoting an improvement in relations with the Soviet Union and the countries of Eastern Europe, bearing in mind that the pursuit of detente must not be allowed to split the Alliance.[4]

In principle, the Harmel two-track policy was not dissimilar to the Dulles–Adenauer position of "negotiating from strength." But the early 1970s offered ground far more fertile for cooperation; "nuclear parity" and "mutually assured destruction" were the watchwords. The most important agreement, SALT I, restricted the deployment of antiballistic missile systems and put a ceiling on the number of land-based and sea-based launchers. At the same time, Chancellor Brandt and Foreign Minister Genscher initiated *Ostpolitik:* the Moscow Treaty (1970), the Warsaw Treaty (1970), the Quadripartite Agreement on Berlin (1971), the Prague Treaty (1973). The Berlin agreements resolved the issue of access routes and normalized inner-city affairs, ending twenty-five years of superpower wrangling over the city's status. The other agreements were non-aggression pacts, the West German government renouncing its claims to Polish territory East of the Oder–Neisse line and to the Czech Sudetenland.[5]

Though the SALT talks and *Ostpolitik* occurred simultaneously, the two were not identical. The SALT talks focused primarily on the American and Russian strategic arsenals. *Ostpolitik* was designed to eliminate potential causes of conflict in Central Europe; there was no sustained effort to reduce the number of warheads on

West German soil. Moreover, other arms control forums—from the Mutual and Balanced Force Reduction (MBFR) talks in Vienna to the Helsinki Conference on Security and Cooperation in Europe (CSCE)—failed to halt the European arms spiral. The West Germans purchased Pershing Ia missiles in 1969, while the Americans stationed F-111 bombers in Britain and installed short-range Lance missiles on the continent. The French deployed short-range Pluton rockets and medium-range missiles. The Soviets implemented the most extensive of these modernization programs, replacing their SS-4 and SS-5 missiles with mobile SS-20 medium-range missiles and the Backfire bomber.[6]

It was Chancellor Schmidt (1974–1982) who most forcefully argued that the American–Soviet arms agreements undermined flexible response doctrine and endangered Western European security. "SALT codifies the nuclear strategic balance between the Soviet Union and the United States," he stated in his Alastair Buchan Memorial Lecture of October 1977. "To put it another way: SALT neutralizes their strategic nuclear capabilities. In Europe this magnifies the significance of the disparities between East and West in nuclear tactical and conventional weapons." Schmidt urged the superpowers to continue their negotiations. But he warned that

> strategic arms limitations confined to the United States and the Soviet Union will inevitably impair the security of the West European members of the alliance vis-à-vis Soviet military superiority in Europe if we do not succeed in removing the disparities of military power in Europe parallel to the SALT negotiations. So long as this is not the case we must maintain the balance of the full range of deterrence strategy. The alliance must, therefore, be ready to make available the means to support its present strategy.[7]

American leaders had already been contemplating several ways of strengthening the link between the U.S. strategic arsenal and NATO's ground forces, including the deployment of the controversial neutron bomb in Europe. In 1979, NATO's Nuclear Planning Group worked out a "two-track" approach to eliminating the Soviet's military advantage in Europe. One track involved arms control negotiations between the superpowers over intermediate-range nuclear forces (INF). If these talks did not produce results, NATO intended to follow a second track: the deployment of ground-launched cruise missiles in West Germany, Britain, Italy, Belgium, Holland, and the stationing of Pershing II missiles in West Germany.[8]

IT was ironic that flexible response doctrine—whose original purpose had been to reduce NATO's dependency on nuclear weapons—became the justification for a nuclear buildup. It was also ironic that Schmidt's name became so closely identified with NATO's decision to deploy Euromissiles. In the 1950s, he had been on the GCND lecture circuit denouncing Adenauer's nuclear policy. As a Bundeswehr reserve officer, he once told his army superiors and his party comrades that he "would disobey if forced to implement an order involving nuclear weapons, regardless of the laws governing this matter."[9]

Like the Bundestag's March 1958 Resolution, NATO's 1979 two-track decision coupled an arms control initiative with the threat of a nuclear buildup. Both tracks promised to eliminate the disparity in military capabilities between NATO and East bloc forces, thereby reassuring Western European governments of America's continued commitment to their defense. But like Adenauer, Schmidt rediscovered that there was a public dimension to the formulation of nuclear strategy. As the superpowers sought an INF accord, Europe experienced the rebirth of an antinuclear crusade, and for the next several years its major cities were the sites of frequent peace rallies. At the center of the debate were West Germans: church leaders, labor groups, grassroots organizers, and Communist sympathizers rekindled the spirit of opposition from the embers of the GCND.

This new antinuclear campaign reenacted the cycle of the Adenauer-era debate. Like the 1953 debate over atomic cannons, the neutron bomb controversy (1977–1978) aroused a core group of nuclear foes who claimed that such "battlefield" weapons increased the risk that any future European war would soon escalate into a nuclear one. (Research on the neutron bomb, ironically, began in the wake of Carte blanche and similar NATO maneuvers of the 1950s, with T. S. Cohen and others arguing that an enhanced radiation warhead would minimize collateral damage in highly populated regions.) A second phase began with NATO's two-track decision and the election of President Reagan (1980–1988). During this phase, opponents of NATO policy attempted to mobilize antinuclear sentiment through manifestos and signature campaigns. The most famous of these initiatives—the "Krefeld Appeal"—was initiated by the German Peace Union and other Communist-backed organizations. Finally, a demonstration phase occurred from 1981 to 1983, peaking in the two Bonn rallies (October 1981 and June 1982) and the "Hot Autumn" Action Week (mid-October 1983).[10] By November, the antinuclear campaign had lost momentum. NATO began stationing its Pershing II and cruise missiles in Western Europe as planned. The Soviets left the INF talks, temporarily precluding any possibility of compromise. Like the GCND campaign, the antinuclear movement found itself isolated and impotent. Attendance at demonstrations dwindled, and peace leaders retired from view.

As in the 1950s, the morality of nuclear weapons became topical within the churches. The Protestant church devoted two Church Assemblies to the peace theme: the June 1981 Hamburg meeting attracted over 50,000 participants, the June 1983 Hanover meeting 200,000. Protestant organizations from the 1950s—the Action Committee for Reconciliation/Peace Service and the Action Committee in the Service of Peace—sponsored the October 1981 Bonn demonstration, which drew a crowd of 300,000. At the Catholic Church Assembly in Düsseldorf (September 1982), several Catholic peace organizations—the *Pax Christi*, the Christians against Atomic Armaments, and the Church Initiative from Below—urged their churches to join forces with Protestant crusaders against the two-track decision.[11]

Following the lead of the CDU/CSU, Catholic bishops gave their blessings to nuclear deterrence, just as they had in the 1950s. A more lively debate occurred within the Protestant church, but even here there was no succession of innovative theological tracts comparable to those of the Adenauer years; the participants only retraced the ground that Gollwitzer, Thielicke, the Rhine Convent, the Brethren, and others had explored twenty-five years earlier. In 1981, the Protestant Council reaffirmed the Heidelberg Theses (1959) as the majority position among Protestants. A year later, the council blocked the Brethren's attempt to reintroduce the Ten Theses (1958) for synodal debate; it did not want to address anew the irresolvable

question of *status confessionis.* Once the Protestant leadership upheld the 1958 Synodal Resolution (the "formula of impotence"), antinuclear activists had no chance of gaining the institutional back-
ing of the church. The Protestant church, in the 1980s as in the
1950s, tolerated the bomb, while offering haven to conscientious
objectors; it avoided direct involvement in politics, while urging its
congregation to explore new paths to peace.[12]

The environmentalist Green Party became the political homeland
for West Germany's antinuclear forces. Comprised of pacifists, socialists, students, and feminists, the Greens opposed the two-track
decision and the presence of America's nuclear arsenal in Western
Europe. Their 1983 party platform stated:

> Humanity can only survive if right takes the place of might. We
> Germans must particularly stress this demand, as any so-called
> "emergency" would bring our destruction. The nuclear "deter-
> rent" has become an ineffective threat, as it implies nuclear self-
> destruction. Peace and disarmament must therefore become the
> maxim of German foreign policy and strategy. . . . The con-
> struction of civil power guided by peace must proceed by im-
> mediately beginning to dissolve the military blocs, in particular
> NATO and the Warsaw Pact. This will create the basis for ov-
> ercoming the partition of Europe and the division of Germany.[13]

In the early 1980s, the Greens experienced some success in state
and local elections, especially in traditional SPD strongholds; after
receiving slightly over 5 percent of the vote in the 1983 federal elections, they entered the Bundestag. Yet even though the Greens were
far more successful than previous antinuclear parties, their ambivalent attitude toward a conventional defense and their tolerance of
Communist members limited the party's electoral attractiveness. The
Greens remained politically isolated, internally fragmented, and domestically impotent during the entirety of the debate over NATO's
two-track decision. The party's sole experiment in government—an
SPD–Green coalition in Hessen—ended in discord in 1987.[14]

The emergence of the Greens as a political force had a pro-
nounced effect on the Social Democrats. On the one hand, the SPD
was the major government party, with a chancellor who com-
manded domestic and international respect. The socialists were

proponents of flexible response doctrine, and their party leaders had been instrumental in the formulation of the 1979 two-track decision. "A policy of peace," stated their defense resolution at the 1982 Munich party convention, "is connected with a policy of 'security and detente,' in accordance with NATO's 1967 Harmel Report. . . . A modernly equipped and trained Bundeswehr is still an essential element of our capability in the NATO alliance."[15] On the other hand, the SPD traditionally opposed a nuclear defense of Europe, favoring instead a buildup of NATO's conventional forces. Since the Ollenhauer era, moreover, the socialists had welcomed pacifists and antinuclear activists to its ranks. Nearly one-quarter of the SPD's 218 Bundestag delegates openly opposed Schmidt's defense policies; they felt that the party's future depended on its ability to reabsorb the Green Party's constituency. Hence, the absence of a consistent policy. As long as Schmidt remained chancellor, the SPD supported the two-track decision; but when the SPD–FDP alliance dissolved in 1982, the SPD took a more pacifist course. At the 1983 Cologne party convention, the socialists reversed themselves on the two-track decision. "The SPD," stated the Cologne resolution, "opposes the stationing of new American medium-range missiles on West German soil."[16]

Labor leaders—with the conspicuous exception of the Metalworkers' Union chairman Georg Benz—kept aloof from the antinuclear movement in the early phases. During Schmidt's chancellorship, the DGB gave cautious support to the two-track decision, laying emphasis on the arms control side of the initiative. "A first step toward general disarmament would be to limit the number of medium-range missiles and to reduce the existing nuclear potential," stated DGB chairman Heinz Vetter at labors' Anti-War Day (September 1, 1981). "It is in the common interest of Europeans that the dangerous threat caused by these weapons be eliminated. This is only possible if the medium-range weapons on both sides get removed. I repeat: whoever says 'Pershing' must also say 'SS-20.' "[17] After the socialist–liberal coalition dissolved in 1982, the DGB adopted a more hostile stance toward NATO policy, becoming the only major West German institution to endorse the peace movement. But the support not only came late, it was also largely symbolic: a flurry of antinuclear resolutions and a five-minute "peace pause" at factories on October 5, 1983. When the issue of a general strike reemerged, labor leaders only dusted off their 1958 resolutions. "The DGB rejects a general strike as a means to hinder the possible stationing of nuclear medium-range missiles. The consultative referendum is also not the appropriate way of dealing with this problem."[18]

In special federal elections in March 1983, the CDU/CSU captured 48.8 percent of the vote, its strongest showing since 1957; the FDP received 6.9 percent. Though the conservatives' popularity dipped below 45 percent in 1987, CDU/CSU Chancellor Helmut Kohl still enjoyed a clear mandate to govern in coalition with a stronger FDP (1987: 9 percent). On the opposition benches sat the Greens with 5 percent of the vote, and the SPD held slightly over 38 percent. For the socialists, the 1983 election was their worst defeat since the Adenauer era; their percentages dipped further in 1987 as the Greens increased to over 8 percent. State elections followed the same pattern. As of April 1987, the SPD controlled only three state governments: Saar, Bremen, and North Rhine-Westphalia. Even the two traditional SPD strongholds—Hamburg and Hessen—went to the CDU/CSU for the first time since 1945.

Since the Dehler era, the FDP has concerned itself more with foreign affairs than defense policy, more with detente than nuclear strategy. "German foreign policy is a peace policy," stated the FDP's resolution at the 1981 Cologne party convention. "It serves the goal of maintaining the peace in Europe and the world."[19] No liberal has ever held the post of defense minister, nor has the FDP articulated a clear position on nuclear issues. Yet because they have remained in power continuously since 1969, the liberals have exerted a moderating influence on the two larger parties. Foreign Minister Genscher worked closely with Chancellor Schmidt in the design and implementation of NATO's two-track decision. After the formation of a conservative-liberal coalition in 1982, Genscher put pressure on CDU/CSU Chancellor Helmut Kohl to accept the "double-zero" option negotiated by the superpowers at Geneva: the elimination of medium-range missiles in Europe, including the SS-20s, Pershing IIs, and cruise missiles.[20]

As in the Adenauer era, CDU/CSU leaders remained West Germany's foremost champions of nuclear deterrence in the 1980s.

"NATO is the cornerstone of peace," stated the conservatives' 1978 program. "We support the close cooperation with our alliance partners. Mutual security requires cooperative efforts beyond defense matters. For deterrence to be effective, the Europeans must make a convincing defense contribution, and the North Americans must not diminish their military presence in Europe or their nuclear umbrella."[21] The conservatives were quick to point out the danger of Soviet SS-20 deployments, lending their complete support to the new NATO buildup. They also resisted the double-zero option, initially agreeing to it only on the condition that the West German Bundeswehr be allowed to retain its 72 Pershing Ia missiles.[22] When Chancellor Kohl finally yielded on the Pershing Ia issue, unconditionally accepting the double-zero plan, he revitalized the tripartisan spirit of compromise within the Bundestag. Equally important, by restoring consensus in NATO, he also removed one of the most formidable roadblocks to an INF agreement at the Reagan-Gorbachev summit of 1987.

The 1950s set the stage for the actors of the 1980s, much as the Adenauer-era conflict was scripted during Weimar. But the themes were no longer chaos and isolation, but parliamentary stability and an unswerving commitment to NATO. Never before had Europe enjoyed forty years of peace: this alone made West Germany's choice irresistible.

NOTES

Prologue

1. Cited in Friedrich Torberg, "Als er zum 3. Male Kanzler wurde," p. 118.
2. "Verbatim Record of the 9th Plenary Meeting of the Nine-Power Conference, 2 October 1954," U.S. State Department, Conference Files 60 D 627, CF 368. Only a portion of this protocol has been made available under the Freedom of Information Act (FOI case no. 8400592). A synopsis is available in "Telegraphic Summary by the United States Delegation," in U.S. Dept. of State, *FRUS 1952–1954*, vol. 5, pt. 2, pp. 1324–25. For the treaties' details, see *Treaty Establishing the European Defense Community and Related Protocols;* Beate Ruhm von Oppen, ed., *Documents on Germany Under Occupation 1945–1954*, pp. 613–48; and "Agreement on Restoration of German Sovereignty," p. 519.
3. Cited by Catherine Kelleher, *Germany and the Politics of Nuclear Weapons*, p. 114.
4. Fritz René Allemann's celebrated book, *Bonn ist nicht Weimar*, explores how the Weimar experience influenced West German politics in the mid-1950s.

Part I

Introduction

1. On NATO's nuclear doctrine, see Raymond Aron, *The Great Debate;* Lawrence Freedman, *The Evolution of Nuclear Strategy;* John Lewis Gaddis, *Strategies of Containment;* Laurence Martin, *NATO and the Defense of the West;* Robert Osgood, *NATO: The Entangling Alliance;* Steven L. Rearden, *The Evolution of American Strategic Doctrine;* David Alan Rosenberg, "The Origins of Overkill"; and David Schwartz, *NATO's Nuclear Dilemmas*. See also three collections published by the Militärgeschichtliches Forschungsamt: *Anfänge westdeutscher Sicherheitspolitik 1945–1956*, vol. 1; *Vorträge zur Militärgeschichte*, vol. 4; and *Verteidigung im Bündnis*.
2. Christian Greiner, "Die alliierten Militärstrategischen Planungen zur Verteidigung Westeuropas 1947–1950," Militärgeschichtliches Forschungsamt, ed., *Anfänge*, 1:119–323.
3. "A Report to the President Pursuant to the President's Directive of January 31, 1950. NSC 68," U.S. Dept. of State, *FRUS 1950*, 1:244.
4. Samuel F. Wells, "Sounding the Tocsin."

5. "A Report to the President," U.S. Dept of State, *FRUS 1950*, 1:250.

6. "Supplementary Report of the Temporary Council Committee, 8th February 1952, Provisional Text," U.S. Dept. of State, *FRUS 1952–1954*, 5:115.

7. "Denkschrift des militärischen Expertenausschusses über die Aufstellung eines Deutschen Kontingents im Rahmen einer übernationalen Streitmacht zur Verteidigung Westeuropas vom 9. October 1950," *Militärgeschichtliche Mitteilungen* (1977), 21:169–72. This document, known as the Himmerod Memorandum, was the blueprint for the Bundeswehr's creation.

8. Cited by Kurt Klotzbach, *Der Weg zur Staatspartei*, p. 212.

9. Cited by Charles Naef, "The Politics of West German Rearmament, 1950–1956," p. 92.

10. Cited by Klaus Knorr, "The Strained Alliance," in Knorr, ed., *NATO and American Security*, p. 4.

11. "Review of Basic National Security Policy, NSC 162/2," in *The Pentagon Papers*, 1:413–29; John Foster Dulles, "The Evolution of Foreign Policy"; and Dulles, "Challenge and Response in United States Policy." For a critique of massive retaliation doctrine, see William W. Kaufmann, ed., *Military Policy and National Security;* Henry Kissinger, *Nuclear Weapons and Foreign Policy;* and Maxwell Taylor, *The Uncertain Trumpet.*

12. John Foster Dulles, "Policy for Security and Peace," p. 358.

13. "Statement by the Secretary of State to the North Atlantic Council, April 23, 1954," U.S. Dept. of State, *FRUS 1952–1954*, 5:511–12.

14. Cited by Osgood, *NATO*, p. 109.

15. The expression was coined by Sir John Slessor in "The Place of the Bomber in British Strategy." On British strategy, see Lawrence Freedman, *Britain and Nuclear Weapons;* Margaret Gowing, *Britain and Atomic Energy, 1939–1945;* John Groom, *British Thinking about Nuclear Weapons;* and Andrew Pierre, *Nuclear Politics: The British Experience.*

16. Cited by Wilfrid Kohl, *French Nuclear Diplomacy*, p. 152. See also Pierre Gallois, *The Balance of Terror;* and Wolf Mendl, *Deterrence and Persuasion.*

17. Christian Greiner, "Nordatlantische Bündnisstrategie und deutscher Verteidigungsbeitrag, 1954 bis 1957," Militärgeschichtliches Forschungsamt, ed., *Vorträge* 4:116–143; Osgood, *NATO*, pp. 116–23; Schwartz, *NATO's Nuclear Dilemmas*, pp. 22–34.

1. The Nuclear Arsenal of Democracy

1. Paul Sethe, "Man muss für alles bezahlen," *FAZ*, July 14, 1950. On West German rearmament, see Joseph Foschepoth, ed., *Kalter Krieg und Deutsche Frage;* Helga Haftendorn, *Sicherheit und Entspannung;* Andreas Hillgruber, *Europa in der Weltpolitik der Nachkriegszeit 1945–1963;* Gunther Mai, *Westliche Sicherheitspolitik im Kalten Krieg;* Robert McGeehan, *The German Rearmament Question;* Militärgeschichtliches Forschungsamt, ed., *Militärgeschichte;* Roger Morgan, *The United States and West Germany 1945–1973;* Charles Naef, "The Politics of West German Rearmament, 1950–1956"; Ernst Nolte, *Deutschland und der Kalte Krieg;* Robert Osgood, *NATO: The Entangling Alliance;* James L. Richardson, *Germany and the Atlantic Alliance;* Klaus von Schubert, *Weiderbewaffnung und Westintegration;* and

Gerhard Wettig, *Entmilitarisierung und Wiederbewaffnung in Deutschland, 1943–1955.* For an excellent overview of the Adenauer era, see Anselm Doering-Manteuffel, *Die Bundesrepublik Deutschland in der Aera Adenauer.*

2. Elisabeth Noelle and Erich Peter Neumann, *The Germans: Public Opinion Polls 1947–1966,* p. 436.

3. "Regierungserklärung vor dem Deutschen Bundestag, 8. November 1950," in Hans-Peter Schwarz, ed., *Konrad Adenauer: Reden 1917–1967,* pp. 199–200.

4. On Adenauer, see Arnulf Baring, *Aussenpolitik in Adenauers Kanzlerdemokratie;* Dieter Blumenwitz, ed., *Konrad Adenauer und seine Zeit,* 2 vols; Helmut Kohl, ed., *Konrad Adenauer 1876–1976;* and Rudolf Morsey and Konrad Repgen, eds., *Adenauer-Studien.*

5. Helga Haftendorn, "Adenauer und die europäische Sicherheit," in Blumenwitz, ed., *Konrad Adenauer und seine Zeit,* p. 95.

6. See Schubert, *Wiederbewaffnung und Westintegration,* p. 42; and Lewis J. Edinger, *Kurt Schumacher,* p. 171.

7. Cited by Hans Speier and W. Phillips Davison, eds., *West German Leadership and Foreign Policy,* p. 2.

8. *New York Times,* August 18, 1950.

9. Kelleher, "German Nuclear Dilemmas, 1954–1966," p. 89.

10. Baring's depiction in *Aussenpolitik in Adenauers Kanzlerdemokratie.*

11. On Heinemann and the German neutralist movement, see Diether Koch, *Heinemann und die Deutschlandfrage;* Peter Molt, "Die neutralistische Opposition"; and Rainer Dohse, *Der Dritte Weg.*

12. On the FDP, see Richard H. Bald, "The Free Democratic Party"; Sebastian Glatzender, *Die Deutschlandpolitik der FDP in der Aera Adenauer;* Jörg M. Gutscher, *Die Entwicklung der FDP;* and Dietrich Wagner, *FDP und Wiederbewaffnung.*

13. Karl Georg Pfleiderer, "Für oder gegen die Verträge," in *Politik für Deutschland,* pp. 83–99; Wagner, *FDP und Wiederbewaffnung,* pp. 106–11.

14. On the SPD and rearmament, see Ulrich Buczylowski, *Kurt Schumacher und die deutsche Frage;* Douglas Chalmers, *The Social Democratic Party of Germany;* Gordon Douglas Drummond, *The German Social Democrats in Opposition, 1949–1960;* Rudolf Hrbek, *Die SPD—Deutschland und Europa;* Kurt Klotzbach, *Der Weg zur Staatspartei;* Udo Loewke, *Für den Fall;* Theo Pirker, *Die SPD nach Hitler;* and Hartmut Soell, *Fritz Erler.*

15. Klotzbach, *Der Weg zur Staatspartei,* pp. 216–17.

16. *Protokoll: 3. ordentlicher Bundeskongress Frankfurt am Main: 4. bis 9. Oktober 1954,* p. 807. On the DGB, see Wolfgang Hirsch-Weber, *Gewerkschaften in der Politik;* Theo Pirker, *Die blinde Macht.* Dieter Schuster, *Die deutschen Gewerkschaften seit 1945;* Hans-Erich Volkmann, "Zur innenpolitischen Diskussion um einen westdeutschen Verteidigungsbeitrag am Beispiel der Gewerkschaften, 1947 bis 1956," Militärgeschichtliches Forschungsamt, ed., *Vorträge,* 4:143–63.

17. On the German Catholic church, see Anselm Doering-Manteuffel, *Katholismus und Wiederbewaffnung.*

18. On the German Protestant church, see Heinz Brunotte, *Die Evangelische Kirche in Deutschland;* Johanna Vogel, *Kirche und Wiederbewaffnung;* and Ina Görlich, "Zum ethischen Problem der Atomdiskussion."

19. Paul Sethe first made the "missed opportunity" argument in *Zwischen Bonn und Moskau* (1956). On the Stalin note, see Hermann Graml, "Die Legende von der

verpassten Gelegenheit"; Hermann-Josef Rupieper, "Zu den sowjetischen Deutsch-landnoten 1952"; and Schubert, *Wiederbewaffnung und Westintegration*, pp. 165–75.

20. *Verhandlungen des Deutschen Bundestages, 1. Wahlperiode, 19. März 1953*, p. 12325.

21. Statistics from Hans Georg Lehmann, *Chronik der Bundesrepublik Deutschland 1945/49 bis 1981*. On the 1953 elections, see Wolfgang Hirsch-Weber and Klaus Schütz, *Wähler und Gewählte*.

22. *Government Declaration by the German Federal Chancellor Dr. Konrad Adenauer before the German Bundestag on 20 October 1953*, p. 7.

23. "The Deputy Undersecretary of State (Matthews) to the Assistant Secretary of Defense for International Security Affairs (Nash), July 30, 1953," and "The Secretary of State to the Embassy in France, September 3, 1953," both in U.S. Dept of State, *FRUS 1952–1954*, vol. 5, pt. 1, pp. 437–40. Dulles stated that deployment was set for mid-September, "assuming no radical upset in German elections."

24. On the West German nuclear debate, see Richard Close, "Nuclear Weapons and West Germany"; Gordon Craig, "Germany and NATO: The Rearmament Debate, 1950–1958," in Klaus Knorr, ed., *NATO and American Security;* Manfred Dormann, *Demokratische Militärpolitik;* Martin Geiling, *Aussenpolitik und Nuklearpolitik;* Kelleher, *Germany and the Politics of Nuclear Weapons;* Kurt Lauk, "Die nuklearen Optionen der Bundesrepublik Deutschland"; Dieter Mahncke, *Nukleare Mitwirkung;* Reinhard Mutz, *Sicherheitspolitik und demokratische Oeffentlichkeit in der BRD;* Hans-Gert Pöttering, *Adenauers Sicherheitspolitik 1955–1963;* Theo Sommer, "The Objectives of Germany," in Alastair Buchan, ed., *A World of Nuclear Powers?;* and Hans Speier, *German Rearmament and Atomic War*. See also A. J. Bacevich, *The Pentomic Era*.

25. "Protokoll der 2. Sitzung des Ausschusses für Fragen der europäischen Sicherheit (6. Ausschuss) am 19. November 1953," PA:VA. (The Defense Committee went under the name of the Committee for Questions of European Security until 1956.)

26. Blank headed the so-called Blank Office; he became West Germany's first defense minister in 1956. Heusinger and Kielmansegg handled political and military questions for the Blank Office.

27. "Protokoll der 2. Sitzung des Ausschusses für Fragen der europäischen Sicherheit (6. Ausschuss) am 19. November 1953," PA:VA.

28. "Stenographisches Protokoll der 15. Sitzung des Ausschusses für Fragen der europäischen Sicherheit, den 12. Juli 1954," PA:VA.

29. "Stenographische Niederschrift der 37. Sitzung des Ausschusses für auswärtige Angelegenheiten in Verbindung mit der 32. Sitzung des Ausschusses für Fragen der europäischen Sicherheit, den 10. Februar 1955," PA:VA.

30. *Ibid.*

31. "Protokoll der 2. Sitzung des Ausschusses für Fragen der europäischen Sicherheit (6. Ausschuss) am 19. November 1953," PA:VA.

32. Stenographisches Protokoll der 23. Sitzung des Ausschusses für Fragen der europäischen Sicherheit am 1. Dezember 1954," PA:VA.

33. *Ibid.*

34. On Bonin, see Heinz Brill, "Das Problem einer wehrpolitischen Alternative"; Hans Speier, *German Rearmament and Atomic War*, pp. 75–88; and Henry Kissinger, *Nuclear Weapons and Foreign Policy*, pp. 286–91.

35. Bogislav von Bonin, "Das Märchen von Sicherheit," *Atomkrieg—Unser Ende*,

p. 7. See also Bonin, "Amerika-Reise 1954: Neue Waffen, neue Organisationsformen in der US-Army (Juni 1954)," BA-MA:BW9/2065.

36. *Der Spiegel*, March 30, 1955, pp. 8–9. A full account of the Bonin controversy in "Stenographische Niederschrift über die 36. Sitzung des Ausschusses für europäischen Sicherheit, 30. März 1955," PA:VA.

37. "Sprechzettel für Herrn Blank (6. März 1955)," BA-MA:BW9/2065.

38. *Verhandlungen des Deutschen Bundestages, 2. Wahlperiode, 25. Februar 1955*, p. 3729.

39. "Stenographisches Protokoll über die 25. Sitzung des Ausschusses für Fragen der europäischen Sicherheit, den 12. Januar 1955," PA:VA, pp. 61–62.

40. *Verhandlungen des Deutschen Bundestages, 2. Wahlperiode, 25. Februar 1955*, p. 3736.

41. "Stenographische Niederschrift, 10. Februar 1955," PA:VA, pp. 14–15.

42. On Carte blanche, see Speier, *German Rearmament and Atomic War*, pp. 144–47 and 182–93; Catherine Kelleher, *Germany and the Politics of Nuclear Weapons*, pp. 34–43; Kissinger, *Nuclear Weapons and Foreign Policy*, pp. 291–97; Edouard Le Ghait, *No Carte Blanche to Capricorn*; A. W. Uhlig, *Atom—Angst oder Hoffnung?*; and O. W., "Luftmanoever 'Carte Blanche' im Kommandobereich Mitteleuropa," *Wehrkunde* (July 1955), pp. 308–10, and (August 1955), pp. 351–52. The press attended the exercises; there were accounts in *The Times*, June 24–29, 1955; *SDZ*, June 29–July 3, 1955; and *NZZ*, June 27 and July 15, 1955.

43. A succinct summary of the military questions being probed by the NATO exercise, in "Abschrift eines Vortrages von Generalmajor Laegeler (Verteidigungsministerium) über carte blanche, 22. August 1955," FNS:BVA Protokolle 1955.

44. *Ibid.* See also Adolf Heusinger, "Die Manoever 'Carte Blanche,'" *Bulletin des Presse- und Informationsamtes* (July 2, 1955); and Wilhelm Ritter von Schramm, "Was lehrt 'Carte Blanche,'" *Rheinischer Merkur*, July 8, 1955.

45. "Verteidigung: Ueberholt wie Pfeil und Bogen," *Der Spiegel*, July 13, 1955, pp. 7–11.

46. Cited in *The Times*, June 29, 1955. Obviously, there is no way to verify or disprove any estimates on the effects of nuclear warfare, so all estimates of the death toll from the Carte blanche exercise will remain speculative. But a sophisticated mathematical study prepared by Carl-Friedrich von Weizsäcker and others, *Kriegsfolgen und Kriegsverhütung*, left little doubt that Germany would cease to function as a viable society in the event of a war even as "limited" as Carte blanche.

47. Weinstein, "Operation Carte Blanche: Ein Alarmzeichen," *FAZ*, June 27, 1955. See also Weinstein, "So stellt man sich den Krieg der Zunkunft vor," *FAZ*, June 21, 1955; "Die Suche nach der grossen Wahrheit," *FAZ*, July 12, 1955; and "Atomkrieg oder Bonin-Plan?" See also Bonin: "Das Märchen von Sicherheit," *Atomkrieg—Unser Ende*, p. 7; "'Carte blanche' letzte Warnung," *Rheinische-Westphälische Nachrichten*, July 23, 1955; and *Opposition gegen Adenauers Sicherheitspolitik*, pp. 21–57. At its December 1954 meeting, NATO decided to invite journalists to future maneuvers in the hope that the public would come to see the virtues of the New Look. See "Allgemeine Grundsätze für die Unterrichtung der Oeffentlichkeit über vorgetäuschte Atom-Operationen bei Manövern and Uebungen (11. Mai 1955)," BAMA:BW9/2479. After Carte blanche, NATO concluded that this practice was unwise.

48. *Verhandlungen des Deutschen Bundestages, 2. Wahlperiode, 28. Juni 1955*, p. 5232.

49. *Ibid.*, p. 5605.

50. *Ibid.* See also Speier's interview of October 5, 1955, with Strauss over Bonin and Carte blanche, in Hans Speier, *From the Ashes of Disgrace*, pp. 288–93.

51. Erler and Schmidt recounted their meeting with Gruenther in "Stenographisches Protokoll der 99. Sitzung des Ausschusses für Verteidigung, den 20. Juni 1956," PA:VA, pp. 53–59.

52. *Verhandlungen des Deutschen Bundestages, 2. Wahlperiode, 6. Juli 1956*, p. 8778.

53. "Radford Seeking an 800,000 Man Cut," *New York Times*, July 13, 1956. On the Radford crisis, see Kelleher, *Germany and the Politics of Nuclear Weapons*, pp. 44–59.

54. *Rheinischer Merkur*, August 10, 1956.

55. Konrad Adenauer, "Lohnt sich der Aufbau der Bundeswehr noch?" *Bulletin* (August 21, 1956). See also: *Bulletin* (July 25, August 2, and August 7, 1956); and *Union in Deutschland*, July 26, 1956.

56. On Adenauer's talk with Allan Dulles, see Konrad Adenauer, *Erinnerungen 1955–1959*, pp. 212–13.

57. "Keine Revolution in Führung und Organisation der Streitkräfte," *Bulletin* (September 25, 1956); and *Rheinischer Merkur*, February 22, 1957. The new SACEUR general, Lauris Norstad, paid indirect tribute to Adenauer's diplomatic skills in a Defense Committee hearing a short time later, stating that for the first time in NATO's eight-year history a major decision had been reversed almost single-handedly. "Stenographisches Protokoll über die 147. Sitzung des Ausschusses für Fragen der europäischen Sicherheit, 21. März 1957," PA:VA.

58. Adenauer, *Erinnerungen 1955–1959*, pp. 212–13. See also "Konrad Adenauers 'new look,' " *Vorwärts* (October 5, 1956).

59. "Stenographisches Protokoll der 111. Sitzung des Verteidigungsausschusses des Deutschen Bundestages, 3. Oktober 1956," PA:VA.

60. "NATO: Vieles hat sich geändert," *Der Spiegel*, November 28, 1956, pp. 11–12; Kelleher, *Germany and the Politics of Nuclear Weapons*, pp. 61–88.

61. "Stenographisches Protokoll über die 147. Sitzung des Ausschusses für Fragen der europäischen Sicherheit, 21. März 1957," PA:VA.

62. "Stenographische Niederschrift, 10. Februar 1955," PA:VA.

63. "Der grosse Prügel," *Der Spiegel*, January 2, 1957, p. 21; similar in Franz Josef Strauss, "Glaubhafte Sicherheit," *Aussenpolitik* (1961), 12:517.

2. The War at Home

1. Speier, *German Rearmament and Atomic War*, p. 257.

2. On the Paulskirche movement, see Eckart Dietzfelbinger, *Die westdeutsche Friedensbewegung 1948 bis 1955*, pp. 182–94.

3. On the Eden Plan, see Anthony Eden, *Full Circle*, pp. 330–46; and Charles Planck, *The Changing Status of German Reunification in Western Diplomacy, 1955–1966*, pp. 10–20.

4. Eden, *Full Circle*, pp. 335–36.

5. "Kurzprotokoll: FDP FS, 28. August 1955," FDP BA:FS Protokolle 1955–56.

6. "FDP: 7.o. Bundesparteitag, 20–21. April 1956 (Würzburg)," FNS: Protokolle, p. D7.

7. The coalition break is outlined in detail by Erich Mende, *Die FDP*, pp. 96–

106. See also FDP BA:FS Protokolle 1955–56, and FNS:GBV Protokolle, esp. "Kurzprotokoll über die Sitzung des GBV der FDP, den 25. Februar 1956." See also "Vorgeschichte zum Koalitionsbruch 1955–56," FNS:EM 2311.

8. FDP leaders discussed their foreign and defense policy during the months April to July 1956. See: "Protokoll der Arbeitstagung des BVAs am 19. April 1956," and "Kurzprotokoll: Sitzung des Arbeitskreises des BVA der FDP am 27. Oktober 1956 in Bonn," FNS:BVA 1956.

9. "Kurzprotokoll: FDP FS, 11. September 1956," FDP BA:FS 1956. See also "Kurzprotokoll: Sitzung des Arbeitskreises des BVA der FDP am 27. Oktober 1956 in Bonn," FNS:BVA 1956.

10. "Das Berlin Programm der Freien Demokraten," FDP 8.o. Bundesparteitag, 24–26. Januar 1957, (Berlin), FNS: Protokolle, pp. 14–15. See also Hans-Dietrich Genscher's "Entwurf einer Wahlplattform, 31. März 1957," FNS:Klausurtagungen.

11. "Rengsdorfer Klausurtagung, 6–7. April 1957," FNS:Klausurtagungen. See especially the two memorandums entitled "Wehrpflicht" and "Rengsdorfer Ergebnisse für die Wahlplattform Aussenpolitik."

12. "Der Besitz von Atomwaffen erhöht die Gefahr," fdk, (May 7, 1957) no. 8/30, pp. 2–4.

13. "Ergebnisprotokoll der Sitzung des BHA am 30. April 1957," FNS:BHA. Citation from attached memorandum, "Aktionsprogramm der Freien Demokratischen Partei."

14. "Grosse Anfrage der Fraktion der SPD, betr. Atomwaffen, 2. April 1957," Verhandlungen des Deutschen Bundestages, 2. Wahlperiode, vol. 50, Drucksache 3347.

15. Adenauer's press conference reprinted in Dokumente zur Deutschlandpolitik, III. Reihe, 3:577–78.

16. Ibid.

17. Carl-Friedrich von Weizsäcker, Der bedrohte Friede, pp. 29–30. The Göttingen 18 controversy will be handled more fully in chapter 3.

18. FAZ, April 24, 1957; Albert Schweitzer, Friede oder Atomkrieg; Adenauer, "Bericht zur politischen Lage," Hans-Peter Schwarz, ed., Konrad Adenauer. Reden, p. 354. In a letter to Karl Bechert (a nuclear physicist and SPD leader), Schweitzer expressed his commitment to SPD politics: "I hear from American sources that Mr. Strauss is doing everything possible to offer you a fait accompli, whereby Germany would receive nuclear weapons from America without allowing you to express your opinion on the matter. Raise a hue and cry, unleash everything. The matter is deadly serious. . . . Yield on nothing. This is something for which the people must take to the streets!" ASD:KB 11.

19. Rheinischer Merkur, April 19 and 26, 1957. See also Bayern-Kurier, April 27, 1957.

20. Vorwärts (April 29 and May 1, 1957); and Welt der Arbeit, April 19, 1957.

21. Verhandlungen des Deutschen Bundestages, 2. Wahlperiode, 10. Mai 1957, p. 12057.

22. Mende's speech of June 6, 1957, "Sicherheit im Atomzeitalter," FNS:Wahlkongress, p. 4. See also Verhandlungen des Deutschen Bundestages, 2. Wahlperiode, 10. Mai 1957, pp. 12098–110.

23. Verhandlungen des Deutschen Bundestages, 2. Wahlperiode, 10. Mai 1957, p. 12073.

24. Ibid., p. 12130.

25. Ibid., p. 12138.

26. K. Popgen, "Finis Germaniae: SPD Wahlsieg 1957," in Blumenwitz, ed., *Konrad Adenauer und seine Zeit*, 2:297.

27. Lehmann, *Chronik der Bundesrepublik Deutschland*, p. 160. For a complete analysis of the elections, see Uwe Kitzinger, *German Electoral Politics*.

28. Lehmann, *Chronik der Bundesrepublik Deutschland*, pp. 159–61. German electoral law gives no representation to parties with less than 5 percent of the vote.

29. Text of Rapacki's speech in Klaus von Schubert, ed., *Sicherheitspolitik der Bundesrepublik Deutschland*, 1:199–205. See also "Rapacki-Plan: Es kommt der Tag," *Der Spiegel*, February 26, 1958, pp. 15–21.

30. Adenauer's comment in *Rheinischer Merkur*, January 24, 1958; Spaak's in *Der Spiegel*, February 26, 1958; and Acheson's in "The Illusion of Disengagement," p. 371.

31. "Grosse Anfrage der Fraktion der FDP betr. Haltung der Bundesregierung auf der NATO-Konferenz am 16. Dezember 1957," *Verhandlungen des Deutschen Bundestages, 3. Wahlperiode, Anlagen*, vol. 55, Drucksache 82.

32. "Antrag der Fraktion der SPD betr. Bemühungen der Bundesrepublik um internationale Entspannung und Einstellung des Wettrüstens," *Ibid.*, Drucksache 54 (neu).

33. *Verhandlungen des Deutschen Bundestages, 3. Wahlperiode, 23. Januar 1958*, pp. 393–95.

34. *Ibid.*, p. 404.

35. "Entschliessungsantrag der Fraktionen der CDU/CSU, DP," *Verhandlungen des Deutschen Bundestages, 3. Wahlperiode, 25. März 1958, Anlagen*, Umdruck 41, p. 1169.

36. *Verhandlungen des Deutschen Bundestages, 3. Wahlperiode, 20. März, 1958*, pp. 875–79.

37. *Ibid.*, p. 880.

38. *Ibid.*, p. 895.

39. *Ibid.*, p. 990.

40. *Ibid.*, pp. 1040–45. Kurt-Georg Kiesinger, a CDU deputy, called Schmidt's speech a "vat of filth poured over this House," p. 1048.

41. Fritz René Allemann, "Wie sag ich's meinem Volke?" *Die Zeit*, March 27, 1958.

42. Cited by Bernhard Röhl, "1958," p. 116.

Part II

Introduction

1. Cited by Michael Howard, *War and the Liberal Conscience*, p. 15.

2. Christopher Duffy, *Borodino and the War of 1812*, p. 135.

3. See Roger Chickering, *Imperial Germany and a World Without War;* and A. C. F. Beales, *The History of Peace*.

4. Martin Niemöller, *Was Niemöller sagt—wogegen Strauss klagt*, p. 5. See also "Stenographisches Protokoll der Sitzung des Verteidigungsausschusses, dem 28. Januar 1959," PA:VA.

5. *Protokoll über den dritten ordentlichen Gewerkschaftstag der Industriegewerkschaft Metall für die Bundesrepublik Deutschland*, pp. 391–92.

6. *Protokoll: 4. ordentlicher Bundeskongress Hamburg 1. bis 6. Oktober 1956*, pp.

884–86. The DGB resolution was originally passed at the 1956 IG Metall congress. See *Protokoll des 4. ordentlichen Gewerkschaftstages der Industriegewerkschaft Metall für die Bundesrepublik Deutschland*, p. 234.

3. The Göttingen Republic: The Nuclear Physics Community

1. Cited by Carl-Friedrich von Weizsäcker, "The Ethical Problems of Modern Strategy," p. 125.

2. Einstein's letter is printed in Morton Grodzins and Eugene Rabinowitch, eds., *The Atomic Age*, p. 12.

3. On the state of Germany's nuclear research, see Alan D. Beyerchen, *Scientists Under Hitler;* David Irving, *The Virus House;* and Robert Jungk, *Brighter Than a Thousand Suns.* See also Weizsäcker, "Die Atomwaffen," *Burschenschaftliche Blätter* (September 1957), 72:198; and Werner Heisenberg, *Der Teil und das Ganze.*

4. Irving, *The Virus House*, pp. 11–16; Beyerchen, *Scientists under Hitler*, pp. 196–98.

5. On the nuclear industry, see Helga Bufe and Jürgen Grumbach, *Staat und Atomindustrie;* Joachim Radkau, *Aufstieg und Krise der deutschen Atomwirtschaft 1945–1975;* and Thomas Stamm, *Zwischen Staat und Selbstverwaltung.*

6. Text in J. Rotblat, *Scientists in the Quest for Peace*, p. 139. For the discussion among German physicists, see "Protokoll über die Mitgliederversammlung des Verbandes Deutscher Physikalischen Gesellschaften, e. V., den 25. September 1955, in Wiesbaden," ASD:KB 21, pp. 3–7.

7. Carl-Friedrich von Weizsäcker, *Der bedrohte Friede*, p. 192.

8. Weizsäcker, "Die Atomwaffen," *Burschenschaftliche Blätter* (September 1957), 72:199. See also Weizsäcker, *Der bedrohte Friede*, p. 34; Werner Heisenberg, *Der Teil und das Ganze*, pp. 300–01; and Wilhelm Walcher in *Vorwärts* (May 17, 1957). The scientists were concerned about "foreign production" because, under the terms of the chancellor's ABC renunciation pledge, West Germany could not produce nuclear weapons on its soil.

9. Weizsäcker, *Der bedrohte Friede*, p. 35.

10. Cited by Otto Hahn, *Mein Leben*, p. 231. The exact text of the group's warning to Strauss has never been printed, but it is similar to the subsequent manifesto. Letter from Weizsäcker to author, November 17, 1981.

11. Weizsäcker: "Die Atomwaffen," *Burschenschaftliche Blätter* (September 1957), 72:199; and *Der bedrohte Friede*, p. 193.

12. Hahn, *Mein Leben*, p. 231.

13. Weizsäcker, *Der bedrohte Friede*, p. 193; Walcher, *Vorwärts* (May 17, 1957).

14. Text in Weizsäcker, *Der bedrohte Friede*, pp. 29–30. The title "Göttingen 18" was a media creation. Most of the scientists were affiliated with the Max Planck Institute at Göttingen. The title also alludes to the "Göttingen 7" manifesto of November 1837, which resulted in the expulsion of seven celebrated professors (including Jacob and Wilhelm Grimm) from their university posts. Unlike the Göttingen 7, none of the eighteen faced reprimand. The Göttingen 18 physicists wrote somewhat contradictory descriptions of the events that led up to their manifesto. Rudolph Fleischmann, "Kernphysik und Atombombe," in Karl Forster, ed., *Kann der atomare Verteidigungskrieg ein gerechter Krieg sein?;* Walter Gerlach, "Der Zwang zum Frieden und die heutigen Naturwissenschaften," *Universitas* (1967), 22:449–57; Otto Hahn, *Mein Leben*, pp. 231–6; Werner Heisenberg, *Der Teil und das Ganze*, pp. 196–311;

Wolfgang Paul, *Vorwärts* (May 10, 1957); Wilhelm Walcher, *Vorwärts* (May 17, 1957). The best descriptions are by Carl-Friedrich von Weizsäcker: "Die Atomwaffen," *Burschenschaftliche Blätter*, vol. 72 (September 1957); *Die Verantwortung der Wissenschaft im Atomzeitalter*; and *Der bedrohte Friede*. See also Hans-Karl Rupp, *Ausserparlamentarische Opposition in der Aera Adenauer*, pp. 73–90.

15. See Konrad Adenauer, "Bericht zur politischen Lage vor dem Bundesparteivorstand der CDU in Hamburg, 11. Mai 1957," Schwarz, ed., *Konrad Adenauer. Reden*, p. 355. A few months after the Göttingen Manifesto's publication, Weizsäcker wrote the SPD leader, Fritz Erler: "The claim of the Göttingen Manifesto that tactical weapons possessed the destructive equivalent of a Hiroshima-size bomb was quite correct regarding the weapons available at that time. We intentionally expressed ourselves in vague terms since the possibility of one-kiloton weapons did not seem impossible to us. That there are such weapons is now well known. We did not know at that time how far one could take this miniaturization, and we still do not know exactly." Weizsäcker's letter to Fritz Erler, November 13, 1958, ASD:FE 147. Scientific laymen, however, would hardly consider the manifesto vaguely worded ("Each tactical atomic warhead today has the equivalent effect of the one that destroyed Hiroshima").

16. See Strauss' comments, "An die falsche Adresse gerichtet," *Bulletin* (April 16, 1957), no. 73; *Die Zeit*, April 18, 1957; and *Der Spiegel*, May 1, 1957, p. 18. Aside from attacking the content of the manifesto, Strauss accused the scientists of intervening in politics in an effort to purge their own consciences. "These things," he told *Der Spiegel*, "slipped away from the hands of the physicists a long time ago."

17. Reprinted in *Junge Kirche* (1957), 17:200. *Neues Deutschland*, the official organ of the East German government, published a bowdlerized version of the Göttingen Manifesto, devoid of such bourgeois phrases as "We profess our allegiance to the freedom that is today safeguarded by the Western world against Communism," and "We do not deny that the mutual fear of thermonuclear bombs makes an essential contribution both to the maintenance of peace in the whole world and to freedom in a part of the world." *Neues Deutschland*, April 13, 14, and 19, 1957.

18. Konrad Adenauer, "Bericht zur politischen Lage," Schwarz, ed., *Konrad Adenauer. Reden.* p. 358.

19. *Ibid.*

20. Konrad Adenauer, "Zur Frage der atomaren Rüstung," *Bulletin* (April 16, 1957); and *Rheinischer Merkur*, April 19, 1957.

21. Adenauer's meeting with the scientists is described in detail in *SDZ*, April 20/21, 1957.

22. *Bulletin* (April 18, 1957); and *Dokumente zur Deutschland Politik: III. Reihe*, 3:619.

23. Adenauer, "Bericht zur politischen Lage," Schwarz, ed., *Konrad Adenauer. Reden*, p. 360.

24. Pascual Jordan, *Physikalisches Denken in der neuen Zeit* (Hamburg: Hanseatische Verlagsanstalt, 1935); and Jordan, *Die Physik des 20 Jahrhunderts* (Brunswick: Friedrich Vieweg, 1936). See also the attack on Jordan in *Vorwärts* (June 21, 1957), and Beyerchen, *Scientists under Hitler*, pp. 129 and 228.

25. Pascual Jordan, *Der gescheiterte Aufstand*, pp. 176–79.

26. Pascual Jordan, "Die Ueberwindung der Gefahr," in *Selbstbehauptung in gefährdeter Freiheit*, p. 24. See also his *Wir müssen die Frieden retten!*, p. 13. His choice of phrases is reminiscent of Fascist code words for Jews.

27. Pascual Jordan, "Die Verantwortung des Wissenschaftler," *Dokumente zur Deutschlandpolitik, III. Reihe*, 3:635.

28. *Ibid.*, p. 634.

29. Jaspers' contributions to the nuclear debate include: "Das Gewissen vor der Bedrohung durch die Atombombe," in *Rechenschaft und Ausblick* (Munich: Piper, 1951); *Die Atombombe und die Zukunft des Menschen: Ein Radiovortrag* (Munich: Piper, 1957)—hereafter *Radiovortrag*; and *Die Atombombe und die Zukunft des Menschen* (Munich: Piper, 1958)—hereafter *Die Atombombe*. Unlike Jordan, Jaspers was not directly involved in party politics. However, he published the *Radiovortrag* in May 1957, partly in response to the Göttingen 18, and he inserted an extended analysis of the Göttingen Manifesto in *Die Atombombe* (pp. 268–77). An edited version of *Die Atombombe* is available in English, *The Atom Bomb and the Future of Man* (Chicago: University of Chicago Press, 1961), but the Göttingen 18 section was not included. Other pertinent books by Jaspers include *Freiheit und Wiedervereinigung: Ueber Aufgaben deutscher Politik* (Munich: Piper, 1960); and *Wahrheit, Freiheit und Friede* (Munich: Piper, 1958). A full discussion of Jaspers' political thought can be found in Rolf Sternberger, "Jaspers und die Staat," in Klaus Piper, ed., *Karl Jaspers*, pp. 133–41.

30. Jaspers, *The Atom Bomb*, p. 4. See also Jaspers: *Radiovortrag*, p. 23; and *Freiheit und Wiedervereinigung*, p. 11.

31. Jaspers, *The Atom Bomb*, p. 118.

32. Jaspers, *Die Atombombe*, p. 277.

33. *Ibid.*, p. 269.

34. *Ibid.* p. 270.

35. *Ibid.*

36. Jaspers, *The Atom Bomb*, p. 132.

37. *Ibid.*, pp. 273–75.

38. Thielicke's contributions to the nuclear discussion include "Der Christ und die Verhütung des Krieges im Atomzeitalter," *Zeitschrift für Evangelische Ethik* (March 1957), 1:1–6; "Abschaffung der Atomwaffen," *Sonntagsblatt*, no. 18 (May 5, 1957); *Die Atomwaffe als Frage an die Christliche Ethik* (Tübingen: J. C. B. Mohr (Paul Siebeck), 1958); and "Gewissen und Verantwortung im Atomzeitalter," *7. Bundesparteitag der CDU. Hamburg 1957* (Hamburg: Sator Werbe, 1957), pp. 100–30. In his memoirs, *Begegnungen und Erfahrungen*, p. 105, he states that the chancellor "very determinedly requested" that he address the CDU convention. Thielicke agreed only after Adenauer "guaranteed him complete freedom to be critical" of government policy.

39. Thielicke, "Gewissen und Verantwortung im Atomzeitalter," pp. 103–04.

40. *Ibid.*, p. 121.

41. *Ibid.*, pp. 123–24.

42. *Ibid.*, pp. 126–27.

43. *Ibid.*

44. Adenauer's remarks, *ibid.*, pp. 130–33. Wolf's remarks in Ernst Wolf, "Theologische Atomdiskussion," *Junge Kirche* (1958), 19:285.

45. Weizsäcker, *Der bedrohte Friede*, p. 194.

46. Werner Kliefoth, "Atomrundschau," *Atomkernenergie* (1957), 2:508. See also G. Burkhardt, "Report on the Activities of the German Pugwash Group," pp. 69–71; and Weizsäcker, *Der bedrohte Friede*, pp. 197–201. In 1961, the German Physics Society surveyed the Göttingen 18 anew. The results were published in "Göttingen

heute," *Physikalische Blätter* (1961), pp. 264–69. Of the sixteen remaining physicists (Paneth and von Laue had died), fifteen answered questionnaires. All said they would sign the document again under similar circumstances. But as Walter Menzel, a SPD leader and nuclear foe, noted: "It is good that the Göttingen professors have once again stepped into the public light, but it is worrying to ascertain that this time the declaration has nowhere near the same resonance as the first time in April 1957," ASD:PV 0811.

47. Weizsäcker's works include *Mit der Bombe leben: Die gegenwärtigen Aussichten einer Begrenzung der Gefahr eines Atomkrieges* (Hamburg: Die Zeit, 1958); *Ethical and Political Problems of the Atomic Age* (London: SCM, 1958); *Der ungesicherte Friede* (Göttingen: Vandenhoeck and Ruprecht, 1969); *Fragen zur Weltpolitik* (Munich: Carl Hanser, 1975); *The Politics of Peril: Economics, Society and the Prevention of War* (New York: Seabury, 1978); *Der Garten des Menschlichen: Beiträge zur geschichtlichen Anthropologie* (Munich: Carl Hanser, 1977); and *Der bedrohte Friede.*

48. Cited by *SDZ*, April 20/21, 1957.

49. Weizsäcker, *Mit der Bombe leben,* p. 6.

50. *Ibid.,* p. 9.

51. *Ibid.,* p. 10. On Teller's talk with Weizsäcker, see Weizsäcker's letter to Fritz Erler, November 13, 1958, ASD:FE 147.

52. Weizsäcker, *Mit der Bombe leben,* p. 10.

53. *Ibid.,* p. 12. Weizsäcker used the term *abgestufte Abschreckung* to describe both "graduated deterrence" and "flexible response." The two concepts, however, are not identical. The former was coined by British strategists, who sought flexibility primarily at the nuclear level. The latter was used by American strategists interested in a doctrine that also allowed for a nonnuclear response.

54. *Ibid.,* p. 16.

55. *Ibid.,* p. 14.

4. Missal Diplomacy: The Protestants and Nuclear Weapons

1. Cited by Roland Bainton, *Christian Attitudes Toward War and Peace.* On just war doctrine, see Albert Marrin, ed., *War and the Christian Conscience;* Franziskus Stratmann, *The Church and War;* Jenny Teichman, *Pacificism and the Just War;* and Michael Walzer, *Just and Unjust Wars.*

2. Theodor G. Tappert, ed., *Selected Writings of Martin Luther, 1523–1526,* p. 439.

3. Martin Niemöller, "Unsere Zukunft," *Reden 1958–1961,* p. 42.

4. Karl Barth, *Eine Schweizer Stimme, 1938–1945,* p. 113.

5. *Evanston Speaks: Reports of the Second Assembly of the World Council of Churches, August 13–15, 1954,* p. 39.

6. *Evanston to New Delhi 1954–1961,* p. 261.

7. On the German Protestant church, see Heinz Brunotte, *Die Evangelische Kirche in Deutschland;* Johanna Vogel, *Kirche und Wiederbewaffnung;* Ina Görlich, "Zum ethischen Problem der Atomdiskussion"; and Michael Weinzierl, "Die Christen und die Problematik des gerechten Krieges im Atomzeitalter," in Friedrich Engel-Janosi, Grete Klingenstein, and Heinrich Lutz, eds., *Gewalt und Gewaltlosigkeit.* A parallel debate occurred on a much smaller scale within the German Catholic church. See Karl Forster, ed., *Kann der atomare Verteidigungskrieg ein gerechter Krieg sein?;*

G. E. Kafka, ed., *Die Katholiken vor der Politik;* Peter Nellen, *Reden und Aufsätze;* "Die atomare Aufrüstung als Gewissensfrage: Ein katholisch-theologisches Gutachten," ASD:GHA 292; and "Bayerischer Rundfunk: Bericht von einer Tagung der Katholischen Akademie in Würzburg, 21.–22. Februar 1959," ASD:PN 7.

8. Helmut Gollwitzer, *Forderung der Freiheit,* p. 287. See also Gollwitzer, "Christ und Atomwaffen," *Stimme der Gemeinde: Sonderdruck* (1958), no. 1, pp. 4–5. At the beginning of his tract, *Die Christen und die Atomwaffen,* he states: "The reflections in this essay are consciously based on the premises that have guided Christians in the past in their participation in the use of force. It does not call this basis into question, but rather demonstrates that the same line of thinking that previously made the participation in warfare possible—if argued correctly and not hypocritically—make it now impossible."

9. Gollwitzer, *Die Christen,* pp. 23–24.

10. *Ibid.,* p. 26; Gollwitzer, "Christ und Atomwaffen," *Stimme der Gemeinde: Sonderdruck* (1958), no. 1, p. 10.

11. Gollwitzer, *Die Christen,* p. 30.

12. *Deutsches Pfarrerblatt,* no. 15 (August 1, 1958); also cited by Erwin Wilkens, "Theologisches Gespräch," in Günther Howe, ed. *Atomzeitalter, Krieg und Frieden,* p. 117.

13. Gollwitzer, *Die Christen,* p. 39; *Stimme der Gemeinde,* p. 12.

14. Gollwitzer, *Forderungen der Freiheit,* p. 347.

15. Gollwitzer, *Die Christen,* p. 4.

16. Helmut Thielicke, "Abschaffung der Atomwaffen," *Sonntagsblatt* (May 5, 1957). See also Heinemann's critique in *Zeitschrift für Evangelische Ethik* (1960), 4:374–75.

17. Thielicke, *Die Atomwaffe als Frage an die Christliche Ethik,* pp. 24–25. See also Thielicke's "Gewissen und Verantwortung im Atomzeitalter," *7. Bundesparteitag der CDU,* p. 121; and "Gedankenführung: Vertrag Thielicke," EZB:BK 6, 2.

18. Thielicke, *Die Atomwaffe als Frage,* p. 15.

19. *Ibid.,* pp. 30 and 35–36.

20. *Ibid.,* pp. 35–36.

21. The two most important books are Ernst Wolf's: *Die Königsherrschaft Christi und der Staat;* and *Christusbekenntnis im Atomzeitalter?* For comprehensive analyses of the Brethren's position see Wilkens, "Theologisches Gespräch," in Howe, ed., *Atomzeitalter, Krieg und Frieden,* pp. 118–25; and Ina Görlich, "Zum ethischen Problem," pp. 186–228. Not just the Brethren, but many churchmen considered Gollwitzer's nuclear pacifism illogical. "I never could agree with you on the theological relevance of the distinction between nuclear and conventional weapons," Weizsäcker wrote to him. "I always found Niemöller's fundamental pacifism more theologically convincing" (Weizsäcker, "Ein Brief," in Andreas Baudis, ed., *Richte unsere Füsse auf den Weg des Friedens,* p. 394.

22. Helmut Simon, "Die frohe Botschaft von der Königsherrschaft Christi in unserer Zeit," *Junge Kirche: Sonderdruck* (1957), no. 21/22, pp. 3–4.

23. Wolf, *Christusbekenntnis,* p. 5.

24. Wolf, *Die Königsherrschaft Christi,* pp. 53–54.

25. "Erklärung des Konvents der Kirchl. Bruderschaft im Rheinland zur atomaren Bewaffnung, Wermelskirchen, Ostern 1957," *Evangelische Stimmen zur Atomfrage,* p. 49.

26. "Erklärung des 'Rheinischen Konvents' vom 30. April 1958," in Heipp, ed.,

Es geht ums Leben!, p. 87. On the Convent, see also *Informationen des Rheinischen Konvents* (September 1958), no. 2; Paul Seifert, "Verlust der Mitte," *Sonntagsblatt* (October 5, 1958); H. Höhler, "Die theologischen Auseinandersetzungen über die Atomwaffen in der Sicht des Rheinischen Konvents (9. September 1959)," LKA:AB 15. For the Brethren's response to the Convent, see Ernst Wolf, "Theologische Atomdiskussion," *Junge Kirche* (1958), 19:287; Hans Iwand, "Die evangelische Kirche," p. 186; and Dieter Linz, "Was tut unserer Kirche Not? *Sonntagsblatt* (September 21, 1958). For more on the Brethren and Convent, see LKA:AB 15 and LKA:KI 9.

27. Walter Künneth, *Rechtfertigung im Atomzeitalter*, pp. 26–27.

28. Künneth, "Die Atomfrage in christlicher Sicht," pp. 32–38. See also Künneth; "Glaubensentscheidung"; and "Atomtheologie heute."

29. Künneth, *Rechtfertigung*, pp. 3 and 13–17.

30. *Ibid.*, pp. 13–17.

31. Künneth, "Die Atomfrage," p. 40.

32. Künneth, "Glaubensentscheidung," p. 25.

33. Hans Asmussen, *Verleugnung der drei Glaubensartikel*, p. 16. For a critique of Asmussen by a Brethren leader, see Wolfgang Schweitzer, "Zu Hans Asmussens 'Gegenthesen,'" *Junge Kirche* (1958), 19:196–97.

34. Simon recounted the misgivings of this Brethren member in a letter to the "Kirchliche Bruderschaft im Rheinland," April 30, 1957, LKA:AB 20.

35. Richard Solberg, *God and Caesar in East Germany*, p. 269.

36. *Ibid.*

37. Otto Dibelius, President of the Protestant church, discussed the tensions within the church at the 1961 synod. Text of speech in ASD:GHA 296; an edited version has been printed: "Bericht des Vorsitzenden des Rates der Evangelischen Kirche in Deutschland, Bischof D. Dr. Dibelius," *KJ* (1961), pp. 22–29.

38. Text in *Verhandlungen des Deutschen Bundestages, 2. Wahlperiode, 6. Juli 1956*, p. 8836.

39. The Protestants' proposed text is cited in *Verhandlungen des Deutschen Bundestages, 2. Wahlperiode, 6. Juli 1956*, pp. 8836–37. On the Protestants' position, see also *Kirche und Kriegsdienstverweigerung;* and Ulrich Scheuner, "Die Frage der Kriegsdienstverweigerung," *Evangelische Welt* (January 1956).

40. "Stenographisches Protokoll der 94. Sitzung des Ausschusses für Verteidigung, 1. Juni 1956," PA:VA.

41. "Denkschrift zur Kriegsdienstverweigerung and zum Friedensdienst," *KJ* (1956), p. 38.

42. The Brethren's request in "Niederschrift über die Verhandlungen der Kammer für öffentliche Verantwortung am 9.12.1955 in Hannover," ASD:GHA 290. The council's response in "7. Sitzung des EKD Rates, 15./16. Dez. 1955," ASD:GHA 290. See also "Niederschrift über die Verhandlungen der Kammer für öffentliche Verantwortung in ihrer Sitzung am 11. Januar 1956 in Bonn," ASD:GHA 290.

43. See the comments by Präses D. Wilm at the Protestant synod, *Berlin 1956: Bericht über die ausserordentliche Tagung der zweiten Synode der EKD von 27.–29. Juli 1956*, p. 59. On the Council's decision to convoke a synod, see "11. Sitzung des EKD Rates, 7./8. Mai 1956," ASD:GHA 290.

44. For the discussion of the Brethren's resolution, *Berlin 1956*, pp. 43–88.

45. *KJ* (1956), p. 21. *Berlin 1956*, pp. 129–34 and 156–73.

46. A full analysis of the controversy in "Bericht des Präsidiums der Synode der EKD über die bei der ausserordentlichen Synodaltagung 27.–29. Juni 1956 veran-

staltete Unterschriftensammlung und ihre Verwendung," ASD:GHA 291. The Brethren tried unsuccessfully for several more years to gain recognition for nuclear conscientious objectors. See "Antrag des Rates der EKD zu #25 Wehrpflichtgesetz (5. Januar 1960)," and "Niederschrift über die 44. Sitzung des Rates der EKiD am 4. und 5. Februar 1960 in Hannover," both in ASD:GHA 294.

47. Hanns Lilje, "Unabhängige Synode," *Sonntagsblatt* (March 17, 1957). Text of treaty in *KJ* (1957), pp. 40–47. See also Renate Maria Heydenreich, "Die Spandauer Synode," p. 173.

48. *Berlin 1958*, p. 307. Also Heydenreich, "Die Synode der EKD Berlin 1958," p. 239.

49. *KJ* (1957), p. 23.

50. *Ibid.*, pp. 48–49.

51. *Ibid.*, p. 49.

52. "Ueberprüfung des Militärseelsorge-Vertrages," ASD:GHA: Kirchl. Angelegenheiten 1960. For more information, see *Berlin 1958*, pp. 284–308 and 456. See also minutes of Protestant Council and other church meetings in ASD:GHA: Kirchl. Angelegenheiten 1959.

53. *KJ* (1958), pp. 17–18.

54. Text in *KJ* (1958), pp. 29–34. On the intra-Brethren discussions over the Ten Theses, see the documents on the Wermelskirchen and Wuppertal meetings in LKA:AB 2, 20, 38, and 52. Before going to the Protestant synod, the Ten Theses first went to the Rhineland synod, where they were rejected in January 1958; see *Verhandlungen der siebten ordentlichen Rheinischen Landessynode*, pp. 163–67. This did not bode well for their chances at the Protestant synod, since the Rhineland was the Brethren's stronghold.

55. Niederschrift über die 28. Sitzung des Rates der E.K.i.D. am 3. und 4. Februar 1958," ASD:GHA Kirchl. Angelegenheiten 292. Not only the Brethren was causing the Council problems. The East Germans were calling Otto Dibelius an "evangelical NATO pope," and claiming he had a "wild passion for conquest, barbaric anti-semitism, and bitter anti-socialist hatred." See Alfred Norden, "Herr der Christen: Diener der Vernichtung," *Neues Deutschland* (April 26, 1958).

56. Erwin Wilkens, "Theologisches Gespräch über die nuklearen Waffen," in Günther Howe, ed. *Atomzeitalter, Krieg und Frieden*, pp. 108–09; and *KJ* (1959), pp. 91–92.

57. Künneth's and Vogel's remarks are summarized in Heydenreich, "Die Synode der EKD Berlin 1958," pp. 234–36.

58. Wolf summarized Weizsäcker's arguments in *Christusbekenntnis im Atomzeitalter?*, pp. 39–41. See also, "Zur Stellungnahme Prof. von Weizsäcker," *Junge Kirche* (1958), 19:312–17.

59. Text in *Berlin 1958*, pp. 455–56.

60. *KJ* (1958), pp. 49–50.

61. *Ibid.*

62. *Berlin 1958*, pp. 256–59.

63. Hanns Lilje, "Nach der Synode," *Sonntagsblatt* (May 11, 1958); and "Die Atomfrage darf die Kirche nicht spalten," *Sonntagsblatt* (April 27, 1958). See also: "Niederschrift über die Synode der Kirchenprovinz Sachsen in Halle/S. vom 1. bis 6. Juni 1958," ASD:GHA: Kirchl. Angelegenheiten 292.

64. Wolf, *Christusbekenntnis*, p. 8; and "Rundbrief (10. Juni 1958)," LKA:AB 20.

65. *KJ* (1958), p. 72; "Erklärung des Arbeitskreises kirchlicher Bruderschaften zur

Berliner Synode," *Stimme der Gemeinde* (July 1958), 10:522; "Stellungnahme zur Synode der EKiD," Heipp, ed., *Es geht ums Leben!*, p. 81. See also Wolfgang Schweitzer, "Zur Atomwaffendiskussion in der Evangelischen Kirche," *Blätter* (1958), 3:668; and "Arbeitskreis kirchlicher Bruderschaft," *Junge Kirche* (1958), 19:361–62.

66. "Theologische Gutachten," *Christusbekenntnis*, pp. 78–90. A full report of the Brethren meetings that produced this document, in "Arbeitskreis kirchlicher Bruderschaften," ASD:GHA: Allg. Korr. 1958.

67. "Verhandlungsniederschrift der 1. Sitzung des EKD-Ausschusses für Atomfragen am 3. Juli 1959 in Hannover," EZB:BK 3,2; Dr. Niemeier, "Tagebuch Nr. 612.III, (3. März 1959)," EZB:BK 3,2. Most of the documents and protocols for the Atom Commission are available in EZB:BK 3,2.

68. *KJ* (1960), pp. 91–95. See also "Verhandlungsniederschrift der 2. Sitzung des EKD-Ausschusses für Atomfragen am 28./29. September 1959 in Stuttgart," EZB:BK 3,2; and Helmut Simon's "Entwurf eines Berichtes an die Synode," LKA:AB 58.

69. The "Heidelberg Theses" are printed in Howe, ed., *Atomzeitalter, Krieg und Frieden*, pp. 226–36. I have paraphrased the main points.

70. Howe's comment, quoted in a letter from Niemeier to the Atom Commission, "Tagebuch, Nr. 2674. III (16 Oktober 1959)," EZB:BK 3,2. Niemeier offers the most detailed description of the concept of "complementarity." For positive reactions, see Walter Künneth, "Atomrüstung und Ethos," *Zeitwende: die Neue Furche* (1961), 32:235–38; and Eberhard Müller, "Einstimmige Synode," *Zeitwende: Die Neue Furche* (1960), 31:260–62.

71. Helmut Simon's letter to Günther Howe, November 25, 1959, EZB:BK 3,2.

72. "Verhandlungsniederschrift der Sitzung des EKD-Ausschusses für Atomfragen am 18./19. Dezember 1959 in Bad Boll," EZB:BK 3,2.

73. "Rundbrief (Dez. 1959)," LKA:AB 20. The Brethren's misgivings over the "complementarity" concept are summarized in "Stellungnahmen zu den Thesen von Prof. D. Helmut Gollwitzer," in Howe, ed., *Atomzeitalter, Krieg und Frieden*, pp. 247–67.

74. Raiser's report in *KJ* (1960), pp. 89–92.

75. "Zweiter Bericht über die Arbeit des vom Rat der EKD eingesetzten Ausschusses für Atomfragen," ASD:GHA 296. See also "Niederschrift über die 14. Sitzung des Rates der EKiD am 11. und 12. Oktober 1962 in Berlin," ASD:GHA 297.

76. Stratmann, *The Church and War*, p. 6.

77. *Berlin 1958*, p. 260; *KJ* (1958), p. 66.

5. The Cold Peace: Ideology and Confrontation in the Antinuclear Movement

1. On the origins of the World Peace Council, see Jürgen von Hahn, "Die Weltfriedensbewegung im Atomzeitalter." On the various Communist-backed organizations, see "Tarnorganisation," ASD:PV 0878. On the Standing Congress, see Kurt Gröbe, ed., *Gelsenkirchener Protokoll . . . und du?* There is also information on the Standing Congress' activities in ASD:SPD-LO Hamburg 515; Bundesarchiv:ZSg1-218/1 and ZSg1-E33; and in its *Kongressdienst*. The Standing Congress justified its existence as a rival to the GCND in "Genesis and History of the Permanent Congress," (February 6, 1960), ASD:PV 0881. On the GCND's attitude to the Standing Congress, see Menzel's correspondence, especially his letter to Reuter of March 11, 1959, ASD:PV 0871. The Protestant church's Brethren also opposed the Standing Congress' activ-

ities; see Forschepiepe's letter to Kloppenburg, April 1, 1958, and Kloppenburg's response, April, 8 both in EZB:BK 6,1.

2. On the British CND, see Christopher Driver, *The Disarmers: A Study in Protest;* Frank Parkin, *Middle Class Radicalism;* and Richard Taylor and Colin Pritchard, *The Protest Makers.* On the German campaign, see Rupp, *Ausserparlamentarische Opposition,* pp. 129–32; and Klotzbach, *Der Weg zur Staatspartei,* pp. 470–71. On the European Federation, see *Europa ruft: Der Europäische Kongress gegen Atomrüstung;* and A. Maass, "Bericht über den Europäischen Kongress in London am 17./18. Januar 1959," ASD:HW 163. There is additional information on the European Federation in ASD:PV 0775, 0820, 0823, 0887.

3. The protocols of first meeting available in "22/II: Schaumburger Hof Godesberg," EZB:BK 6,2; and "Aktennotiz: Hauptabteilung Organisation und Werbung, 25. Februar 1958," DGB:Atom.

4. "Protokoll über die Besprechung mit den Landesbezirksvorsitzenden betreffend Fortführung der Aktion KdA in Düsseldorf am 1. April 1958," DGB:Atom.

5. The GCND's manifesto and a list of those who signed it is available in *Blaubuch: Dokumentation über den Widerstand gegen die atomare Aufrüstung der Bundesrepublik,* pp. 11–12. See also Arbeitsausschuss 'Kampf dem Atomtod,' *Kampf dem Atomtod.*

6. "Empfehlung: Sicherheitsausschuss beim Parteivorstand (28. Februar)," ASD:EO 113; "Kurzprotokoll über die Sitzung des Sicherheitsausschusses beim Parteivorstand (28. Februar 1958)," ASD:FE 138. See also "Arbeitsausschuss: Volksbefragung KAMPF DEM ATOMTOD," (1958), and "Protokoll: 19. Sitzung des Bundesvorstandes, 4. März 1958," both in DGB:Atom; see also two mimeographed letters from Fritz Erler to party members and German citizens, April 16 and May 10, 1958, ASD:FE 148. "It's been a long time," Ollenhauer told SPD delegates at the party convention, "since we've hit the streets for such a good cause and in such good company." *Protokoll der Verhandlungen des Parteitages der Sozialdemokratischen Partei Deutschlands vom 18. bis 23. Mai 1958 in Stuttgart,* p. 47.

7. "Bericht über die Entwicklung des Vorbereitenden Ausschusses NRW 'KdA' 17. April 1958"; and "Ergebnisprotokoll über die Sitzung des Arbeitsausschusses NRW 'KdA' in Düsseldorf am 17. Mai 1958," both in ASD:PV 0820.

8. "Bericht über die bisherige Arbeit des Ausschusses," and "Bisherige Arbeiten des zentralen Arbeitsausschusses 'KdA,'" both in ASD:PV 01493. See also Rupp, *Ausserparlamentarische Opposition,* pp. 175–77.

9. On GCND–CNA relations, see ASD:PV 0881. For the CNA's manifesto, see *Die Kultur* (April 15, 1958) and *Blaubuch,* p. 135. Members were drawn largely from three organizations headed by H. W. Richter: the "Gruppe 47," the "Club republikanischer Publizisten," and the "Grünwalder Kreis." (Hans-Jochen Vogel—the SPD's chancellor-candidate in 1983—was a cofounder of the Grünwalder Kreis; but he did not join the CNA). On the structure and goals of the CNA, see "Satzung des Komitees gegen Atomrüstung, e. V., 2. Juni 1958," and Ludwig Linsert's letter to the DGB-Landesbezirk Bayern, April 24, 1958, both in DGB:KgA; and Linsert's letter to Willi Richter, July 7, 1958, DGB:Atom I.

10. See Brandt's comments in "Besprechung Arbeitsausschuss 'Gegen den Atomtod' am 21. April 1958," in MR:Ausschuss KdA bis 1961. A full discussion of Brandt's attitude in Abraham Ashkenasi, *Reformpartei und Aussenpolitik.*

11. This was part of the text of Resolution 23, "Zur politischen Lage," FNA:LA 1952–1960 (no. 16.).

12. The tensions within the Berlin GCND were discussed at various DGB and Bonn Central Committee meetings. "Protokollarische Notizen aus der Sitzung des Ausschusses 'KdA' mit den Beauftragten der Landesausschüsse, den 26. April 1958 in Bonn," ASD:PV 0886; and "Protokoll der 65. Sitzung des GBV, dem 28. April 1958," and "Protokoll der 22. Sitzung des BV, dem 6. Mai 1958," both in DGB:GBV.

13. These statistics are from Rupp, *Ausserparlamentarische Opposition*, pp. 289–96, with the following exceptions: Hamburg estimates from *Hamburger Echo*, April 18, 1958; Munich estimates from DGB:KgA; Bielefeld and Wuppertal estimates from J. Naber's letter to GCND, May 29, 1958, ASD:PV 0820. In only one case—the Wuppertal demonstration of April 22—are my figures lower than Rupp's. He estimated a 15,000-strong attendance, based on the *Blaubuch* (which gave no source). According to Naber, only 4,000 attended.

14. Menzel told Berlin GCND leaders that overall the GCND "found its greatest resonance on the universities." See "Protokoll: Berliner Ausschuss 'Gegen den Atomtod,' 29. September 1958," MR:Ausschuss KdA bis 1961.

15. Rupp, *Ausserparlamentarische Opposition*, pp. 291–95; and Naber's letter to GCND, May 29, 1958, ASD:PV:0820

16. On CNA strategy, see "Protokoll über die Besprechung mit den Landesbezirksvorsitzenden betreffend Fortführung des Aktion KdA in Düsseldorf am 1. April 1958," DGB:Atom. On attendance figures, see Rupp, *Ausserparlamentarische Opposition*, p. 294; "Bericht über die erste öffentliche Kundgebung des KgA DGB-Landesbezirk Bayern, 24. April 1958," and S. Bussjäger's letter to Linsert, May 29, 1958, both in DGB:KgA.

17. When DGB leaders discussed the demonstration wave at their October meeting, Reuter admitted that "the high point of the first actions was already over by May." Reuter's comments in "Protokoll der 7. Sitzung des BA am 8. Oktober 1958," DGB:GBV. See also Menzel's letter to Szczesny, February 26, 1960, ASD:PV 0815.

18. A tally of Rupp's statistics yields around 420,000, but there are a number of gaps. Rupp, *Ausserparlamentarische Opposition*, pp. 289–96.

19. "Aktennotiz, 25. Februar 1958," DGB:Atom; Bucher's letter to Menzel, April 17, 1958, EZB:BK 6,2; and "Ergebnisprotokoll der Sitzung des GBVs am 25. April 1958," FNS:GBV.

20. "FDP 9.o. Bundesparteitag 28./29. März 1958," FNS:Protokolle, A1-140; and the executive board minutes of February 28, March 27, and April 18, 1958, FNS:GBV.

21. "Ergebnisprotokoll der Sitzung des GBV's der FDP am 28. Februar 1958," FNS:GBV.

22. Quotes from Werner Stephan's letter to FDP state organizations, April 19, 1958; and Reinhold Maier's and Stephan's letter to FDP state chairmen, April 22, 1958, FNS:GBV. On the FDP's decision, see "Ergebnisprotokoll der Sitzung des GBVs der FDP am 18. April 1958," and Gerhard Daub's "Entwurf einer Entschliessung des BVs der FDP vom 18. April 1958," both in FNS:GBV. See also "Rundschreiben Nr. A 10/58 (30. April 1958), FDP LV NRW," WDS:Landtagswahl 1958.

23. "Entwurf: Entschliessung über die Haltung der FDP zur Volksbefragung über die atomare Bewaffnung der Bundeswehr"; "Entwurf einer Entschliessung des BV der FDP vom 18. April 1958"; and "Ergebnisprotokoll der Sitzung des GBVs der FDP am 18. April 1958," all in FNS:GBV. See also "Vermerk, 4. April 1958," FNS:TDA Aussenpolitik 1958. For Meier's and Mende's comments on the referendum, see "FDP 9.o. Bundesparteitag 28./29. März 1958," FNS:Protokolle, A1–140, pp. I/A20–21 and II/33–51. Their reservations rested on Articles 20, 38, and 70 of the Basic Laws.

24. Döring's comment at a meeting where FDP policy was under discussion, "Sitzung des Landesausschusses am 16. April 1958 in Dortmund," WDS: Sitzung des Landesausschusses. A complete list of FDP attitudes from state to state in "Volksbefragung über Atomrüstung (7 Mai 1958)," FNS:TDA Verteidigungspolitik. See also "Rundschreiben Nr. 30," ASD:WM R27.

25. See Werner Stephan's letter to FDP state leaders, April 19, 1958; and "Ergebnisprotokoll der Sitzung des GBVs der FDP am 18. April 1958," both in FNS:GBV. Also "Parlamentarische Entscheidungen statt Volksbefragung," *fdk*, no. 9/30 (April 22, 1958).

26. "Entwurf eines Gesetzes zur Volksbefragung wegen einer atomaren Ausrüstung der Bundeswehr," *Verhandlungen des Deutschen Bundestages, Anlagen, 3. Wahlperiode*, vol. 57, Drucksache 303. On the state referenda, see ASD:WM R27; and "Volksbefragung: Kabinettstod gegen Atomtod," *Der Spiegel*, April 16, 1958, pp. 15–18.

27. *Verhandlungen des Deutschen Bundestages, 3. Wahlperiode, 24–25. April 1958*. SPD's position, pp. 1412–20, 1476–80, and 1506–08. CDU/CSU's position, pp. 1421–30, 1431–33, and 1448–56. FDP's position, pp. 1433–37. The voting results, p. 1746.

28. "Gesetz über einer Volksbefragung bezüglich der Ausrüstung der Bundeswehr mit Atomwaffen," *Bayerischer Landtag: 127. Sitzung, den 24. April 1958: Beilage 3360*. SPD's position, pp. 4363–69. CSU's position (Seidel's speech), pp. 4360–63.

29. The results of the various state resolutions and debates are in ASD:WM R27.

30. "Mit dem Grundgesetz nicht vereinbar," *Bulletin* (May 7, 1958) no. 83. See also *Die Welt*, June 5, 1958; *FAZ*, April 25, 1958; and "Volksbefragung: Wer fragt?" *Der Spiegel*, May 21, 1958, pp. 15–17.

31. "Volksbefragung: Der Atomkram," *Der Spiegel* (May 28, 1958), p. 27.

32. On Adenauer's injunction, see *Bundesverfassungsgericht: 2BvQ 1/58* (May 27, 1958). On the Hamburg and Bremen decisions, see the *Bundesverfassungsgericht: 2BvF 3/58* and *2BvF 6/58* (July 30, 1958); on the Hessen decision, *2BvQ 1/58* (July 30, 1958). Article 65 gives the chancellor authority over political matters; Article 73 accords the federal government exclusive control over defense and foreign policy; and Article 87 regulates civilian–military relations. The justices of the German Supreme Court (Bundesverfassungsgericht) were selected by parliament; they served twelve-year terms. The Supreme Court was the final arbiter on matters concerning West Germany's constitution, known as the Basic Laws (Grundgesetz).

33. On the SPD's attitude, see Menzel's letter to Bonn Central Committee, March 25, 1958, DGB:Atom. On Riemeck's appeal, see *Blaubuch*, pp. 26–28; Erich Rüttel, "Gewerkschaften vor der Entscheidung," *Blätter* (1958), 3:168–72; and Leo Weismantel, "Was ist gemeint?" *Blätter* (1958), 3:172–75. "The trade unions are the only institution that Adenauer still hears and fears," said Riemeck, in explaining the genesis of the appeal (ASD:GHA:Allg. Korr. 1958). See also Rupp, *Ausserparlamentarische Opposition*, pp. 165–68; and *Blaubuch*, pp. 38–62. The Buildingworkers Union declared that they would protect the right of workers not to engage in the construction of nuclear missile sites. The declaration was, however, largely symbolic, since the U.S. army had a ready supply of American construction workers. See the discussion in "Protokoll: 19. Sitzung des BVs am 4. März 1958"; and "Protokoll der ausserordentlichen Sitzung des BVs am 28. März 1958 in Hamburg," DGB:GBV.

34. *Jahrbuch der öffentlichen Meinung 1958–1964*, p. 375.

35. Letters in DGB:Schriftverkehr-Ost. This quote is from a letter to the DGB from Deutsches Hydriewerk Rodeben, March 27, 1958. See also "Appell an alle Arbeiter

und Gewerkschaftler Deutschlands," *Dokumentation der Zeit* (1958), no. 165, pp. 11–12; and "Vorschläge des FDGB und des DGB zum gemeinsamen Handeln gegen die atomare Aufrüstung Westdeutschlands," *Dokumentation der Zeit* (1958), no. 168, pp. 13–14.

36. Rupp, *Ausserparlamentarische Opposition,* pp. 286–87, has reprinted the two falsified letters. See also "Protokoll der 64. Sitzung des GBV, dem 21. April 1958," DGB:GBV

37. "Protokoll der ausserordentlichen Sitzung des GBVs am 28. März 1958 in Hamburg," DGB:GBV.

38. *Ibid.*

39. Hermann Grote, "Gewerkschaften und Generalstreik: Persönlich: 28.3.58," DGB:Atom. See also the testimony of other legal experts, "Protokoll der ausserordentlichen Sitzung des BVs am 28. März 1958 in Hamburg," DGB:GBV.

40. "Protokoll der ausserordentlichen Sitzung des BVs am 28. März 1958 in Hamburg," DGB:GBV. See also *dpa-Meldung* (March 30, 1958).

41. "Protokoll über die Besprechung mit den Landesbezirksvorsitzenden betreffend Fortführung der Aktion KdA in Düsseldorf am 1. April 1958," DGB:Atom.

42. *Ibid.* See also "Atom-Proteste: Wie es die ÖTV befahl," *Der Spiegel,* April 30, 1958, pp. 25–26. Complete documentation on the Hamburg demonstration in ASD:SPD-LO Hamburg 514.

43. *Hamburger Echo,* April 18 and May 2, 1958; *Metall,* no. 9 (May 1, 1958); "Maifeier: Fussball gegen Atomtod," *Der Spiegel,* April 30, 1958, pp. 29–30; and "Mai am Kwai," *Der Spiegel,* May 7, 1958, p. 13. See also "Protokoll der 66. Sitzung des GBV, dem 5. Mai 1958," DGB:GBV.

44. "Protokollarische Notizen aus der Sitzung des Ausschusses 'KdA' mit den Beauftragten der Landesausschüsse, den 26. April 1958," ASD:PV 0886. Follow-up discussions occurred at the April 28 and May 6 meetings of the DGB executive board, DGB:GBV.

45. Quote from Menzel's report to the Bonn Central Committee concerning Richter's meeting with the ICFTU. "Protokollarische Notizen über die Sitzung des zentralen Arbeitsausschusses KdA am 10. Juli 1958 in Bonn," EZB:BK 6,1.

46. *Vorwärts* (July 21, 1958).

47. Döring's remarks and the FDP's party plank in "Sitzung des Landesausschusses am 16. April 1958 in Dortmund," WDS:Landtagswahl 1958. See also "Der Landesverband NRW der SPD hat zur Frage einer eventuellen Koalition nach den Landtagswahlen diesen Standpunkt," WDS:Landtagswahl 1958.

48. A good analysis of the CDU's campaign strategy in "Erlahmende Kampagne gegen den Atomtod in Westdeutschland," *NZZ,* July 27, 1958. Public opinion polls bespoke a favorable outcome for the CDU. A majority of West German citizens favored the Bundeswehr (51 percent). Voters preferred the CDU to SPD by 46 percent to 39 percent in July 1958. Even those in favor of a nuclearized Bundeswehr had risen (from 15 percent to 21 percent) despite the SPD's campaign; see *Jahrbuch der öffentlichen Meinung 1958–1964,* pp. 422 and 470–71. In the 1957 federal elections, a whopping 54 percent of North Rhine-Westphalian voters had voted for the CDU.

49. "Bundeskanzler Dr. Adenauer auf der Grosskundgebung der CDU in Krefeld, 21. Juni 1958," KAS (Rhöndorf); and "Dr. Adenauer bittet zum Tee," *SDZ,* April 19/20, 1958. See also Adenauer's comments on the GCND, "Bundeskanzler Dr. Adenauer auf der Wahlgrosskundgebung der CDU in Dortmund, 18. Mai 1958," KAS (Rhöndorf).

50. Statistics from *Vorwärts* (July 11, 1958).

51. "Protokoll der 7. Sitzung des BA am 8. Oktober 1958," DGB:GBV.

52. "Protokoll der 26. Sitzung des BV, den 2. September 1958," DGB:GBV.

53. Maass' letter to Menzel, January 6, 1959, ASD:PV 0884. "Protokoll der 7. Sitzung des BA am 8. Oktober 1958," DGB:GBV.

54. Menzel's letter to Ollenhauer, March 20, 1959, ASD:PV 0807. See also "Bericht vor dem Parteipräsidium am Montag, dem 25. Mai 1959," ASD:PV 01493.

55. "Bericht zur Landtagswahl in NRW am 6. Juli 1958," WDS:Wahlberichte 1951–1968. See also the discussion by FDP leaders in "Ergebnisprotokoll der Sitzung des GBV der FDP am 11. Juli 1958 in Frankfurt," FNS:GBV 1958; and "Kurzprotokoll über die Sitzung des BVA am 30. Juli 1958," FNS:BVA Protokolle 1957–1963.

56. *Vorwärts* (July 18, 1958).

57. Hans Kroll, *Lebenserinnerungen eines Botschafters*, pp. 389–90.

58. Ernst Nolte, *Deutschland und der Kalte Krieg*, p. 474.

59. Ashkenasi, *Reformpartei und Aussenpolitik*, p. 161.

60. Kurt L. Shell and Nils Diederich, "Die Berliner Wahl vom 7. Dezember 1958," *Zeitschrift für Politik* (1960), 7:274–81. Full analysis of elections, pp. 258–64.

61. Cited by Ashkenasi, *Reformpartei und Aussenpolitik*, p. 162–63.

62. On the student organizations, see Manfred Rexin's letter to Menzel, August 7, 1958, ASD:PV 0821; and the memo by Rexin and Skriver, "Zur Situation der studentischen Bewegung gegen die Atomrüstung in der Bundesrepublik und West-Berlin," ASD:PV 0880. See also "Rundbrief (11. Mai 1958)," by Jürgen Habermas, and other documents in Bundesarchiv:ZSg1-E/68. On the various groups around *konkret*, see ASD:PV 0878. See also Meinhof and Seifert, "Unruhe in der Studentenschaft," *Blätter* (1958), 3:524–26; Meinhof's "Was wird aus Deutschland?"ASD:PV 0821; and the newsletter *argument* (Münster). On *konkret*, see the autobiography of its editor, Klaus Rainer Röhl, *Fünf Finger sind keine Faust*, and Klotzbach, *Der Weg zur Staatspartei*, p. 459.

63. W. Gessler's letter to local student committees, October 1, 1958, MR:KdA I: Allgemeines Material. At the July meeting of the coordinating committee, Röhl stated that he "would be prepared, if necessary under oath, to declare that his journal received no financial assistance from Communist groups or individuals." See "Studentische Ausschüsse gegen Atomrüstung: Protokoll der Konferenz vom 26. Juli 1958 in Frankfurt," ASD:PV 0821. In his memoirs, *Fünf Finger*, he admitted otherwise.

64. "Studentische Ausschüsse gegen Atomrüstung: Protokoll der Konferenz vom 11. Oktober 1958 in Frankfurt," ASD:PV 0821. See also "Studentische Ausschüsse gegen Atomrüstung: Protokoll der Konferenz vom 11. November 1958 in Frankfurt," ASD:PV 0821. See also Maass' "Bericht eines Telefongesprächs mit dem Genossen W.v.K. [W. von Knoeringen]," (January 7, 1959), ASD:PV 0882.

65. Havemann's letter to West Berlin student leaders, January 3, 1959, MR: Studentenkongress: Presseberichte (Ost). On the Humboldt Congress, see "Zusammenfassung der Aussprache im Senatssitzungssaal der Humboldt-Universität am 3. Januar 1959," ASD:PV 0821. See also *konkret*, no. 1 (January 1, 1959) and no. 2 (January 2, 1959).

66. Röhl, *Fünf Finger*, p. 143.

67. *Ibid.*, pp. 143–44. For a detailed summation of the course of events, see the unpublished text of a speech given by Manfred Rexin in May 1982, "Kampf dem Atomtod;—damals und heute: Rolf Schroers in der APO der Adenauer Aera" (copy from Rexin).

68. "Beschlüsse des Plenums am 4. Januar 1959: Zusatzresolutionen," ASD:PV 0882.

69. *Neues Deutschland*, January 6, 1959; *Berliner Zeitung*, January 4, 5, and 6, 1959; *Junge Welt*, January 5, 1959; *Neue Zeit*, January 6, 1959.

70. Röhl, *Fünf Finger*, p. 145.

71. *Bildzeitung*, January 5, 1959; *Vorwärts*, January 9, 1959; *SDZ*, January 5, 1959; *FR*, January 5, 1959; *Die Zeit*, January 9 and 17, 1959.

72. Schmidt's speech cited in *Berliner Stimme* (January 10, 1959). See also *Vorwärts* (January 9, 1959). "Was the congress Communist controlled and infiltrated, as was claimed afterwards?" Röhl asked rhetorically in his memoirs. "In the final analysis, only a tram ride separates us from our peace friends in East Berlin. Was our final resolution—the sensational one that Erich Kuby still today believes he helped formulate—actually prepared in East Berlin? Those are questions, aren't they. We had no time to ride over there, and it would have been unnecessary anyway. We did a little bit on our own." Röhl, *Fünf Finger*, p. 145.

73. *Konkret's* position was defended by Oswald Hüller in "Erklärung zur Atomrüstung und zum Berliner Studentenkongress," ASD:SPD-LV Berlin 325; and by Erich Kuby in a letter to W. Gessler and M. Rexin, January 14, 1959, ASD:PV 0882. Kuby states that the congress saved the student movement from sliding into the "social democratic swampland of the yes/no." For the GCND–SPD position, see Rexin's and Skriver's analysis, "Vorschläge zur Reorganisation des Berliner Arbeitsausschusses 'Gegen den Atomtod,'" ASD:SPD-LV Berlin 325. An initial meeting took place on January 20. "Studentenausschuss gegen Atomrüstung an der Freien Universität Berlin: Mitgliederversammlung am 20. Januar 1959," ASD:PV 0882.

74. "Kompromiss-Antrag von Manfred Rexin, 28. Februar 1958," ASD:PV 0882.

75. The *konkret*-backed resolution is quoted in full by Rexin in a letter to Gessler, March 5, 1959, ASD:PV 0882.

76. See Rexin's "Rundschreiben: An alle Studentenausschüsse gegen Atomrüstung," (no date); and his letter to Gessler, February 23, 1959, both in ASD:PV 0882. See also "Zur Situation der studentischen Bewegung gegen die Atomrüstung in der Bundesrepublik und West-Berlin," ASD:PV 0880.

77 Röhl, *Fünf Finger*, p. 150. On *konkret's* activities, see "Rundschreiben 3/SS 59: Studentische Ausschüsse gegen Atomrüstung: Zentrale, 2. Mai 1959," ASD:PV 0821.

78. Maass' letter to Menzel, January 6, 1959, ASD:PV 0884.

79. Beermann, "Bericht über meine Gespräche in Paris, 5. Mai 1959," ASD:FE 138.

Part III

Introduction

1. Dean Acheson, "The Practice of Partnership," p. 252.

2. Cited by Schwartz, *NATO's Nuclear Dilemmas*, p. 58.

3. *Ibid.*, pp. 75–81; Kelleher, *Germany and the Politics of Nuclear Weapons*, pp. 136–43.

4. On the MLF, see Schwartz, *NATO's Nuclear Dilemmas*, pp. 82–135; John D. Steinbruner, *The Cybernetic Theory of Decision*; and Alastair Buchan, "The Multi-

lateral Force." German reactions are handled best by Kelleher, *Germany and the Politics of Nuclear Weapons*, pp. 228–69.

5. On flexible response doctrine, see Schwartz, *NATO's Nuclear Dilemmas*, pp. 136–92; Gaddis, *Strategies of Containment*, pp. 198–236; and Kelleher, *Germany and the Politics of Nuclear Weapons*, pp. 157–227.

6. Schwartz, *NATO's Nuclear Dilemmas*, pp. 146–50. Two of the most important works of this period were Henry Kissinger, *Nuclear Weapons and Foreign Policy*, and Maxwell Taylor, *The Uncertain Trumpet*.

7. "Remarks by Secretary McNamara, NATO Ministerial Meeting, 5 May 1962. Restricted Session," p. 18. Declassified on August 17, 1979, under the Freedom of Information Act.

8. *Ibid.*, p. 25.

6. The Young Adenauerians

1. On the SPD, see Ashkenasi, *Reformpartei und Aussenpolitik;* Chalmers, *The Social Democratic Party of Germany;* Edwin Czerwick, *Oppositionstheorien und Aussenpolitik;* Joachim Hütter, *SPD und nationale Sicherheit;* Klotzbach, *Der Weg zur Staatspartei;* Theo Pirker, *Die SPD nach Hitler;* Schellenger, *The SPD in the Bonn Republic;* and Lothar Wilker, *Die Sicherheitspolitik der SPD 1956–1966.*

2. On Beermann, see Drummond, *The German Social Democrats*, pp. 228–33; Klotzbach, *Der Weg zur Staatspartei*, pp. 467–83; and Eckardt Opitz, "Friedrich Beermann und die Wehrpolitik der SPD von 1955 bis 1959." See also Beermann's letter to Ollenhauer, December 3, 1953, ASD:EO 3; his letter to Erler, February 6, 1956, ASD:FE 137; also Beermann, "Besuch bei der Bundeswehr, Juli/August 1956," FNA:Vb 3/4:Atom; "Bericht über die sozialdemokratische Wehrpolitik: Zur Vorlage für den Parteitag 1956," ASD:FE 138; and "Wehrfrage und Wahlkampf (7. Juni 1956)," ASD:FE 137.

3. Beermann, "Die Auswirkungen der bisherigen Verteidigungspolitik der SPD (22. Februar 1958)," ASD:FE 138. See also two other Beermann memoranda, "Die militärische Verteidigung der Bundesrepublik" and "Landesverteidigung," both in ASD:FE 138.

4. Beermann, "Die Auswirkungen." In 1960, Beermann warned again that the SPD's "accent on antinuclear politics" would "boomerang" on the party in the next elections. Beermann's letter to Erler, January 25, 1960, ASD:FE 143.

5. Lichtenstein recapitulates Beermann's remarks in "Ergebnis eines Gespräches zwischen Redakteur Kurt Lichtenstein (*Westfälische Rundschau*) und Erwin Welke," ASD:EO 114. See also "Aktennotiz, 3. Februar 1958,"ASD:EO 114; "Gespräch mit Herrn Gumbel, Leiter der Personalabteilung im Bundesministerium für Verteidigung, am 30. Juni 1958," ASD:FE 137; and "SPD-Wehrgutachten: Messer im Rücken," *Der Spiegel*, February 26, 1958, pp. 22–27.

6. "Empfehlung: Sicherheitsausschuss beim Parteivorstand (28. Februar)," ASD:EO 113; "Kurzprotokoll über die Sitzung des Sicherheitsausschusses beim Parteivorstand (28. Februar 1958)," ASD:FE 138; and *Protokoll der Verhandlungen des Parteitages der Sozialdemokratischen Partei Deutschlands vom 18. bis 23. Mai 1958 in Stuttgart*, pp. 485–88.

7. Hartmut Soell, *Fritz Erler–Eine politische Biographie*, 222–25. See also Erler, "Unser Verhältnis zur Bundeswehr," *SPD-Pressedienst* P/XIII/247 (October 29, 1958);

Erler, "Sozialdemokratie und Bundeswehr," *SPD-Pressedienst* P/XIII/247 (October 17, 1958); and Beermann's letter to Erler, October 17, 1958, ASD:FE 138.

8. *Protokoll der Verhandlungen des Ausserordentlichen Parteitages der Sozialdemokratischen Partei Deutschlands vom 13.–15. November 1959 in Bad Godesberg*, p. 16.

9. "Beschluss-Protokoll der gemeinsamen Sitzung des Innen- und Sicherheitsausschusses beim Parteivorstand (30. Januar 1959)," ASD:FE 138.

10. *Protokoll vom 13.–15. November 1959 in Bad Godesberg*, pp. 138–39.

11. Erler, "SPD und atomare Ausrüstung der Bundeswehr," ASD:FE 138. Same in ASD:EO 9.

12. "Beschluss-Protokoll der gemeinsamen Sitzung des Innen- und Sicherheitsausschusses beim Parteivorstand (30. Januar 1959)," ASD:FE 138.

13. Erler, "Notizen für ein Gespräch mit Adolf Arndt (14. Dezember 1958)," ASD:FE 138. He made similar comments in "Kurzprotokoll über die Sitzung des Sicherheitsausschusses beim Parteivorstand, den 5. März 1959," ASD:FE 138.

14. Text of the "Home Defense" plank in *Protokoll vom 13.–15. November 1959 in Bad Godesberg*, pp. 16–17. See Also Jesco von Puttkamer, "Landesverteidigung," *Vorwärts* (December 4, 1959).

15. The complete text of the SPD's Plan for Germany is available in Schubert, ed., *Sicherheitspolitik der Bundesrepublik Deutschland*, 2: 522–25.

16. Drummond, *The German Social Democrats*, p. 251.

17. Soell, *Fritz Erler*, p. 380.

18. Drummond, *The German Social Democrats*, pp. 258–60; and Klotzbach, *Der Weg zur Staatspartei*, pp. 474–75.

19. Schmidt's speech in *Verhandlungen des Deutschen Bundestages, 3. Wahlperiode, 5. November 1959*, pp. 4758–67.

20. *Ibid.*

21. *Vorwärts* (May 27, 1960). Cited by Klotzbach, *Der Weg zur Staatspartei*, p. 499.

22. Wehner's speech in *Verhandlungen des Deutschen Bundestages, 3. Wahlperiode, 30. Juni 1960*, pp. 7052–61.

23. *Ibid.*, pp. 7040–41.

24. *Ibid.*, p. 7089.

25. *Ibid.*, p. 7083. See also Freiherr von Guttenberg, *Gemeinsame Aussenpolitik?*

26. Erler's remark to Willi Gasper during the Saarland Rundfunk's "Aus dem Zeitgeschehen" series. Printed in *SPD-Pressemitteilungen und Informationen*, no. 204/60 (July 22, 1960).

27. This was an untitled 34-point memorandum, dated July 12, 1960, which Erler sent to Wehner, Knoeringen, and Ollenhauer. It is available in ASD:FE 138 and ASD:EO 9. Many of Erler's arguments can be found in Erler, "Sicherheitspolitik," *SPD-Pressedienst* P/XV/168 (July 27, 1960).

28. Erler's 34-point memorandum, July 12, 1960, ASD:FE 138, p. 3.

29. *Ibid.*

30. Erler's letter to Ollenhauer, July 13, 1960, ASD:FE 138.

31. Helmut Schmidt, *Verteidigung oder Vergeltung*.

32. *Ibid.*, p. 218.

33. *Ibid.*, p. 40. The Cuban missile crisis a year later confirmed his surmisal.

34. *Ibid.*, p. 215.

35. See Schmidt's remarks, "Kurzprotokoll über die Sitzung des Sicherheitsausschusses beim Parteivorstand, 4. November 1960," ASD:FE 138. It is "absolutely im-

perative," Schmidt noted, "that we strengthen the West's conventional capability." See also "Empfehlung des Sicherheitsausschusses des Parteivorstandes aus seiner Sitzung am 4. November 1960," ASD:FE 138.

36. "Wie wollen Sie gewinnen, Herr Brandt?" *Der Spiegel,* November 23, 1960, pp. 30–43. Brandt's position is also explained in Erler's letter to Ollenhauer, September 10, 1960, ASD:EO 5.

37. Text of Hanover resolution, *Protokoll der Verhandlungen und Anträge vom Parteitag der Sozialdemokratischen Partei Deutschlands in Hannover 21. bis 25. November 1960,* p. 715.

38. *Ibid.,* p. 75. See also "Was wollte Erich?" *Der Spiegel,* November 30, 1960, pp. 23–26.

39. Schmidt's remark was recorded by the GCND's business manager, Alexander Maass, in a letter to Menzel, January 30, 1961, ASD:PV 0884.

40. Schmidt's letter to Erler, December 14, 1961, ASD:FE 58.

41. *Protokoll der Verhandlungen und Anträge vom Parteitag, Hannover 1960,* p. 140.

42. *Ibid.,* p. 182.

43. *Ibid.,* pp. 117–20 and 170–80.

44. See Erler's comments in the manuscript text of "Unter uns gesagt," Deutsches Fernsehen, 7 Dezember 1960/2135, ASD:FE 16.

45. For a detailed analysis on the Schmidt-Ollenhauer strife, see Soell, *Fritz Erler,* pp. 413–26; and Erler's press interviews, ASD:FE 16.

46. See Karl Blöcher, *Der Widerstandskampf der westdeutschen Bevölkerung gegen Remilitarisierung und atomare Aufrüstung;* Deutsches Institut für Zeitgeschichte, *Das Wiedererstehen des Militarismus in Westdeutschland 1945–1960;* Karl Heinz Lehmann, *Revisionismus und Antikommunismus im Dienst der atomaren Aufrüstung;* Hermann Matern, *Der Parteitag der SPD und die Politik der SED.* This is also essentially the position taken by Rupp, *Ausserparlamentarische Opposition;* Pirker, *Die SPD nach Hitler;* Karl A. Otto, *Vom Ostermarsch zur APO;* and the editors of *Blätter für deutsche und internationale Politik.*

47. On the Standing Congress–DFU relationship, see "Kommuniqué über die Tagung des Präsidiums des 'Ständigen Kongresses aller Gegner der atomaren Aufrüstung in der Bundesrepublik' am 4./5. Februar 1961," ASD:PV 0878. Election statistics from Lehmann, *Chronik der Bundesrepublik Deutschland,* pp. 162–64.

48. "Kurzprotokoll über die Sitzung des Sicherheitsausschusses beim PV, den 5. März 1959," ASD:FE 138.

49. See the exchange of letters, Heinemann to Ollenhauer (December 12, 1960, and February 3, 1961) and Ollenhauer to Heinemann (January 30, 1961), in ASD:EO 12. Same in ASD:WM R28. See also Heinemann's article, "Neue Kräfte—neue Wege," *Politische Verantwortung* (February 1961), 5(1/2):1.

50. "Ergebnisprotokoll der Sitzung des GBV der FDP am 11. Juli 1958 in Frankfurt," FNS:GBV 1958.

51. Döring's speech cited in "Ergebnisprotokoll der Sitzung des BV am 11. und 13. Dezember 1958 in Bonn," FNS:GBV 1958.

52. See especially "Kurzprotokoll über die Klausurtagung am 16. Juni 1960 in Frankfurt/Main," and "Entwurf eines aussenpolitischen Kommuniqués für die Klausurtagung der FDP in Fr/M.," both in FNS:GBV 1960. See also Max Becker, "Gedanken zu einer gemeinsamen Aussenpolitik," *fdk,* no. 11/46 (June 1, 1960); and Erich Mende, "FDP-Parteivorsitzender zur Gemeinsamen Aussenpolitik," *fdk,* no. 11/

Movement in West Germany"; Wynfred Joshua, "Soviet Manipulation of the European Peace Movement"; Hans Rattinger, "The Federal Republic of Germany: Much Ado About (Almost) Nothing," in Gregory Flynn and Hans Rattinger, eds., *The Public and Atlantic Defense,* pp. 101–74; and Günther Schmid, *Sicherheitspolitik und Friedensbewegung.*

11. Risse-Kappen, "Gesellschaftlicher Konsens," pp. 71–78.

12. On the churches' peace politics, see "The Preservation, Promotion and Renewal of Peace," *EKD Bulletin* (October 1981); "Das Bekenntnis zu Jesus Christus wird missbraucht, wenn es politisch verwendet wird," *FAZ,* September 21, 1982; *Reformierter Bund* (1982); *Kirche und Frieden* (1982); and *Frieden wahren fördern und erneuern* (1984). See also Günther Baadte, ed., *Frieden stiften;* and Thomas Risse-Kappen, *Christen Zur Friedensdiskussion.*

13. *Die Grünen: The Programme of the German Green Party,* p. 26.

14. On the Green Party, see Elim Papadakis, *The Green Movement in West Germany;* and Petra Kelly, *Fighting for Hope.*

15. *SPD Parteitag: April 1982, München,* p. 4.

16. *SPD Ausserordentlicher Parteitag: November 1983, Köln,* p. 7.

17. Heinz O. Vetter, "Initiative für den Frieden: Rede auf der Veranstaltung des DGB zum Antikriegstag am 1. September 1981 in Düsseldorf," reprinted in Gerhard Leminsky and Bernd Otto, *Politik und Programmatik des Deutschen Gewerkschaftsbundes.*

18. "Stellungnahme des Deutschen Gewerkschaftsbundes zur Friedens- und Sicherheitspolitik, 1983," *Ibid.,* p. 95. On the DGB, see also *Antikriegstag 1981* (1981); *Materialien zum Kongress* (1981); and Thomas Walter, ed., *Gewerkschaften und Demokratie.*

19. Risse-Kappen, "Gesellschaftlicher Konsens," p. 124.

20. On the FDP, see *Ibid.,* pp. 122–131. On the double-zero option, see *New York Times,* June 5, 1987.

21. "Grundsatzprogramm der Christlich Demokratischen Union Deutschlands, 26. Bundesparteitag Ludwigshafen, 23–25. Oktober 1978," in Heiner Geissler, ed., *Grundwerte in der Politik,* p. 167.

22. See W. Schönbohm, *Die CDU wird moderne Volkspartei; Die Geschichte der CDU* (1980); Risse-Kappen, "Gesellschaftlicher Konsens," pp. 112–22; and *New York Times,* June 5, 1987.

SELECTED BIBLIOGRAPHY

Archival Sources

Konrad Adenauer Stiftung, Rhöndorf (KAS):
  Reden, Interviews, Aufsätze 1955–1963
Archiv der sozialen Demokratie, Bonn (ASD):
  Karl Bechert Nachlass (KB)
  Fritz Erler Nachlass (FE)
  Gustav Heinemann Archiv (GHA):
    Kirchliche Angelegenheiten
    Allgemeine Korrespondenz
  Walter Menzel Nachlass (WM)
  Peter Nellen Nachlass (PN)
  Erich Ollenhauer Nachlass (EO)
  Parteivorstand Bestand (PV)
  SPD-LO Hamburg
  SPD-LV Berlin
  Helene Wessel Nachlass (HW)
Archiv des DGB-Bundesvorstandes, Düsseldorf (DGB-Archiv):
  Atom
  Atom-Gegner
  Ausschuss Kampf dem Atomtod westlich
  DGB Bundesausschuss Protokolle 1956–60
  Frankfurt am Main 1958
  Komitee gegen Atomrüstung, Bayern (KgA)
  Protokolle Bundesvorstand
  Protokolle Gesamt Bundesvorstand 1956–1960 (GBV)
  Schriftverkehr-Ost
  Zustimmungs-Erklärung 1958
Bundesarchiv, Koblenz:
  Zeitschrift-Sammlung (ZS)
Bundesarchiv-Militärarchiv, Freiburg (BA–MA):
  Bundeswehr 2 (BW2)
  Bundeswehr 9 (BW9)
Wolfgang Döring Stiftung, Landesverband FDP Düsseldorf (WDS):
  Landtagswahl 1958
  Sitzungen des Landesausschusses
  Wahlberichte 1951–1968

Selected Bibliography

Evangelisches Zentralarchiv, Berlin (EZB):
   Büro Kloppenburg: Atombewaffnung (BK)
   Sammlung Friederich Sigmund-Schultze
FDP Bundestag Archiv, Bonn (FDP BA):
   Fraktionssitzung: Protokolle (FS)
Institut für Zeitgeschichte, Munich:
   Christel Küpper Nachlass
Landeskirchenamt, Archiv der Evangelischen Kirche im Rheinland, Düsseldorf (LKA):
   Akten der Kirchlichen Bruderschaft im Rheinland (AB)
   Karl Immer Nachlass (KI)
Franz Neumann Archiv, Berlin (FNA):
   Landesausschuss (LA)
   Vb 3/4:Atom
Parlamentsarchiv, Abteilung Wissenschaftliche Dokumentation des Deutschen Bundestages, Bonn (PA):
   Protokolle des Verteidigungsausschusses des Deutschen Bundestages (VA)
Politisches Archiv der Friedrich Naumann Stiftung, Bonn (FNS):
   Aussenpolitischer Ausschuss: Protokolle 1954–1959
   Aussen- und Deutschlandpolitik 1958–1963
   Bundesgeschäftsführung Korrespondenz mit Bundesvorstand
   Bundeshauptausschuss Protokolle 1955–1961 (BHA)
   Bundesparteitage 1955–1961
   Bundesverteidigungsausschuss Protokolle (BVA)
   Bundesvorstand (Gesamt) Protokolle 1955–1961 (GBV)
   Thomas Dehler Archiv (TDA)
      Aussenpolitik
      Verteidigungspolitik
   Klausurtagung 1958–1961
   Erich Mende Bestand 1955–1961 (EM)
   Wahlkongress
Presse-Ausschnitt-Archiv des Deutschen Bundestages, Bonn
Manfred Rexin Papers, private collection of Manfred Rexin, West Berlin (MR):
   Ausschuss Kampf dem Atomtod bis 1961
   Kampf dem Atomtod I: Allgemeines Material
   Studentenkongress: Presseberichte (Ost)
Zeitungsausschnitt-Archiv des Presse- und Informationsamtes der Bundesregierung, Bonn

Books, Articles, Manuscripts

Abenheim, Donald. "A Valid Heritage: The Policy of Military Tradition in the Emergence of the Bundeswehr, 1950–1965." Ph.D. dissertation, Stanford University, 1985.
Acheson, Dean. "The Illusion of Disengagement." *Foreign Affairs* (April 1958), 36:371–82.
——"The Practice of Partnership." *Foreign Affairs* (January 1963), 41:247–60.
——*Present at the Creation.* New York: Norton, 1969.
Adenauer, Konrad. *Erinnerungen.* Stuttgart: Deutsche Verlags-Anstalt, 1965–68.

"Agreement on Restoration of German Sovereignty." *Department of State Bulletin* (October 11, 1954), 30:517–19.

Alexander, H. G. "Germany Before the Elections." *The Political Quarterly* (1961), 32:168–81.

Allemann, Fritz René. *Bonn ist nicht Weimar.* Cologne and Berlin: Kiepenheuer and Witsch, 1956.

——"Wehrminister Strauss." *Die Politische Meinung* (1956), 1:51–56.

Almeida, J. A. "Pius XII und der Atomkrieg." Ph.D. dissertation, University of Freiburg, 1961.

Antikriegstag 1981: DGB: Frieden durch Abrüstung! Düsseldorf: DGB-Bundesvorstand, 1981.

Arbeitsausschuss 'Kampf dem Atomtod,' ed. *Kampf dem Atomtod.* Stuttgart: Druck Schwäbische Tagwacht, 1958.

Aron, Raymond. *The Great Debate: Theories of Nuclear Strategy.* Garden City, N.Y.: Doubleday, 1965.

Ashkenasi, Abraham. *Reformpartei und Aussenpolitik: Die Aussenpolitik der SPD Berlin–Bonn.* Cologne and Opladen: Westdeutscher Verlag, 1968.

Asmussen, Hans. *Krieg und Frieden.* Osnabrück: A. Fromm, 1961.

——*Verleugnung der drei Glaubensartikel: Eine Antwort an die kirchlichen Bruderschaften.* Munich: Evangelischer Presseverband für Bayern, 1958.

Atomare Kampfmittel und christliche Ethik: Diskussionsbeiträge deutscher Katholiken. Munich: Kösel, 1960.

Baadte, Günther, ed. *Frieden stiften: Die Christen zur Abrüstung.* Munich: Beck, 1984.

Bacevich, A. J. *The Pentomic Era: The U.S. Army Between Korea and Vietnam.* Washington, D.C.: National Defense University Press, 1986.

Bainton, Roland H. *Christian Attitudes Toward War and Peace: A Historical Survey and Critical Re-evaluation.* New York: Abingdon Press, 1960.

Bald, Richard H. "The Free Democratic Party (FDP) and West German Foreign Policy, 1949–1959." Ph.D. dissertation, University of Michigan, 1963.

Baring, Arnulf. *Aussenpolitik in Adenauers Kanzlerdemokratie: Bonns Beitrag zur Europäischen Verteidigungsgemeinschaft.* Munich: R. Oldenbourg, 1969.

——*Machtwechsel: Die Aera Brandt-Scheel.* Stuttgart: Deutsche Verlags-Anstalt, 1982.

Barth, Karl. *Eine Schweizer Stimme, 1938–1945.* Zürich: Evangelischer Verlag, 1945.

Baudis, Andreas, ed. *Richte unsere Füsse auf den Weg des Friedens: Helmut Gollwitzer zum 70. Geburtstag.* Munich: Chr. Kaiser, 1979.

Bauer, Karl. *Deutsche Verteidigungspolitik, 1948–1967: Dokumente und Kommentare.* Boppard am Rhein: Harald Boldt, 1968.

Bayerischer Landtag: Stenographische Berichte. Munich, 1958.

Beales, A. C. F. *The History of Peace: A Short Account of the Organised Movements for International Peace.* New York: Dial Press, 1931.

Bechert, Karl. *Deutsche Politik im Schatten der Atomdrohung.* Bonn: Arbeitsausschuss 'Kampf dem Atomtod,' n.d. [1958?].

——*Gefahren der Radioaktivität: Droht Dir der Atomtod?* Dortmund: Westfalendruck, 1957.

——*Der Wahnsinn des Atomkrieges.* Düsseldorf: Eugen Diederichs, 1956.

Below, Fritz. *Armee und Soldat im Atomzeitalter.* Karlsruhe: Stahlberg, 1957.

Benz, Wolfgang, Günter Plum, and Werner Röder. *Einheit der Nation: Diskussionen und Konzeptionen zur Deutschlandpolitik der grossen Parteien seit 1945.* Stuttgart: Frommann-Holzboog, 1978.

Selected Bibliography

Berghahn, V. R. *Modern Germany: Society, Economy, and Politics in the Twentieth Century.* Cambridge: Cambridge University Press, 1982.

Berlin 1956: Bericht über die ausserordentliche Tagung der zweiten Synode der EKD. Hanover: EKD, 1957.

Berlin 1958: Bericht über die Tagung der zweiten Synode der EKD. Hanover: EKD, 1959.

Beyerchen, Alan D. *Scientists Under Hitler: Politics and the Physics Community in the Third Reich.* New Haven: Yale University Press, 1977.

Beyme, Klaus von. *The Political System of the Federal Republic of Germany.* New York: St. Martin's Press, 1982.

Biedenkopf, Kurt. "Domestic Consensus, Security and the Western Alliance." In *Defence and Consensus: The Domestic Aspects of Western Security.* Adelphi Papers 183 and 184. London: International Institute for Strategic Studies, 1983.

Blaubuch: Dokumentation über den Widerstand gegen die atomare Aufrüstung der Bundesrepublik. Düsseldorf: Friedenskomitee der Bundesrepublik, 1958.

Blöcher, Karl. *Der Widerstandskampf der westdeutschen Bevölkerung gegen Remilitarisierung und atomare Aufrüstung.* Berlin: Ministerium für Nationale Verteidigung, 1959.

Blumenwitz, Dieter, ed. *Konrad Adenauer und seine Zeit: Politik und Persönlichkeit des ersten Bundeskanzlers.* 2 vols. Stuttgart: Deutsche Verlags-Anstalt, 1976.

Bond, Brian. *War and Society in Europe, 1870–1970.* Oxford: Oxford University Press, 1984.

Bonin, Bogislav von. *Atomkrieg—Unser Ende.* Recklinghausen: J. Bauer, 1955.

——*Opposition gegen Adenauers Sicherheitspolitik: Eine Dokumentation.* Heinz Brill, ed. Hamburg: Verlag Neue Politik, 1976.

Bonn 10.10.81: Friedensdemonstration für Abrüstung und Entspannung in Europa. Berlin: Lamuv, 1981.

Born, Hegwig. *Der Christ im Atomzeitalter.* Munich: Komitee gegen Atomrüstung, n.d. [1959?].

Born, Hegwig and Max Born. *Der Luxus des Gewissens: Erlebnisse und Einsichten im Atomzeitalter.* Munich: Nymphenburger Verlagshandlung, 1969.

Born, Max. *Physik und Politik.* Göttingen: Vandenhoeck & Ruprecht, 1960.

——*Von der Verantwortung des Naturwissenschaftlers: Gesammelte Vorträge.* Munich: Nymphenburger Verlagshandlung, 1965.

Boutwell, Jeffrey. "Politics and the Peace Movement in West Germany." *International Security* (Spring 1983), 7:72–92.

Brenner, Otto. "Die Unabhängigkeit und Einheit der Gewerkschaften." *Die neue Gesellschaft* (1958), 5:329–32.

Brill, Heinz. "Das Problem einer wehrpolitischen Alternative für Deutschland. Die Auseinandersetzungen um die wehrpolitischen Alternativvorschläge des Obersten Bogislav von Bonin." Ph.D. dissertation, University of Göttingen, 1977.

Brückner, Peter. *Ulrike Marie Meinhof und die deutschen Verhältnisse.* Berlin: Klaus Wagenbach, 1976.

Brunotte, Heinz. *Die Evangelische Kirche in Deutschland.* Gütersloh: Gerd Mohn, 1964.

Buchan, Alastair. "The Multilateral Force: A Study in Alliance Politics." *International Affairs* (October 1964), 40:619–37.

Buchbinder, Heinrich. *Landesverteidigung im Atomzeitalter.* Zürich: Schweizerische Bewegung gegen Atomare Aufrüstung, 1966.

Buczylowski, Ulrich. *Kurt Schumacher und die deutsche Frage.* Stuttgart: Seewald, 1973.

Büscher, Wolfgang, Peter Wensierski, and Klaus Wolschner, eds. *Friedensbewegung in der DDR: Texte 1978–1982.* Hattingen: Scandica, 1982.

Bufe, Helga and Jürgen Grumbach. "Der Griff nach der Atommacht: Zur Rolle des F. J. Strauss bei der Schaffung eines atomaren Potentials der BRD." *Blätter für deutsche und internationale Politik* (1979), 24:1439–62.

——*Staat und Atomindustrie: Kernenergiepolitik in der BRD.* Cologne: Pahl-Rugenstein, 1979.

Bundesverfassungsgericht: Protokolle. Karlsruhe, 1958.

Bundy, McGeorge, George F. Kennan, Robert S. McNamara, and Gerard Smith. "Nuclear Weapons and the Atlantic Alliance." *Foreign Affairs* (Spring 1982), 60:753–68.

Burkhardt, G. "Report on the Activities of the German Pugwash Group." *Proceedings of the Tenth Pugwash Conference on World Affairs.* London: Pugwash, 1962.

Buteux, Paul. *The Politics of Nuclear Consultation in NATO, 1965–1980.* Cambridge: Cambridge University Press, 1983.

Calleo, David. *The Atlantic Fantasy.* Baltimore: Johns Hopkins University Press, 1970.

Chalmers, Douglas. *The Social Democratic Party of Germany: From Working-Class Movement to Modern Political Party.* New Haven: Yale University Press, 1964.

Chickering, Roger. *Imperial Germany and a World Without War: The Peace Movement and German Society 1892–1914.* Princeton: Princeton University Press, 1975.

Close, Richard. "Nuclear Weapons and West Germany." Ph.D. dissertation, University of Massachusetts, 1967.

Czerwick, Edwin. *Oppositionstheorien und Aussenpolitik: Eine Analyse sozialdemokratischer Deutschlandpolitik 1955 bis 1966.* Königstein in Taunus: Anton Hain, 1981.

"Denkschrift des militärischen Expertenausschusses über die Aufstellung eines Deutschen Kontingents im Rahmen einer übernationalen Streitmacht zur Verteidigung Westeuropas vom 9. Oktober 1950." *Militärgeschichtliche Mitteilungen* (1977), 21:168–90.

DePorte, A. W. *Europe Between the Superpowers: The Enduring Balance.* New Haven: Yale University Press, 1979.

Deutsche Chronik 1945 bis 1970: Daten und Fakten aus beiden Teilen Deutschlands. 2 vols. Freudenstadt: Eurobuch Verlag August Lutzeyer, 1971.

Deutsches Institut für Zeitgeschichte. *Das Wiedererstehen des Militarismus in Westdeutschland 1945–1960.* Berlin: Volk und Wissen Volkseigener, 1962.

Dietzfelbinger, Eckart. *Die westdeutsche Friedensbewegung 1948 bis 1955: Die Protestaktionen gegen die Remilitarisierung der Bundesrepublik Deutschland.* Cologne: Pahl-Rugenstein, 1984.

Doering-Manteuffel, Anselm. *Die Bundesrepublik Deutschland in der Aera Adenauer: Aussenpolitik und innere Entwicklung 1949–1963.* Darmstadt: Wissenschaftliche Buchgesellschaft, 1983.

——*Katholismus und Wiederbewaffnung: Die Haltung der deutschen Katholiken gegenüber der Wehrfrage 1948–1955.* Mainz: Matthias-Grünewald, 1981.

Dohse, Rainer. *Der Dritte Weg: Neutralitätsbestrebungen in Westdeutschland zwischen 1945 und 1955.* Hamburg: Holsten, 1974.

Dokumente zur Deutschlandpolitik: III. Reihe. Vols. 2–4. Ernest Deuerlein, ed. Bonn: Bundesministerium für Gesamtdeutsche Fragen, 1961–1969.

Selected Bibliography

Dormann, Manfred. *Demokratische Militärpolitik: Die alliierte Militärstrategie als Thema deutscher Politik 1949–1968.* Freiburg: Rombach, 1970.

Dorn, Wolfram, ed. *Mehrheitsmacher oder Mehr? 30 Jahre liberale Politik in der Bundesrepublik Deutschland.* Essen: Rathaus Verlagsgesellschaft, 1979.

Dorn, Wolfram and Friedrich Henning, eds. *Thomas Dehler: Begegnungen-Gedanken-Entscheidigungen.* Bonn: Liberal-Verlag, 1977.

Dorn, Wolfram and Wolfang Wiedner. *Der Freiheit gehört die Zukunft: Wolfgang Döring: Eine politische Biographie.* Bonn: Liberal-Verlag, 1974.

Dräger, Heinrich, Hellmuth Heye, and Franz Sackmann. *Probleme der Verteidigung der BRD.* Berlin: E. S. Mittler, 1959.

Driver, Christopher. *The Disarmers: A Study in Protest.* London: Hodder and Stoughton, 1964.

Drummond, Gordon Douglas. *The German Social Democrats in Opposition, 1949–1960: The Case Against Rearmament.* Norman: University of Oklahoma Press, 1982.

Duffy, Christopher. *Borodino and the War of 1812.* London: Seeley Service, 1972.

Dulles, John Foster. "Challenge and Response in United States Policy." *Foreign Affairs* (October 1957), 36:25–43.

——"The Evolution of Foreign Policy." *Department of State Bulletin* (January 25, 1954), 30:107–10.

——"Policy for Security and Peace." *Foreign Affairs* (April 1954), 32:353–64.

Eberlein, Klaus D. "Die Wahlentscheidung vom 17. September 1961, ihre Ursachen und Wirkung." *Zeitschrift für Politik* (1962), 9:237–57.

Eden, Anthony. *Full Circle: The Memoirs of Anthony Eden.* London: Cassell, 1960.

Edinger, Lewis J. *Kurt Schumacher: A Study in Personality and Political Behavior.* Stanford: Stanford University Press, 1965.

——*West German Politics.* New York: Columbia University Press, 1986.

Engel-Janosi, Friedrich, Grete Klingenstein, and Heinrich Lutz, eds. *Gewalt und Gewaltlosigkeit: Probleme des 20. Jahrhunderts.* Munich: R. Oldenbourg, 1977.

Erler, Fritz. *Politik für Deutschland: Eine Dokumentation.* Stuttgart: Seewald, 1968.

——*Ein Volk sucht seine Sicherheit.* Frankfurt am Main: Europäische Verlagsanstalt, 1961.

——"The Struggle for German Reunification." *Foreign Affairs* (April 1956), 34:380–93.

——"Umrüstung." *Aussenpolitik* (1957), 8:12–20.

Erler, Hans. *Fritz Erler contra Willy Brandt: Demokratie oder Volksfront in Europa.* Stuttgart: Seewald, 1976.

Europa ruft: Der Europäische Kongress gegen Atomrüstung: London 17.–18. Januar 1959. Munich: Komitee gegen Atomrüstung, 1959.

Europäische Sicherheit: Grundgedanken, Probleme und Tatsachen in militärischer und politischer Sicht. Vol. 5 of *Europa-Union Deutschland.* Bonn: H. Köllen, 1958.

European Security Study Report. Strengthening Conventional Deterrence in Europe. New York: St. Martin's Press, 1983.

Evangelische Stimmen zur Atomfrage. Hanover: Verlag des Amtsblattes der Evangelischen Kirche in Deutschland, 1958.

Evanston Speaks: Reports of the Second Assembly of the World Council of Churches, August 13–15, 1954. Geneva: WCC, 1954.

Evanston to New Delhi 1954–1961: Report of the Central Committee to the Third Assembly of the World Council of Churches, New Delhi. Geneva: WCC, 1961.

Flynn, Gregory and Hans Rattinger, eds. *The Public and Atlantic Defense*. London: Rowman & Allanheld, 1985.

Forster, Karl, ed. *Kann der atomare Verteidigungskrieg ein gerechter Krieg sein?* Munich: Karl Zink, 1960.

Foschepoth, Joseph, ed. *Kalter Krieg und Deutsche Frage: Deutschland im Widerstreit der Mächte 1945–1952*. Göttingen: Vandenhoeck and Ruprecht, 1985.

Freedman, Lawrence. *Britain and Nuclear Weapons*. London: Macmillan, 1980.

——*The Evolution of Nuclear Strategy*. New York: St. Martin's Press, 1981.

——"NATO Myths." *Foreign Policy* (Winter 1981/82), no. 45, pp. 48–68.

Frieden wahren fördern und erneuern: Eine Denkschrift der Evangelischen Kirche in Deutschland. Gütersloh: Gütersloher Verlag, 1984.

Fursdon, Edward. *The European Defence Community: A History*. New York: St. Martin's Press, 1980.

Gaddis, John Lewis. "Containment: A Reassessment." *Foreign Affairs* (July 1977), 55:873–87.

——*Strategies of Containment: A Critical Appraisal of Postwar American National Security Policy*. New York: Oxford University Press, 1982.

Gallois, Pierre. *The Balance of Terror: Strategy for the Nuclear Age*. Boston: Houghton Mifflin, 1961.

Garthoff, Raymond L. *Détente and Confrontation: American–Soviet Relations from Nixon to Reagan*. Washington, D.C.: Brookings Institution, 1985.

Geiling, Martin. *Aussenpolitik und Nuklearpolitik*. Cologne: Böhlau, 1975.

Geissler, Heiner, ed. *Grundwerte in der Politik: Analysen und Beiträge zum Grundsatzprogramm der Christlich Demokratischen Union Deutschlands*. Frankfurt am Main: Ullstein, 1979.

Gerstenmaier, Eugen. *Streit und Friede hat seine Zeit: Ein Lebensbericht*. Frankfurt am Main: Propyläen, 1981.

Geschichte der CDU: Programm und Politik der Christlich Demokratischen Union Deutschlands seit 1945. Bonn: CDU-Bundesgeschäftsstelle, 1980.

Glasstone, Samuel, ed. *The Effects of Nuclear Weapons*. U.S. Department of Defense: U.S. Atomic Energy Commission, April 1962.

Glatzender, Sebastian J. *Die Deutschlandpolitik der FDP in der Aera Adenauer: Konzeptionen in Entstehung und Praxis*. Baden-Baden: Nomos, 1980.

Görlich, Ina. "Zum ethischen Problem der Atomdiskussion: Verlauf der Atomdiskussion in der Bundesrepublik Deutschland und Versuch einer Darstellung der durch sie aufbrechenden ethischen Probleme." Ph.D. dissertation, University of Freiburg, 1966.

Gollwitzer, Helmut. *Die Christen und die Atomwaffen*. Munich: Chr. Kaiser, 1957.

——*Forderungen der Freiheit: Aufsätze und Reden zur politischen Ethik*. Munich: Chr. Kaiser, 1962.

——"'Komplementäre' Entscheidungen." *Stimme der Gemeinde* (1959), 11:771–74.

Gollwitzer, Helmut, Heinrich Vogel, and Fritz Heidler. *Christliche Glaube und atomare Waffen*. Berlin: Evangelische Verlagsanstalt, 1959.

Government Declaration by the German Federal Chancellor Dr. Konrad Adenauer before the German Bundestag on 20 October 1953. Bonn: Press and Information Office, 1953.

Gowing, Margaret. *Britain and Atomic Energy, 1939–1945*. London: Macmillan, 1964.

Graml, Hermann. "Die Legende von der verpassten Gelegenheit. Zur sowjetischen

Notenkampagne des Jahres 1952." *Vierteljahrshefte für Zeitgeschichte* (1981), 29:307–41.

Gress, David. *Peace and Survival: West Germany, the Peace Movement, and European Security.* Stanford: Hoover Institution Press, 1985.

Grodzins, Morton and Eugene Rabinowitch, eds. *The Atomic Age: Scientists in National and World Affairs.* New York: Simon and Schuster, 1963.

Gröbe, Kurt, ed. *Gelsenkirchener Protokoll . . . und du?* Hamburg: Präsidium des "Ständigen Kongresses" aller Gegner der Atomaren Aufrüstung in der Bundesrepublik, 1958.

Groom, John. *British Thinking About Nuclear Weapons.* London: Frances Pinter, 1974.

Grosser, Alfred. *The Federal Republic of Germany: A Concise History.* Nelson Aldrich, tr. New York: Frederick Praeger, 1963.

——*Germany in Our Time: A Political History of the Postwar Years.* Paul Stephenson, tr. London: Pall Mall Press, 1971.

——*The Western Alliance: European–American Relations since 1945.* Michael Shaw, tr. New York: Vintage Books, 1982.

Grosser, Alfred and Jürgen Seifert, eds. *Die Spiegel Affäre.* 2 vols. Olten and Freiburg: Walter, 1966.

Die Grünen: The Programme of the German Green Party. London: Heretic Books, 1983.

Gutscher, Jörg Michael. *Die Entwicklung der FDP von ihren Anfängen bis 1961.* Meisenheim am Glan: Anton Hain, 1967.

Guttenberg, Karl-Theodor Freiherr zu. *Gemeinsame Aussenpolitik? Eine Antwort auf Herbert Wehner.* Bonn: Bundesgeschäftsstelle der CDU, 1960.

Haftendorn, Helga. *Abrüstungs- und Entspannungspolitik zwischen Sicherheitsbefriedigung und Friedenssicherung: Zur Aussenpolitik der BRD 1955–1973.* Düsseldorf: Bertelsmann Universitätverlag, 1974.

——*Sicherheit und Entspannung: Zur Aussenpolitik der Bundesrepublik Deutschland 1955–1982.* Baden-Baden: Nomos, 1983.

Hahn, Dietrich, ed. *Otto Hahn in der Kritik.* Munich: Heinz Moos, 1981.

Hahn, Jürgen von. "Die Weltfriedensbewegung im Atomzeitalter." *Europa-Archiv* (1954), 9:6807–21.

Hahn, Otto. *Erlebnisse und Erkenntnisse.* Düsseldorf: Econ, 1975.

——*Mein Leben.* Munich: Bruckmann, 1968.

Hahn, Walter F. *Between Westpolitik and Ostpolitik: Changing West German Security Views.* Beverly Hills: SAGE, 1975.

Hammerschmidt, Helmut, ed. *Zwanzig Jahre danach: Eine deutsche Bilanz 1965.* Munich: Kurt Desch, 1965.

Hanrieder, Wolfram F. *West German Foreign Policy 1949–1963.* Stanford: Stanford University Press, 1967.

Harbsmeier, Götz. "Kirchenspaltende Atomwaffen." *Junge Kirche* (1958), 19:132–34.

Hassel, Kai-Uwe von. "The Search for Consensus: Organizing Western Defense." *Foreign Affairs* (January 1965), 43:209–16.

Healy, Denis. *A Neutral Belt in Europe?* Fabian Tract 311. London: Fabian Society, 1958.

Heinemann, Gustav. *Reden und Schriften.* Frankfurt am Main: Suhrkamp, 1975–77.

——"Kein Ja zur Atomwaffen." *Atomzeitalter* (July 1960), 7:73.

——*Verfehlte Deutschlandpolitik—Irreführung und Selbsttäuschung: Artikel und Reden.* Frankfurt am Main: Stimme-Verlag, 1966.

Heipp, Günther, ed. *Es geht ums Leben! Der Kampf gegen die Bombe 1945–1965: Eine Dokumentation.* Hamburg: Herbert Reich, 1965.

Heisenberg, Elisabeth. *Das politische Leben eines Unpolitischen: Erinnerungen an Werner Heisenberg.* Munich: R. Piper, 1980.

Heisenberg, Werner. *Der Teil und das Ganze: Gespräche im Umkreis der Atomphysik.* Munich: R. Piper, 1969.

Herken, Gregg. *The Winning Weapon: The Atomic Bomb in the Cold War, 1945–1950.* New York: Vintage Books, 1982.

Herrmann, Horst. "Der Ausschuss 'Kampf dem Atomtod' und die SPD-Führung." *Beiträge zur Zeitgeschichte* (1959), 2:86–91.

Hessische Stiftung Friedens- und Konfliktforschung, ed. *Unsere Bundeswehr? Zum 25jährigen Bestehen einer umstrittenen Institution.* Frankfurt am Main: Suhrkamp, 1981.

Heusinger, Adolf. *Reden 1956–1961.* Boppard am Rhein: H. Boldt, 1961.

Heydenreich, Renate Maria. "Die Spandauer Synode." *Junge Kirche* (1958), 18:172–86.

——"Die Synod der EKD Berlin 1958." *Junge Kirche* (1959), 19:233–41.

Hiepe, Richard. *Künstler gegen Atomkrieg.* Munich: n.p., 1959.

Hillgruber, Andreas. *Europa in der Weltpolitik der Nachkriegszeit 1945–1963.* Munich: Oldenbourg, 1979.

Hintergründe der Atomdebatte im Bundestag. Bonn: Vorstand der SPD, 1957.

Hirsch-Weber, Wolfgang. *Gewerkschaften in der Politik: Von der Massenstreikdebatte zum Kampf um das Mitbestimmungsrecht.* Cologne: Westdeutscher Verlag, 1959.

Hirsch-Weber, Wolfgang and Klaus Schütz. *Wähler und Gewählte: Eine Untersuchung der Bundestagswahlen 1953.* Berlin: F. Vahlen, 1957.

Hochhuth, Rolf. *Soldiers: An Obituary for Geneva.* Robert David MacDonald, tr. New York: Grove Press, 1968.

Hoffman, Stanley. "NATO and Nuclear Weapons: Reason and Unreason." *Foreign Affairs* (Winter 1981/82), 60:327–46.

Holloway, David. *The Soviet Union and the Arms Race.* New Haven: Yale University Press, 1983.

Holm, Hans-Henrik and Nikolaj Petersen, eds. *The European Missile Crisis: Nuclear Weapons and Security Policy.* London: Frances Pinter, 1983.

Howard, Michael. *Disengagement in Europe.* Harmondsworth, England: Penguin Books, 1958.

——"Reassurances and Deterrences: Western Defense in the 1980s." *Foreign Affairs* (Winter 1982/83), 61:309–24.

——*War and the Liberal Conscience.* New Brunswick, N.J.: Rutgers University Press, 1978.

Howe, Günther, ed. *Atomzeitalter, Krieg und Frieden.* Witten and Berlin: Eckart, 1959.

——*Die Christenheit im Atomzeitalter: Vorträge und Studien.* Stuttgart: Ernst Klett, 1970.

Hrbek, Rudolf. *Die SPD—Deutschland und Europa: Die Haltung der Sozialdemokratie zum Verhältnis von Deutschland-Politik und West-Integration 1945–1957.* Bonn: Europa Union, 1972.

Selected Bibliography

Hütter, Joachim. *SPD und nationale Sicherheit: Internationale und innenpolitische Determinanten des Wandels der sozialdemokratischen Sicherheitspolitik 1959–1961.* Meisenheim am Glan: Anton Hain, 1975.

Hughes, Emmet John. *The Ordeal of Power.* New York: Dell Books, 1964.

Hunter, Robert E., ed. *NATO: The Next Generation.* Boulder, Colo: Westview Press, 1984.

Huntington, Samuel P. *The Common Defense: Strategic Programs in National Politics.* New York: Columbia University Press, 1961.

——"Conventional Deterrence and Conventional Retaliation in Europe." *International Security* (Winter 1983/84), 8:32–56.

Irving, David. *The Virus House: Germany's Atomic Research and Allied Countermeasures.* London: W. Kimber, 1967.

Iwand, Hans. "Die evangelische Kirche und der Protest gegen die atomare Bewaffnung." *Blätter für deutsche und internationale Politik* (1958), 3:185–87.

Jacobsen, Hans-Adolf, ed. *Drei Jahrzehnte Aussenpolitik der DDR.* Munich: R. Oldenbourg, 1979.

Jacobsen, Hans-Adolf and Otto Stenzl, eds. *Deutschland und die Welt: Zur Aussenpolitik der Bundesrepublik 1949–1963.* Munich: dtv-dokumente, 1964.

Jahrbuch der öffentlichen Meinung 1958–1964. Allensbach: Verlag der Demoskopie, 1965.

Janning, Josef, Hans-Josef Legrand, and Helmut Zander, eds. *Friedensbewegungen: Entwicklung und Folgen in der Bundesrepublik Deutschland, Europa und den USA.* Cologne: Wissenschaft und Politik, 1987.

Jansen, Thomas. "Abrüstung and Deutschland-Frage. Die Abrüstungsfrage als Problem der deutschen Aussenpolitik." Ph.D. dissertation, University of Bonn, 1968.

Jaspers, Karl. *The Atom Bomb and the Future of Man.* E. B. Ashton, tr. Chicago: University of Chicago Press, 1961.

——*Die Atombombe und die Zukunft des Menschen.* Munich: R. Piper, 1958.

——*Die Atombombe und die Zukunft des Menschen: Ein Radiovortrag.* Munich: R. Piper, 1957.

——*Freiheit und Wiedervereinigung: Ueber Aufgaben deutscher Politik.* Munich: R. Piper, 1960.

——"Das Gewissen vor der Bedrohung durch die Atombombe." In *Rechenschaft und Ausblick.* Munich: R. Piper, 1951.

——*Wahrheit, Freiheit, und Friede.* Munich: R. Piper, 1958.

Jordan, Pascual. *Der gescheiterte Aufstand–Betrachtungen zur Gegenwart.* Frankfurt am Main: Vittorio Klostermann, 1956.

——*Die Physik des 20. Jahrhunderts: Einführung in den Gedankeninhalt der modernen Physik.* Brunswick: Friedrich Vieweg, 1936.

——*Physikalisches Denken in der neuen Zeit.* Hamburg: Hanseatische Verlagsanstalt, 1935.

——"Die Ueberwindung der Gefahr." In *Selbstbehauptung in gefährdeter Freiheit.* Kiel: Verlag für Landespolitik, 1958.

——*Wir müssen den Frieden retten!* Cologne: Verlag Staat und Gesellschaft, 1957.

Joshua, Wynfred. "Soviet Manipulation of the European Peace Movement." *Strategic Review* (Winter 1983), 11:9–18.

Juling, Peter. *Programmatische Entwicklung der FDP 1946 bis 1969: Einführung und Dokumente.* Meisenheim am Glan: Anton Hain, 1977.

Jungk, Robert. *Brighter Than a Thousand Suns*. Harmondsworth, England: Penguin Books, 1964.

Kaack, Heino. *Zur Geschichte und Programmatik der Freien Demokratischen Partei: Grundriss und Materialien*. Meisenheim am Glan: Anton Hain, 1976.

Kafka, G. E., ed. *Die Katholiken vor der Politik*. Freiburg: Herder, 1958.

Kahn, Helmut Wolfgang. "Strauss und der Griff nach der Atommacht." *Blätter für deutsche und internationale Politik* (1979), 24:1195–1218.

Kaiser, Karl, Georg Leber, Alois Mertes, and Franz-Josef Schulze. "Nuclear Weapons and the Preservation of Peace: A German Response to No First Use." *Foreign Affairs* (Summer 1982), 60:1157–70.

Kaltefleiter, Werner and Robert Pfaltzgraff, eds. *The Peace Movements in Europe and the United States*. London: Croom Helm, 1985.

Kaufmann, William W., ed. *Military Policy and National Security*. Princeton: Princeton University Press, 1956.

Kelleher, Catherine McArdle. "German Nuclear Dilemmas, 1954–1966." Ph.D. dissertation, MIT, 1967.

——*Germany and the Politics of Nuclear Weapons*. New York: Columbia University Press, 1975.

Kelly, Petra. *Fighting for Hope*. Boston: South End Press, 1984.

Kennan, George F. *Memoirs 1925–1950*. Boston: Little, Brown, 1967.

——*Russia, the Atom, and the West*. London: Harper, 1958.

——"The Sources of Soviet Conduct." *Foreign Affairs* (July 1947), 25:562–82.

Kirche und Frieden: Kundgebungen und Erklärungen aus den deutschen Kirchen und der Oekumene. Hanover: EKD, 1982.

Kirche und Kriegsdienstverweigerung: Ratschlag des Rates der Evangelischen Kirche in Deutschland mit Begründung und Dokumentarischem Anhang. Munich: Chr. Kaiser, 1956.

Kirchliches Jahrbuch für die Evangelische Kirche in Deutschland. Joachim Beckmann, ed. Gütersloh: Carl Bertelsmann, 1950–1962.

Kissinger, Henry. *Nuclear Weapons and Foreign Policy*. New York: Harper, 1957.

——*The Troubled Partnership: A Reappraisal of the Atlantic Alliance*. New York: McGraw-Hill, 1965.

Kitzinger, Uwe. *German Electoral Politics: A Study of the 1957 Election Campaign*. Oxford: Clarendon Press, 1960.

——"West Germany: A Pre-Election Survey." *The World Today* (1961), 17(3): 110–22.

Klein, Peter. "Für kernwaffenfreie Zonen in aller Welt: Zusammenstellung und Erläuterung der Pläne für die Schaffung atomwaffenfreier Zonen." *Deutsche Aussenpolitik* (1964), 9:137–47.

——"Schattenboxen im westdeutschen Wahlkampf." *Deutsche Aussenpolitik* (1961), 6:903–16.

——"Westdeutsche Parteien—Kernwaffen und Sicherheit." *Deutsche Aussenpolitik* (1966), 11:1435–48.

Klotzbach, Kurt. *Der Weg zur Staatspartei: Programmatik, praktische Politik und Organisation der deutschen Sozialdemokratie 1945 bis 1965*. Berlin and Bonn: J. H. W. Dietz, 1982.

Knorr, Klaus, ed. *NATO and American Security*. Princeton: Princeton University Press, 1959.

Selected Bibliography

Knorr, Lorenz. *Geschichte der Friedensbewegung in der Bundesrepublik.* Cologne: Pahl-Rugenstein, 1983.
Koch, Dieter. *Heinemann und die Deutschlandfrage.* Munich: Chr. Kaiser, 1972.
Kohl, Helmut, ed. *Konrad Adenauer 1876–1976.* Stuttgart: Belser, 1976.
Kohl, Wilfrid. *French Nuclear Diplomacy.* Princeton: Princeton University Press, 1971.
Kopp, Fritz. *Chronik der Wiederbewaffnung in Deutschland.* Cologne: Markus, 1958.
Krippendorff, Ekkehart and Volker Rittberger, eds. *The Foreign Policy of West Germany: Formation and Contents.* London: SAGE, 1980.
Kroll, Hans. *Lebenserinnerungen eines Botschafters.* Cologne: Kiepenheuer and Witsch, 1967.
Künneth, Walter. "Die Atomfrage in christlicher Sicht: Die politischen Aspekte der Berliner Synode." *Die Politische Meinung* (1958), 3:31–40.
——"Atomrüstung und Ethos." *Zeitwende: Die Neue Furche* (1961), 32:234–44.
——"Atomtheologie heute." *Evangelisch-Lutherische Kirchenzeitung* (1958), no. 16, pp. 263–68.
——"Glaubensentscheidung." *Der Christ im Atomzeitalter: Vorträge auf der Theologischen Tagung des Rheinischen Konvents im Januar 1959,* pp. 23–26. Stuttgart: Evangelisches Verlagswerk, 1959.
——*Rechtfertigung im Atomzeitalter: Kritische Anfrage an Helmut Gollwitzer.* Munich: Claudius, 1958.
Kurscheid, Raimund. *Kampf dem Atomtod! Schriftsteller im Kampf gegen eine deutsche Atombewaffnung.* Cologne: Pahl-Rugenstein, 1981.
Laquer, Walter. *Europe since Hitler: The Rebirth of Europe.* Harmondsworth, England: Penguin, 1982.
Lauk, Kurt J. "Die nuklearen Optionen der Bundesrepublik Deutschland: Die Sicherheit der Bundesrepublik im Kräftefeld der nuklearen Strategien der westlichen Nuklearmächte." Ph.D. dissertation, University of Kiel, 1977.
Leber, Georg. *Vom Frieden.* Stuttgart: Seewald, 1979.
Le Ghait, Edouard. *No Carte Blanche to Capricorn: The Folly of Nuclear War Strategy.* New York: Bookfield House, 1960.
Lehmann, Hans Georg. *Chronik der Bundesrepublik Deutschland 1945/49 bis 1981.* Munich: C. H. Beck, 1981.
Lehmann, Karl Heinz. *Revisionismus und Antikommunismus im Dienst der atomaren Aufrüstung: Eine notwendige Auseinandersetzung mit der militärpolitischen Konzeption der rechten SPD-Führung.* Berlin: Deutscher Militärverlag, 1961.
Leminsky, Gerhard and Bernd Otto. *Politik und Programmatik des Deutschen Gewerkschaftsbundes.* Cologne: Bund-Verlag, 1984.
Lettau, Reinhard, ed. *Die Gruppe 47: Bericht, Kritik, Polemik: Ein Handbuch.* Neuwied: Hermann Luchterhand, 1967.
Lilge, Herbert. *Deutschland von 1955–1963: Von den Pariser Verträgen bis zum Ende der Aera Adenauer.* Hanover: Verlag für Literatur und Zeitgeschehen, 1965.
Löwenthal, Richard and Hans-Peter Schwarz, eds. *Die zweite Republik: 25. Jahre Bundesrepublik Deutschland—Eine Bilanz.* Stuttgart: Seewald, 1974.
Loewke, Udo. *Für den Fall, dass . . . : Die Haltung der SPD zur Wehrfrage, 1949–1955.* Hanover: Verlag für Literatur und Zeitgeschehen, 1969.
Luchtenberg, Paul, ed. *Geschichte des deutschen Liberalismus.* Cologne and Opladen: Westdeutscher Verlag, 1966.
Lutherische Stimmen zur Frage der Atomwaffen: Wilhelm Andersen, Friedrich-Wilhelm Kantzenbach, Georg F. Vicedom. Munich: Chr. Kaiser, 1958.

McGeehan, Robert. *The German Rearmament Question: American Diplomacy and European Defense after World War II.* Urbana, Ill.: University of Illinois Press, 1971.

Mahncke, Dieter. *Nukleare Mitwirkung: Die Bundesrepublik Deutschland in der Atlantischen Allianz, 1954–1970.* Berlin: Walter de Gruyter, 1972.

Mahncke, Dieter and Karl Carstens. *Westeuropäische Verteidigungskooperation.* Munich: R. Oldenbourg, 1972.

Mai, Gunther. *Westliche Sicherheitspolitik im Kalten Krieg: Der Korea-Krieg und die deutsche Wiederbewaffnung 1950.* Boppard am Rhein: Harald Boldt, 1977.

Marrin, Albert, ed. *War and the Christian Conscience: From Augustine to Martin Luther King, Jr.* Chicago: Henry Regnery, 1971.

Martin, Laurence. *NATO and the Defense of the West: An Analysis of America's First Line of Defense.* New York: Holt, Rinehart and Winston, 1985.

Materialien zum Kongress: Abrüstung ist das Gebot der Stunde. Düsseldorf: DGB-Bundesvorstand, 1981.

Matern, Hermann. *Der Parteitag der SPD und die Politik der SED: Zur Herstellung der Aktionseinheit der deutschen Arbeiterklasse im Kampf gegen die atomare Aufrüstung und für die Bildung einer Konföderation beider deutschen Staaten.* Berlin: Dietz, 1958.

Mayne, Richard. *The Recovery of Europe: From Devastation to Unity.* New York: Harper and Row, 1970.

Mearsheimer, John. *Conventional Deterrence.* Ithaca, N.Y.: Cornell University Press, 1983.

Mechtersheimer, Alfred. *Rüstung und Frieden: Der Widersinn der Sicherheitspolitik.* Munich: Wirtschaftsverlag Langen-Müller, 1982.

——*Zeitbombe NATO: Auswirkungen der neuen Strategien.* Cologne: Eugen Diederich, 1984.

Meinhof, Ulrike. "Der Studentenkongress gegen Atomrüstung in Berlin." *Blätter für deutsche und internationale Politik* (1959), 4:51–52.

Meinhof, Ulrike and Jürgen Seifert. "Unruhe in der Studentenschaft." *Blätter für deutsche und internationale Politik* (1958), 3:524–26.

Meissner, Boris, ed. *Moskau Bonn: Die Beziehung zwischen der Sowjetunion und den Bundesrepublik Deutschland 1955–1973: Dokumentation.* Cologne: Verlag Wissenschaft und Politik, 1975.

Mende, Erich. *Die FDP: Daten, Fakten, Hintergründe.* Stuttgart: Seewald, 1972.

Mendl, Wolf. *Deterrence and Persuasion: French Nuclear Armament in the Context of National Policy, 1945–1969.* New York: Praeger, 1970.

Miksche, Ferdinand Otto. *The Failure of Atomic Strategy and a New Proposal for the West.* London: Faber, 1959.

Militärgeschichtliches Forschungsamt, ed. *Anfänge westdeutscher Sicherheitspolitik 1945–1956.* Munich: Oldenbourg, 1982.

——*Militärgeschichte seit 1945: Aspekte der deutschen Wiederbewaffnung bis 1955.* Boppard am Rhein: Harald Boldt, 1975.

——*Verteidigung im Bündnis: Planung, Aufbau und Bewährung der Bundeswehr 1950–1972.* Munich: Bernard und Graefe Verlag für Wehrwesen, 1975.

——*Vorträge zur Militärgeschichte: Entmilitarisierung und Aufrüstung in Mitteleuropa 1945–1956,* vol. 4. Herford: E. S. Mittler, 1983.

Molt, Peter. "Die neutralistische Opposition." Ph.D. dissertation, University of Heidelberg, 1955.

Selected Bibliography

Morgan, Roger. *The United States and West Germany 1945–1973: A Study in Alliance Politics.* London: Oxford University Press, 1974.
——*West European Politics since 1945: The Shaping of the European Community.* London: B. T. Batsford, 1972.
Morgan, Roger and Caroline Bray, eds. *Partners and Rivals in Western Europe: Britain, France, and Germany.* Shaftesbury, England: Blackmore Press, 1986.
Morsey, Rudolf and Konrad Repgen, eds. *Adenauer-Studien.* 4 vols. Mainz: Matthias-Grünewald, 1971–77.
Mulley, F. W. *The Politics of Western Defense.* New York: Praeger, 1962.
Mushaben, Joyce Marie. "Cycles of Peace Protest in West Germany: Experiences from Three Decades." *West European Politics* (January 1985), 18:24–40.
Mutz, Reinhard. *Sicherheitspolitik und demokratische Oeffentlichkeit in der BRD: Probleme der Analyse, Kritik und Kontrolle militärischer Macht.* Munich: R. Oldenbourg, 1978.
Nachrüstungsdebatte im Deutschen Bundestag: Protokoll einer historischen Entscheidung. Hamburg: Rowohlt, 1984.
Naef, Charles Robert. "The Politics of West German Rearmament, 1950–1956." Ph.D. dissertation, Rutgers University, 1979.
Nein zum nuklearen Selbstmord: Der Kreuzzug des Gewissens. Bonn-Venusberg: Arbeitsausschuss "Kampf dem Atomtod," 1958.
Nellen, Peter. *Die Pflicht des Gewissens: Eine Rede vor dem Bundestag zur Wehrpflichtdebatte.* Darmstadt: Georg-Büchner-Verlag, n.d. [1956?].
——*Reden und Aufsätze.* Heinz Robert Schlette, ed. Düsseldorf: Patmos, 1980.
——*Sieben Moraltheologen: Ausblicke im Atomzeitalter.* Nuremberg: Glock und Lutz, 1958.
Nerlich, Uwe. "Die nuklearen Dilemmas der Bundesrepublik Deutschland." *Europa-Archiv* (1965), 17:637–52.
Nerlich, Uwe, ed. *Soviet Power and Western Negotiating Policies.* 2 vol. Cambridge, Mass.: Ballinger, 1983.
Niemöller, Martin. *Gottes Gebot im Atomzeitalter.* Darmstadt: Stimme-Verlag, 1958.
——*Martin Niemöller zur atomaren Rüstung: Zwei Reden.* Darmstadt: Stimme-Verlag, 1959.
——*Reden 1958–1961.* Frankfurt am Main: Stimme-Verlag, 1961.
——*Was Niemöller sagt—wogegen Strauss klagt: Niemöllers Kasseler Rede vom 25. Januar 1959 in vollen Wortlaut.* Darmstadt: Stimme-Verlag, 1959.
——"Wo steht die Kirche 1958?" *Stimme der Gemeinde* (1958), 10:65–74.
Noack, Paul. *Das Scheitern der Europäischen Verteidigungsgemeinschaft: Entscheidungsprozess vor und nach dem 30. August 1954.* Düsseldorf: Droste, 1977.
Noelle, Elisabeth and Erich Peter Neumann. *The Germans: Public Opinion Polls, 1947–1966.* Gerard Finan, tr. Allensbach: Verlag für Demoskopie, 1967.
Nolte, Ernst. *Deutschland und der Kalte Krieg.* Munich: R. Piper, 1975.
"Off-the-Record Meeting on Cuba, October 16, 1962." Transcript in JFK Library. Boston Mass.
Opitz, Eckardt."Friedrich Beermann und die Wehrpolitik der SPD von 1955 bis 1959." *Die neue Gesellschaft* (1977), 24:869–72.
Osgood, Robert E. *NATO: The Entangling Alliance.* Chicago: University of Chicago Press, 1962.
Otto, Karl A. *Vom Ostermarsch zur APO: Geschichte der Ausserparlamentarischen Opposition in der Bundesrepublik 1960–70.* Frankfurt am Main: Campus, 1977.

Papadakis, Elim. *The Green Movement in West Germany*. New York: St. Martin's Press, 1984.

Parkin, Frank. *Middle Class Radicalism: The Social Bases of the British Campaign for Nuclear Disarmament*. Manchester, England: Manchester University Press, 1968.

Pentagon Papers. Gravel Edition. Vol. 1. Boston: Beacon, 1971–72.

Pfleiderer, Karl Georg. *Politik für Deutschland*. Stuttgart: Deutsche Verlags-Anstalt, 1961.

Picht, Georg, ed. *Studien zur politischen und gesellschaftlichen Situation der Bundeswehr*. 3 vols. Witten: Eckart, 1965.

Pierre, Andrew J. *Nuclear Politics: The British Experience with an Independent Strategic Force 1939–1970*. London: Oxford University Press, 1972.

Pierre, Andrew J., ed. *Nuclear Weapons in Europe*. New York: Council on Foreign Relations, 1984.

Piper, Klaus, ed. *Karl Jaspers: Werk und Wirkung*. Munich: R. Piper, 1963.

Pirker, Theo. *Die blinde Macht: Die Gewerkschaftsbewegung in Westdeutschland*. 2 vols. Munich: Mercator, 1960.

——*Die SPD nach Hitler: Die Geschichte der Sozialdemokratischen Partei Deutschlands 1954–1964*. Munich: Rütten and Loening, 1965.

Planck, Charles R. *The Changing Status of German Reunification in Western Diplomacy, 1955–1966:* Baltimore: Johns Hopkins University Press, 1967.

Pöttering, Hans-Gert. *Adenauers Sicherheitspolitik 1955–1963: Ein Beitrag zum deutsch-amerikanischen Verhältnis*. Düsseldorf: Droste, 1975.

"Preservation, Promotion and Renewal of Peace: A Memorandum of the Evangelical Church of Germany." *EKD Bulletin*. Special Issue. October 1981.

Pridham, Geoffrey. *Christian Democracy in West Germany: The CDU/CSU in Government and Opposition, 1945–1976*. New York: St. Martin's Press, 1977.

Protokoll: 3. ordentlicher Bundeskongress Frankfurt a. M. 4. bis. 9. Oktober 1954. Düsseldorf: Deutscher Gewerkschaftsbund, 1954.

Protokoll über den dritten ordentlichen Gewerkschaftstag der Industriegewerkschaft Metall für die Bundesrepublik Deutschland: Hannover vom 13. bis 18. September 1954. Frankfurt am Main: IG Metall, 1954.

Protokoll: 5. ordentlicher Bundeskongress Stuttgart: 7. bis 12. September 1959. Düsseldorf: Deutscher Gewerkschaftsbund, 1959.

Protokoll: 5. ordentlicher Gewerkschaftstag der Industriegewerkschaft Metall für die Bundesrepublik Deutschland: Nürnberg von 15. bis 20. September 1958. Frankfurt am Main: IG Metall, 1958.

Protokoll der Verhandlungen des Ausserordentlichen Parteitages der Sozialdemokratischen Partei Deutschlands vom 13.-15. November 1959 in Bad Godesberg. Bonn: Vorstand der SPD, 1959.

Protokoll der Verhandlungen des Parteitages der Sozialdemokratischen Partei Deutschlands vom 20. bis 24. Juli 1954 in Berlin. Bonn: Vorstand der SPD, 1954.

Protokoll der Verhandlungen des Parteitages der Sozialdemokratischen Partei Deutschlands vom 10. bis 14. Juli 1956 in München. Bonn: Vorstand der SPD, 1956.

Protokoll der Verhandlungen des Parteitages der Sozialdemokratischen Partei Deutschlands vom 18. bis 23. Mai 1958 in Stuttgart. Bonn: Vorstand der SPD, 1958.

Protokoll der Verhandlungen und Anträge vom Parteitag der Sozialdemokratischen Partei Deutschlands in Hannover 21. bis 25. November 1960. Bonn: Vorstand der SPD, 1960.

Selected Bibliography

Protokoll des 6. ordentlichen Gewerkschaftstages der Industriegewerkschaft Metall für die Bundesrepublik Deutschland: Berlin 17. bis 22. Oktober 1960. Frankfurt am Main: IG Metall, 1960.

Protokoll: 4. ordentlicher Bundeskongress Hamburg 1. bis 6. Oktober 1956. Düsseldorf: Deutscher Gewerkschaftsbund, 1956.

Prokotoll des 4. ordentlichen Gewerkschaftstages der Industriegewerkschaft Metall für die Bundesrepublik Deutschland in der Westfalenhalle Dortmund vom 10. bis 15. September 1956. Frankfurt am Main: IG Metall, 1956.

Radkau, Joachim. *Aufstieg und Krise der deutschen Atomwirtschaft 1945–1975.* Reinbek bei Hamburg: Rowohlt, 1983.

Raketenbasen im Westdeutschland? Einstellung der Oeffentlichkeit zur Errichtung von Raketenbasen in der Bundesrepublik. Bielefeld: EMNID, 1958.

Rearden, Steven L. *The Evolution of American Strategic Doctrine: Paul Nitze and the Soviet Challenge.* Boulder, Colo.: Westview, 1984.

Reformierter Bund: Das Bekenntnis zu Jesus Christus und die Friedensverantwortung der Kirche. Gütersloh: Gütersloher Verlag, 1982.

"Remarks by Secretary McNamara, NATO Ministerial Meeting, 5 May 1962. Restricted Session." Declassified on August 17, 1979, under the Freedom of Information Act.

Rettet die Freiheit. *Rettet die Freiheit: Grundungskongress, Köln, 29. Februar 1959.* Berlin: Vorstand 'Rettet die Freiheit,' 1959.

——*Verschwörung gegen die Freiheit: Die kommunistische Untergrundarbeit in der Bundesrepublik.* Munich: Komitee 'Rettet die Freiheit,' n.d.

Rexin, Manfred. "Kampf dem Atomtod;—damals und heute: Rolf Schroers in der APO der Adenauer Aera." Speech of May 1982. Copy from Rexin, West Berlin.

Richardson, James L. *Germany and the Atlantic Alliance: The Interaction of Strategy and Politics.* Cambridge: Harvard University Press, 1966.

Risse-Kappen, Thomas. *Christen zur Friedensdiskussion: Analyse und synoptische Dokumentation von Stellungnahmen aus den Kirchen in der Bundesrepublik Deutschland.* Frankfurt am Main: HSFK-Report, 1982.

——"Gesellschaftlicher Konsens und internationale Kompatibilität: Anforderung und Entscheidungen zur westdeutschen Sicherheitspolitik, 1977–1984." Ph.D dissertation, University of Frankfurt, 1986.

Röhl, Bernhard. "1958—Jahr der bedeutenden Bundestagsdebatten über Wiedervereinigung und Atomrüstung." *Vorgänge* (1979), 18(39):113–17.

Röhl, Klaus Rainer. *Fünf Finger sind keine Faust.* Cologne: Kiepenheuer & Witsch, 1974.

Rosenberg, David Alan. "The Origins of Overkill: Nuclear Weapons and American Strategy, 1945–1960." *International Security* (Spring 1983), 7:3–71.

——" 'A Smoking Radiating Ruin at the End of Two Hours': Documents on American Plans for Nuclear War with the Soviet Union, 1954–1955." *International Security* (Winter 1981/82), 6:3–38.

Rotblat, J. *Scientists in the Quest for Peace: A History of the Pugwash Conferences.* Cambridge: MIT Press, 1972.

Rubin, Hans Wolfgang, ed. *Freiheit, Recht und Einigkeit: Zur Entspannungs- und Deutschlandpolitik der Liberalen.* Baden-Baden: Nomos, 1980.

Ruhm vom Oppen, Beate, ed., *Documents on Germany Under Occupation 1945–1954.* London: Oxford University Press, 1955.

Rupieper, Hermann-Josef. "Zu den sowjetischen Deutschlandnoten 1952: Das Gespräch Stalin-Nenni." *Vierteljahrshefte für Zeitgeschichte* (1985), 33:547–57.

Rupp, Hans-Karl. *Ausserparlamentarische Opposition in der Aera Adenauer: Der Kampf gegen die Atombewaffnung in den fünfziger Jahren.* Cologne: Pahl-Rugenstein, 1970.

——*Politische Geschichte der Bundesrepublik Deutschland.* Stuttgart: W. Kohlhammer, 1978.

Schellenger, Harold Kent. *The SPD in the Bonn Republic: A Socialist Party Modernizes.* The Hague: Martinus Nijhoff, 1968.

Schmid, Günther. *Sicherheitspolitik und Friedensbewegung: Der Konflikt um die "Nachrüstung."* Munich: Günter Olzog, 1982.

Schmidt, Helmut. *The Balance of Power: Germany's Peace Policy and the Super Powers.* Edward Thomas, tr. London: William Kimber, 1971.

——*Beiträge.* Stuttgart: Seewald, 1967.

——*Defense or Retaliation: A German View.* Edward Thomas, tr. New York: Praeger, 1962.

——"Grundzüge und Kontinuität der US-Strategie." *Wehr und Wirtschaft* (1965), 9:108–10.

——"The 1977 Alastair Buchan Memorial Lecture." *Survival* (January/February 1978), 20:2–10.

——*Verteidigung oder Vergeltung: Ein deutscher Beitrag zum strategischen Problem der NATO.* Stuttgart: Seewald, 1961.

Schneider, Franz Paul, ed. *Dokumente zum Göttingen Manifest.* Fulda: "Fränkischer Kreis," 1957.

Schneider, Herbert. "Lanze und Schwert ergeben kein Schild." Bonn, 1958. Manuscript at Deutscher Bundestag Bibliothek.

——"Schwert und Schild: Gedanken zum Aufbau der Verteidigung der Bundesrepublik im Rahmen und in Ergänzung der NATO-Verteidigung." Bonn, 1956. Manuscript at Deutscher Bundestag Bibliothek.

Schoenbaum, David. *The Spiegel Affair.* Garden City, N.Y.: Doubleday, 1968.

Schönbohm, W. *Die CDU wird moderne Volkspartei.* Stuttgart: Klett-Cotta, 1985.

Schöps, Joachim. *Die Spiegel Affäre des Franz Josef Strauss.* Reinbeck bei Hamburg: Rowohlt, 1983.

Schollwer, Wolfgang. "Tagebücher." Vol. 4. Manuscript in possession of Wolfgang Schollwer, Foreign Office, Bonn.

——*Der Weg zur Entspannung: Deutschlandpolitik der F.D.P. seit 1952.* Bonn: Bundesgeschäftsstelle der FDP, 1972.

——*Deutschlandpolitik der F.D.P.: Daten und Dokumente von 1945 bis heute.* Bonn: Bundesgeschäftsstelle der FDP, 1972.

Schubert, Klaus von. *Wiederbewaffnung und Westintegration: Die innere Auseinandersetzung um die militärische und aussenpolitische Orientierung der Bundesrepublik 1950–1952.* Stuttgart: Deutsche Verlags-Anstalt, 1970.

Schubert, Klaus von, ed. *Sicherheitspolitik der Bundesrepublik Deutschland: Dokumentation 1945–1977.* 2 vols. Cologne: Verlag Wissenschaft und Politik, 1978–1979.

Schuster, Dieter. *Die deutschen Gewerkschaften seit 1945.* Stuttgart: W. Kohlhammer, 1973.

Schwartz, David. *NATO's Nuclear Dilemmas.* Washington, D.C.: Brookings Institution, 1983.

Schwarz, Hans-Peter. "Adenauer und Europa." *Vierteljahrshefte für Zeitgeschichte* (1979), 27:471–523.

Selected Bibliography

——"Die Politik der Westbindung oder die Staatsraison der Bundesrepublik." *Zeitschrift für Politik* (1975), 22:307–37.

——*Vom Reich zur Bundesrepublik: Deutschland im Widerstreit der aussenpolitischen Konzeptionen in den Jahren der Besatzungsherrschaft 1945–1949.* Neuwied: Klett-Cotta, 1980.

Schwarz, Hans-Peter, ed. *Konrad Adenauer: Reden 1917–1967: Eine Auswahl.* Stuttgart: Deutsche Verlags-Anstalt, 1975.

Schwarz, Klaus-Dieter, ed. *Sicherheitspolitik: Analysen zur politischen und militärischen Sicherheit.* Bad Honnef-Erpel: Osang, 1976.

Schweitzer, Albert. *Friede oder Atomkrieg.* Munich: C. H. Beck, 1958.

——*Das Problem des Friedens in der heutigen Welt.* Munich: C. H. Beck, 1954.

Sethe, Paul. *Zwischen Bonn und Moskau.* Frankfurt am Main: Heinrich Scheffler, 1956.

Shell, Kurt L. and Nils Diederich. "Die Berliner Wahl vom 7. Dezember 1958." *Zeitschrift für Politik* (1960), 7:241–81.

Sicherheit in Europa: Die Vorschläge für Rüstungsbeschränkung und Abrüstung 1955–1965. Munich: R. Oldenbourg, 1968.

Siegler, Heinrich, ed. *Dokumentation zur Abrüstung und Sicherheit von 1943 bis 1959.* Bad Godesberg: Siegler, 1960.

——*Wiedervereinigung und Sicherheit Deutschlands.* Bonn: Verlag für Zeitarchive, 1964.

Sigal, Leon. *Nuclear Forces in Europe: Enduring Dilemmas, Present Prospects.* Washington, D.C.: Brookings Institution, 1984.

Skalweit, Peter W. "Die Strategische Verteidigungskonzeption von Franz Josef Strauss und Helmut Schmidt." *Gegenwartskunde* (1970), 19:263–81.

Slessor, Sir John. "The Place of the Bomber in British Strategy." *International Affairs* (July 1953), 23:302–08.

Soell, Hartmut. *Fritz Erler—Eine politische Biographie.* 2 vols. Berlin: J. H. W. Dietz, 1976.

Solberg, Richard. *God and Caesar in East Germany: The Conflict of Church and State in East Germany since 1945.* New York: MacMillan, 1961.

Sommer, Theo. "Deutsche Nuklearpolitik." *Oesterreichische Zeitschrift für Aussenpolitik* (1967), 7:26–39.

——"The Objectives of Germany." In Alastair Buchan, ed., *A World of Nuclear Powers?* pp. 39–54. Englewood Cliffs, N.J.: Prentice-Hall, 1966.

Sommer, Theo, ed. *Denken an Deutschland.* Hamburg: Nannen-Verlag, 1966.

Sozialdemokratie und Bundeswehr. Berlin and Hanover: n.p., 1957.

SPD Ausserordentlicher Parteitag: Beschlüsse zu Europa Friedens- und Sicherheitspolitik: 18./19. November 1983, Köln. Bonn: SPD Vorstand, 1983.

SPD Parteitag: Beschlüsse zur Aussen-, Friedens- und Sicherheitspolitik, 19.–23. April 1982, München. Bonn: SPD Vorstand, 1982.

Speidel, Hans. *Aus unserer Zeit: Erinnerungen.* Berlin: Ullstein, 1977.

Speier, Hans. *From the Ashes of Disgrace.* Amherst: University of Massachusetts Press, 1981.

——*German Rearmament and Atomic War: The Views of German Military and Political Leaders.* Evanston, Ill.: Row, Peterson, 1957.

——"German Rearmament and the Old Military Elite." *World Politics* (January 1954), no. 2, pp. 147–68.

Speier, Hans and W. Phillips Davison, eds. *West German Leadership and Foreign Policy*. Evanston, Ill.: Row, Peterson, 1957.

Stamm, Thomas. *Zwischen Staat und Selbstverwaltung: Die deutsche Forschung im Wiederaufbau 1945–1965*. Cologne: Verlag Wissenschaft und Politik, 1981.

Steinbruner, John D. *The Cybernetic Theory of Decision: The New Dimension of Political Analysis*. Princeton: Princeton University Press, 1974.

Steinbruner, John D. and Leon V. Sigal, eds. *NATO and the No-First-Use Question*. Washington, D.C.: Brookings Institution, 1983.

Stratmann, Franziskus. *The Church and War: A Catholic Study*. New York: Garland, 1971.

Strauss, Franz Josef. *Bundestagsreden*. Bonn: AZ Studio, 1968.

——"Glaubhafte Sicherheit durch Abschreckung." *Aussenpolitik* (1961), 12:515–20.

——*The Grand Design: A European Solution to German Reunification*. New York: Praeger, 1966.

——"Verteidigungskonzeption im atomaren Zeitalter." *Politisches Jahrbuch der CDU/CSU* (1960), 4:51–55.

Tappert, Theodor, ed. *Selected Writings of Martin Luther 1523–1526*. Philadelphia: Fortress Press, 1967.

Taylor, Maxwell. *The Uncertain Trumpet*. New York: Harper, 1960.

Taylor, Richard and Colin Pritchard. *The Protest Makers: The British Nuclear Disarmament Movement of 1958–1965, Twenty Years On*. Oxford: Pergamon Press, 1980.

Teichman, Jenny. *Pacifism and the Just War*. Oxford: Basil Blackwell, 1986.

Thielicke, Helmut. *Die Atomwaffe als Frage an die Christliche Ethik*. Tübingen: J. C. B. Mohr (Paul Siebeck), 1958.

——*Begegnungen und Erfahrungen*. Wuppertal: R. Brockhaus, 1977.

——"Der Christ und die Verhütung des Krieges im Atomzeitalter." *Zeitschrift für Evangelische Ethik* (1957), 1:1–6.

——"Gewissen und Verantwortung im Atomzeitalter." *7. Bundesparteitag der CDU. Hamburg 1957*. Hamburg: Sator Werbe, 1957.

Thies, Wallace J. *The Atlantic Alliance, Nuclear Weapons and European Attitudes: Reexamining the Conventional Wisdom*. Berkeley: Institute of International Studies, 1983.

Tönnies, Norbert. *Der Weg zu den Waffen: Die Geschichte der deutschen Wiederbewaffnung 1949–1961*. Rastatt: Pabal, 1961.

Torberg, Friedrich. "Als er zum 3. Male Kanzler wurde: Adenauer und die Intellektuellen." *Die Politische Meinung* (November/December 1975), 20:113–21.

Treaty Establishing the European Defense Community and Related Protocols. Office of the U.S. Special Representative in Europe, Paris, January 26, 1953.

Uhlig, A. W. *Atom:Angst oder Hoffnung? Die Lehren des ersten Atommanövers der Welt*. Munich: Isar, 1955.

U.S. Dept. of State. *FRUS (Foreign Relations of the United States) 1950*. Vol. 1. Washington, D.C.: GPO, 1977.

——*FRUS 1951*. Vol. 3. Washington, D.C.: GPO, 1981.

——*FRUS 1952–1954*. Vol. 5. Washington, D.C.: GPO, 1983.

Verhandlungen der siebten ordentlichen Rheinischen Landessynode. Mülheim: Carl Blech, 1958.

Selected Bibliography

Verhandlungen des Deutschen Bundestages: Stenographische Berichte: 1. Wahlperiode 1949. Bonn, 1950–1953.

Verhandlungen des Deutschen Bundestages: Stenographische Berichte: 2. Wahlperiode 1953. Bonn, 1953–57.

Verhandlungen des Deutschen Bundestages: Stenographische Berichte: 3. Wahlperiode 1957. Bonn, 1957–1961.

Vogel, Bernhard, and Peter Haungs. *Wahlkampf und Wählertradition: Eine Studie zur Bundestagswahl von 1961.* Cologne and Opladen: Westdeutscher Verlag, 1965.

Vogel, Heinrich. *Um die Zukunft des Menschen im atomaren Zeitalter.* Berlin: Lettner, 1960.

Vogel, Johanna. *Kirche und Wiederbewaffnung.* Göttingen: Vanderhoeck and Ruprecht, 1978.

Vom Herrengeheimnis der Wahrheit: Festschrift für Heinrich Vogel. Berlin: Lettner, 1962.

Wagner, Dietrich. *FDP und Wiederbewaffnung.* Boppard am Rhein: Harald Boldt, 1978.

Walter, Thomas, ed. *Gewerkschaften und Demokratie: Analysen zum DGB-Grundsatzprogramm 1981.* Walberberg: Institut für Gesellschaftswissenschaften, 1982.

Walther, Christian, ed. *Atomwaffen und Ethik: Der deutsche Protestantismus und die atomare Aufrüstung 1954–1961: Dokumente und Kommentare.* Munich: Chr. Kaiser, 1981.

Walzer, Michael. *Just and Unjust Wars: A Moral Argument with Historical Illustrations.* New York: Basic Books, 1977.

Weber, Hermann. *Kleine Geschichte der DDR.* Cologne: Verlag Wissenschaft und Politik, 1980.

Weber, Werner and Richter Wehner Jahn. *Synopse zur Deutschlandpolitik 1941 bis 1973.* Göttingen: Otto Schwartz, 1973.

Weinstein, Adelbert. "Atomkrieg oder Bonin-Plan? Irgendeine Form der Neutralität." *Deutsche Volks-Zeitung,* July 30, 1955.

——*Keiner kann den Krieg gewinnen: Strategie oder Sicherheit?* Bonn: Schimmelsbusch, 1955.

——"Strategie oder Sicherheit? Gedanken zur deutschen Verteidigungs-Konzeption." *Aussenpolitik* (1955), 6:233–40.

Weizsäcker, Carl-Friedrich von. *Atomenergie und Atomzeitalter: Zwölf Vorlesungen.* Frankfurt am Main: Fischer Bücherei, 1957.

——*Der bedrohte Friede: Politische Aufsätze 1945–1981.* Munich: Carl Hanser, 1981.

——*Der Garten des Menschlichen: Beiträge zur geschichtlichen Anthropologie.* Munich: Carl Hanser, 1977.

——*Ethical and Political Problems of the Atomic Age.* London: SCM Press, 1958.

——"The Ethical Problems of Modern Strategy." In *Problems of Modern Strategy,* pp. 121–38. New York: Praeger, 1970.

——*Fragen zur Weltpolitik.* Munich: C. Hanser, 1975.

——*Mit der Bombe leben: Die gegenwärtigen Aussichten einer Begrenzung der Gefahr eines Atomkrieges.* Hamburg: Die Zeit, 1958.

——*The Politics of Peril: Economics, Society and the Prevention of War.* New York: Seabury Press, 1978.

——*Der ungesicherte Friede.* Göttingen: Vandenhoeck and Ruprecht, 1969.

——*Die Verantwortung der Wissenschaft im Atomzeitalter.* Göttingen: Vandenhoeck and Ruprecht, 1963.

——*Wege in der Gefahr: Eine Studie über Wirtschaft, Gesellschaft und Kriegsverhütung.* Munich: Carl Hanser, 1976.

Weizsäcker, Carl-Friedrich von, ed. *Kriegsfolgen und Kriegsverhütung.* Munich: Carl Hanser, 1971.

Wells, Samuel F. "Sounding the Tocsin: NSC 68 and the Soviet Threat." *International Security* (Fall 1979), 4:116–58.

Wettig, Gerhard. *Entmilitarisierung und Wiederbewaffnung in Deutschland, 1943–1955.* Munich: R. Oldenbourg, 1967.

Wilker, Lothar. *Die Sicherheitspolitik der SPD 1956–1966: Zwischen Wiedervereinigungs- und Bündnisorientierung.* Bonn–Bad Godesberg: Verlag Neue Gesellschaft, 1977.

Wolf, Ernst, et al. *Christusbekenntnis im Atomzeitalter?* Munich: Chr. Kaiser, 1959.

Wolf, Ernst and Werner Schmauch. *Die Königsherrschaft Christi und der Staat.* Munich: Chr. Kaiser, 1958.

Wolfe, Thomas W. *Soviet Power and Europe, 1945–1970.* Baltimore: Johns Hopkins University Press, 1970.

Zimmerman, Friedrich, ed. *Anspruch und Leistung: Widmungen für Franz Josef Strauss.* Stuttgart: Seewald, 1980.

Newspapers, Journals, Magazines

argument (Münster)
Das Argument (West Berlin)
Atomkernenergie (Munich)
Atomzeitalter (Bonn)
Aussenpolitik (Stuttgart)
Bayern-Kurier (Munich)
Berliner Stimme
Berliner Zeitung
Bildzeitung (Berlin)
Blätter für deutsche und internationale Politik (Cologne)
Bulletin des Presse- und Informationsamtes der Bundesregierung (Bonn)
Burschenschaftliche Blätter (Bad Nauheim)
Die Debatte
Department of State Bulletin (U.S.)
Deutsche Aussenpolitik (East Berlin)
Deutsche Volks-Zeitung
Deutsches Allgemeines Sonntagsblatt
Deutsches Pfarrerblatt
DGB-Pressedienst (Düsseldorf)
Dokumentation der Zeit (East Berlin)
EKD-Bulletin
Europa-Archiv (Frankfurt and Bonn)
Evangelische Welt
Evangelisch-Lutherische Kirchenzeitung (Munich)
Foreign Affairs
Foreign Policy

Selected Bibliography

Frankfurter Allgemeine Zeitung [FAZ]
Frankfurter Hefte
Frankfurter Rundschau [FR]
Frei Demokratische Korrespondenz [fdk]
Gegenwartskunde
Gewerkschaftliche Monatshefte
International Affairs
International Security
Hamburger Echo
Junge Kirche (Dortmund)
Junge Welt
Kirchliches Jahrbuch (KJ)
Kongressdienst (Hamburg)
konkret (Hamburg)
Die Kultur
Metall
Militärgeschichtliche Mitteilungen
Der Monat (West Berlin)
Die neue Gesellschaft (Bielefeld)
Neue Zeit
Neue Zürcher Zeitung (NZZ)
Neues Deutschland (East Berlin)
New York Times
Oesterreichische Zeitschrift für Aussenpolitik
Das Parlament
Physikalische Blätter (Mosbach)
Political Quarterly
Die Politische Meinung (Cologne)
Politische Verantwortung
Die Quelle (Cologne)
Rheinisch-Westfälische Nachrichten (Düsseldorf)
Rheinischer Merkur
SPD-Pressedienst (Bonn)
SPD-Pressemitteilungen und Informationen
Der Spiegel (Hamburg)
Stimme der Gemeinde (Darmstadt)
Strategic Review
Süddeutsche Zeitung (SDZ)
Survival
The Times (London)
Union in Deutschland
Universitas
Vierteljahrshefte für Zeitgeschichte
Vorgänge
Vorwärts (Bad Godesberg)
Wehrkunde
Die Welt (Hamburg)
Welt der Arbeit (Cologne)
Werk-Hefte Katholischer Laien (Munich)

Wochenbericht der Aktionsgemeinschaft gegen die atomare Aufrüstung der Bundesrepublik
The World Today
Die Zeit (Hamburg)
Zeitschrift für Evangelische Ethik (Gütersloh)
Zeitschrift für Politik
Zeitwende: Die Neue Furche (Hamburg)

INDEX

Index